SAINTS AND SCRIBES

Saints and Scribes

Medieval Hagiography in
Its Manuscript Context

Pamela Gehrke

UNIVERSITY OF CALIFORNIA PRESS
Berkeley • Los Angeles • London

UNIVERSITY OF CALIFORNIA PUBLICATIONS IN MODERN PHILOLOGY

Editorial Board: Samuel G. Armistead, Jean-Pierre Barricelli,
Hinrich Seeba, Jon Snyder, Harold E. Toliver

Volume 126

UNIVERSITY OF CALIFORNIA PRESS
BERKELEY AND LOS ANGELES, CALIFORNIA

UNIVERSITY OF CALIFORNIA PRESS, LTD.
LONDON, ENGLAND

© 1993 BY THE REGENTS OF THE UNIVERSITY OF CALIFORNIA
PRINTED IN THE UNITED STATES OF AMERICA

Library of Congress Cataloging-in-Publication Data

Gehrke, Pamela.
   Saints and scribes: medieval hagiography in its manuscript
context / Pamela Gehrke.
      p.   cm. — (University of California publications in modern
philology; v. 126)
   Includes bibliographical references.
   ISBN 0-520-09771-8 (pbk.: alk. paper)
   1. French poetry—To 1500—Criticism, Textual. 2. Christian
saints—Legends—Criticism, Textual. 3. Christian poetry, French—
Criticism, Textual. 4. Christian saints in literature.
5. Manuscripts, Medieval—France. 6. Manuscripts, French—France.
7. Transmission of texts. 8. Christian hagiography. 9. Scriptoria—
France. 10. Literary form.   I. Title. II. Series.
PQ155.R4G44   1993
841'.109382—dc20   92-27741
                                                                           CIP

The paper used in this publication meets the minimum requirements of
American National Standard for Information Sciences—Permanence of
Paper for Printed Library Materials, ANSI Z39.48-1984. ∞

To Wayne

Doing ethnography is like trying to read
(in the sense of "construct a reading of")
a manuscript—foreign, faded, full of ellipses,
incoherencies, suspicious emendations,
and tendentious commentaries, but written
not in conventionalized graphs of sound
but in transient examples of shaped behaviors.

Geertz, *The Interpretation of Cultures*

Contents

List of Figures, viii
List of Tables, ix
Acknowledgments, x

Chapter 1.	Introduction: Selection of Examples and Theoretical Frame	1
Chapter 2.	Confession and Penance: Sincere Observance as a Means of Salvation	12
Chapter 3.	"Literature in the True Sense": Aristocratic Virtues and Textual Travels	54
Chapter 4.	Pious Hermits and Magical Helpers: Alternative Solutions for Spiritual Problems	86
Chapter 5.	Saint Francis and the Mother of God: An Ascetic Ideal for the Laity	124
Chapter 6.	Conclusion: Codicology and Reception History in the Interpretation of Pious Vernacular Literature	161

Bibliography, 169

List of Figures

1.	Paris, B.N. f. fr. 2162: f. 9r (hand 1)	33
2.	Paris, B.N. f. fr. 2162: f. 13r (hand 2)	34
3.	Paris, B.N. f. fr. 2162: f. 83r (hand 3)	35
4.	Paris, B.N. f. fr. 2162: f. 93r (hand 4)	36
5.	Paris, B.N. f. fr. 2162: f. 95r (hand 5)	37
6.	Paris, B.N. f. fr. 2162: f. 98r (hand 6)	38
7.	Paris, B.N. f. fr. 2162: f. 105r (hand 7)	39
8.	Paris, B.N. f. fr. 2162: f. 122v (hand 8)	40
9.	Paris, B.N. f. fr. 2162: Page layout, long lines (ff. 1r-77v)	41
10.	Paris, B.N. f. fr. 2162: Page layout, two columns (ff.77v-136v)	42
11.	Paris, B.N. f. fr. 1374: f. 38v (hand 1)	71
12.	Paris, B.N. f. fr. 1374: f. 69r (hand 2)	72
13.	Paris, B.N. f. fr. 1374: f. 91r (hand 3, cryptogram)	73
14.	Paris, B.N. f. fr. 1374: f. 134v (hand 4)	74
15.	Paris, B.N. f. fr. 1374: f. 171v (hand 5)	75
16.	Paris, B.N. f. fr. 1374: f. 180r (hand 6)	76
17.	Paris, B.N. f. fr. 1374: f. 123v (sketch)	77
18.	Paris, B.N. f. fr. 1374: Page layout	78
19.	Berkeley, Bancroft Library UCB 106: f. 66r	105
20.	Berkeley, Bancroft Library UCB 106: Page layout, verse section	106
21.	Berkeley, Bancroft Library UCB 106: Page layout, prose section	107
22.	Paris, B.N. f. fr. 2094: f. 31r (hand 1)	141
23.	Paris, B.N. f. fr. 2094: f. 68r (hand 2)	142
24.	Paris, B.N. f. fr. 2094: f. 186r (hand 3)	143
25.	Paris, B.N. f. fr. 2094: f. 171v (sketch)	144
26.	Paris, B.N. f. fr. 2094: f. 209r (doodles)	145
27.	Paris, B.N. f. fr. 2094: Page layout, ff. 1r-50v	146
28.	Paris, B.N. f. fr. 2094: Page layout, ff. 51r-171v	147
29.	Paris, B.N. f. fr. 2094: Page layout, ff. 172r-221v	148

List of Tables

1. Genres Occurring Most Frequently in the Subpopulation   5
2. B.N. f. fr. 2162, Organization of the Volume   43
3. B.N. f. fr. 1374, Organization of the Volume   79
4. UCB 106, Organization of the Volume   108
5. UCB 106, Detail of Painted Decoration   111
6. UCB 106, Contents of the *Vie des Pères*   114
7. B.N. f. fr. 2094, Organization of the Volume   149
8. B.N. f. fr. 2094, Contents of the *Vie des Pères*   152

Acknowledgments

I have benefited from the generous assistance of many in the course of this study, which began as a seminar project. I would like to express my gratitude to Professor Hans Ulrich Gumbrecht for stimulating the discussions that helped me shape the idea in its early development and for his insightful and reassuring comments at various junctures.

Fellowships from the French government and from the Regents of the University of California made it possible for me to consult manuscripts at the Bibliothèque Nationale and files at the Section Romane of the Institut de Recherche et d'Histoire des Textes in Paris during the first phase of research.

I especially appreciate the kind interest and provocative suggestions of Miss Marie-Thérèse d'Alverny and Mr. Ezio Ornato and of Professors Bernard Cerquiglini, Ian Short, and Jean Rychner, who gave generously of their time to discuss the project with me during my year abroad. I am grateful to the staffs of the Bibliothèque Nationale and the Institut de Recherche et d'Histoire des Textes for their assistance, and particularly to Miss Anne-Françoise Labie of the Section Romane. For his help in the course of my examination of the manuscript UCB 106 I am indebted to Mr. Anthony Bliss of the Bancroft Library.

I would like to express my appreciation to Professors Carol Clover and Charles Faulhaber for their careful reading and valuable suggestions. During the summer of 1988 I participated in an NEH seminar at Berkeley, where I was able to discuss the project with others interested in similar issues; I am particularly grateful to Professor Anne Middleton for reading and commenting on chapter 5. Finally, I owe special thanks to Professor Joseph Duggan, who has supported my endeavors with indispensable advice and encouragement at every stage.

1
Introduction
Selection of Examples and Theoretical Frame

In their effort to reach a medieval author's original writings, textual critics have regarded the scribe as an impediment. The editor would prefer him to be transparent, leaving no trace of his own ideology, taste, knowledge, or skill. If the scribe is intelligent, he annoys the scholar by making conscious emendations, while the blunders of a less gifted copyist arouse contempt even though they can be useful in establishing stemmata. When the focus of literary study shifts away from the histories of individual works, however, the scribe appears in a different aspect. He was as much a member of his society and a transmitter of his culture as any author, and his creation is as much a historical artifact as any of the works he transmits.

It is not the skills, mentalities, and milieux of a specific author that are highlighted in this study, but rather those of a handful of anonymous copyists. The period under consideration is not that of the texts' composition, but that of their reception and transmission by these scribes. Although no genre definition limits the corpus of texts, hagiography provides a focus. The investigation combines textual analysis with codicological evidence to uncover the principles of inclusion observed by scribes collecting assorted works into single manuscript volumes.

There have been some isolated studies of this kind. For example, an examination of Latin hagiographic manuscripts in one monastic library reveals superficially by the order of contents, marginalia, and physical details whether each might have been used in the mass (a calendar of feast days) or for private reading (arrangement by specific themes) (Dolbeau 1979). Conclusions about medieval pedagogy appear in a discussion of page layouts and methods of presentation in manuscripts of Latin grammars (Holtz 1977). A study of one Middle French manuscript containing several texts leads to speculations about the principles of inclusion, the potential audience, and the relationship between the scriptorium and its client (Ross 1952). Jean-Claude Schmitt has surveyed collections of exempla to relate patterns of inclusion and arrangement to the practices of the various religious orders producing the manuscripts (1977).

More recently, Sylvia Huot has addressed the question in her fine study on the development of literary anthologies in the thirteenth and fourteenth centuries (1987). Focusing on courtly lyric, lyrical romance, and *dit*, she traces the rise of the "single-author codex," which culminated in the poetic compilations of Machaut and Froissart. Her argument depends on the assumption that most codices are "carefully organized literary constructs" (ibid., 5), and in her first chapter she calls attention to the scribal voices in eight separate narrative and didactic collections. She goes on to demonstrate the evolution of the poet from singer to writer, "an author figure who subsumes narrator, compiler, lyric poet, and protagonist" (ibid., 337).

The proposition that principles of inclusion existed is fundamental also to this study. Some medieval collections have explicit unifying devices, and often whole blocks of texts are transmitted together in a manuscript tradition. Collections of *fabliaux* and tales such as those found in the work known as the *Vie des Pères*,[1] though less stable than those attributed to authors such as Marie de France, Gautier de Coinci, and Nicole Bozon, clearly reflect the collectors' consciousness of text types. The thirteenth-century manuscripts of the William cycle represent not just a collection of *chansons de geste*, but a standard sequence of texts. Other combinations appear to be randomly selected, and editors occasionally comment on unaccountable juxtapositions. But even a miscellaneous collection has been put together for *some* reason, and its contents might have been as carefully selected as those of a grouping that is homogeneous according to modern conceptions of genre.

A number of questions arise concerning what works were available to a scribe preparing a given manuscript. Did he make selections from a large collection all in one place? Did he travel in search of materials? Did models circulate among scribes and scriptoria? What role did oral transmission play in the compilation process? Might a scribe simply copy down every text that came into his hands, or all that he found in a library he happened to visit?

Research on medieval book ownership and commerce would add a valuable dimension to studies such as the one I have undertaken, and the answers to these questions would be helpful to the analysis of literary manuscripts. Such answers might go a long way toward substantiating — or disproving — the hypothesis that scribes observed principles of inclusion. Given the improbability of our ever being able to ascertain exactly what materials were or were not available to a scribe, however, I am obliged to concede the possibility of accidental combinations. Randomness may be implied by the possibility that the scribe had access to limited materials and copied everything available. It seems unlikely, however, that this occurred very often. If it had, there should be numerous examples surviving of single-text manuscripts or of miscellaneous groups of texts copied

---

[1] See below, pp. 86-88.

together. Having surveyed the contents of hundreds of manuscripts, I find this not to be the case.

For convenience, in this book the word "scribe" is used to refer not just to the copyist, but also to the person or persons responsible for the combination of texts in any given manuscript. In some cases this will have been the copyist himself, while in others one or more copyists worked at the behest of a client, a patron, or the director of a scriptorium who may have requested, for example, a collection of specified works, of works of a particular type, or of works containing certain kinds of material. I also distinguish between the "work" and its versions, each a different text (Zumthor 1972a, 73).

Unless otherwise specified, quotations are cited from the manuscript, with line references to the published version, when available. I have added modern punctuation and capitalized verse and sentence initials and proper nouns. Diacritical marks are supplied, but I have not normalized, corrected, or emended the texts. Italics represent resolutions of scribal abbreviations. Obvious scribal errors are signaled by [*sic*], and brackets enclose additions where I have conjectured to fill a gap. Lines of verse are represented as they appear in the manuscript.

Since the study treats entire manuscripts rather than individual texts, I am obliged to rely to a greater than usual degree on past scholarship, which varies enormously not only in quality, but also in critical orientation. It is on the topics most crucial to my concerns — manuscript traditions, scribal and authorial language, and literary analysis — that textual critics provide the most uneven illumination, and many of the works under consideration have never appeared in modern editions. It is beyond the scope of this project to undertake new research on individual works.

Focusing on individual cases, the study attempts to reconstruct the process of selection and principles of inclusion observed for each combination of texts. This leads in turn to conclusions concerning the nature of medieval hagiography, which embraces a wide variety of themes as well as forms. Having selected as examples manuscripts that contain at least one saint's life, I am in a position to contribute to the accessibility of this rich corpus by suggesting categories that might be useful to the modern historian of the Middle Ages. Before beginning the analysis of the manuscripts, however, it is necessary first to describe and explain my selection of examples, and then to provide a theoretical framework for the articulation of my observations.

In the first phase of research I took as my starting point the traditionally defined saint's life. Using published catalogues,[2] lists of manuscripts in published editions of

---

[2] A survey of the catalogues for libraries likely to own manuscripts containing Old French was made at the Institut de Recherche et d'Histoire des Textes, which has a large reference collection for codicology. Catalogues with subject indexes were searched for saints' lives, and others were scanned for manuscripts dating to the thirteenth century. The survey included major European university, national, and municipal libraries. Forty-three of the manuscripts in the subpopulation are found in the *Catalogue des manuscrits*

saints' lives, and the files of the Institut de Recherche et d'Histoire des Textes in Paris, I compiled a list of thirteenth-century vernacular manuscripts containing one or more texts labeled "vie de saint" and written in verse.[3] This subpopulation of eighty-three manuscripts approaches comprehensiveness, but it is neither exhaustive nor positively defined: the texts were labeled at different times and perhaps according to different criteria, and manuscript dating is usually approximate and sometimes equivocal. The chronological and generic restrictions were intended to identify a manageable quantity of manuscripts that would be somehow representative of the corpus of medieval manuscripts as a whole.

To continue with the scientific model for settling on a representative sample from the subpopulation, I should have developed a typology of combinations and selected a manuscript of each type for close analysis. My survey of manuscript contents in the subpopulation, however, confirms the inappropriateness of the scientific model for this purpose. While I have made a distinction between manuscripts containing only pious works and those that have at least one text of a secular genre,[4] there is too great a variety among the combinations of texts to yield any meaningful typology based on generic distinctions. An attempt to group them according to textual combination simply produces as many categories as there are manuscripts.

Table 1 provides a summary description of the subpopulation according to contents, listing the number of codices containing one or more examples of each genre. Many of the genre designations are tenuous, especially for pious works. Some genres were easily recognizable by the cataloguers, but others were no doubt misunderstood owing to the discontinuity in literary tradition. Medieval works often bore misleading labels, if any (cf. Fowler 1982, 142-47).

All the manuscripts are predominantly literary, as opposed to liturgical or documentary. With a few exceptions, and excluding rubrics and marginalia, they are also all predominantly in the vernacular. Most of the texts found in combination with saints' lives are narrative. The principal exceptions are sermons and didactic and scientific

---

français: Ancien fonds (1867-95) and other Bibliothèque Nationale catalogues; significant numbers are also held by the British Museum (nine), the libraries of Oxford and of Cambridge (seven), the Bibliothèque l'Arsenal in Paris (six), and the regional public libraries of France (seven).

[3] Factitious collections, consisting of texts copied separately and bound together at a later date, have been excluded from the subpopulation.

[4] It might be argued that what we now consider secular works were no less pious than others generically identified as hagiographic. That a medieval audience would have recognized this distinction, however, is reflected in prologues recommending the speaker's text over any number of "fictional" genres. For example, the prologue to the *Pater Noster* gloss in B.N. f. fr. 2162 identifies it as a prayer ("orison") rather than a "lai/ conte, fauble, ne auenture" (f. 119ra14-15); the *Quinze signes du jugement* in B.N. f. fr. 2094 complains that men would rather hear about Roland and Oliver than about the Passion (f. 195ra21-24).

Table 1

Genres Occurring Most Frequently in the Subpopulation

Genre	Number of Manuscripts			
	Large Miscellanies	Secular	Pious	Total
Saints' lives	8	21	46	83[a]
Marian miracles	4	1	19	24
Tales from the *Vie des Pères*	2	7	11	20
Sermons	0	1	7	8
Prayers	2	3	4	9
Biblical adaptations	5	4	10	19
Miscellaneous pious works	6	7	23	36
Romances	5	11	0	16
Chansons de geste	1	2	0	3
Fabliaux	5	2	0	7
Chronicles	2	3	0	5
Scientific works	3	5	4	12
Didactic works	4	6	7	17
Lyric poems	2	4	0	6
Plays	0	1	0	1

[a] 75 plus 8 *libelli*

literature, with a smattering of prayers, psalms, lyric, and religious drama. *Chansons de geste* occur in only a few of the manuscripts; chronicles, romances, and biblical adaptations are much more common. Short verse narratives commonly referred to as *contes dévots* occur more frequently than any other genre. These include Marian miracles, tales of the *Vie des Pères*, and parables.

Many hagiographic texts in verse come down to us in manuscripts containing very large collections of material. A few contain as many as seventy or eighty items, both long and short. No two of these manuscripts are alike; each has a particular character that implies its function. Most are combinations of religious and secular works, but a few contain predominantly devotional texts. The great *fabliaux* manuscripts B.N. f. fr. 837, 1553, and 19152 all contain saints' lives in verse.

Some codices are limited to one saint's life or to a series of texts concerning one saint. Such a genre exists among Latin hagiographic manuscripts, but the vernacular verse examples certainly served vastly different purposes. A Latin *libellus* might "certify" the relics possessed by a monastery, while the metrical French version of a later period would be of particular interest to laymen named for or otherwise personally connected with the saint.[5]

Most manuscripts containing vernacular verse saints' lives have somewhere between five and twenty items each, and among these there are nearly twice as many collections of religious texts as there are manuscripts containing one or more secular works.

The distribution of genres among large miscellanies, secular collections, and pious collections raises certain questions for eventual consideration. Tales from the *Vie des Pères* appear more often in secular manuscripts than do Marian miracles, an otherwise closely related genre. When *fabliaux* occur with saints' lives, it is most often in very large collections. Didactic and scientific works are distributed relatively evenly. The pattern of distribution will become more intelligible as the various principles of inclusion come to light.

Other than Marian miracles, works of a single author, and tales of the *Vie des Pères*, there are no combinations of texts copied together from one manuscript to another. Certain works have affinities that might draw various versions of them together in more than one manuscript. For example, the life of Saint Margaret occurs in books of hours (e.g., New York, Pierpont Morgan 754, and Paris, Arsenal 570), and the legends of the prostitute saints Thaïs, Mary the Egyptian, and Mary Magdalene are found together with each other and with other texts advocating a rejection of worldly pleasure (e.g., Paris, B.N. f. fr. 19525 and 23112). The life of Saint Alexis, *Li ver de Couloigne*, and a

---

[5] A *libellus* is a codex containing a single saint's life or the "dossier" of one saint, including, for example, his or her biography along with a record of miracles and a report on the translation of his or her relics. Of the eight vernacular *libelli* in this subpopulation five are concerned with insular saints: three with Saint Edward the Confessor, one with Saint Thomas Becket, and one with Saint Alban.

Introduction

parable from *Barlaam et Josaphat* called the *Dit de l'unicorne* are found together (along with diverse other texts) in two manuscripts, B.N. f. fr. 2162 and B.N. f. fr. 12471.

The subpopulation I have just described can be regarded as a representative corpus, since the use of the saint's life as a reference point is not wholly arbitrary. It has a relatively stable traditional generic definition, providing a uniform point of reference and control. While it was widely distributed in the thirteenth century, thus ensuring a broad sample, for modern audiences it barely passes as literature, and yields a spectrum of texts less subject to aesthetic expectations and more valuable as evidence. The boundaries of the thirteenth century define a specific period of vernacular textual *mouvance* in writing. Twelfth-century manuscripts reflect distinct transmission conditions not pertaining to the problem of collection (see Short and Woledge 1981); in my survey of manuscript catalogues during the first phase of research I observed that fourteenth-century manuscripts reflect a relatively consistent tradition of textual combination, perhaps due to the establishment of commercial vernacular book production.

I have alluded to the great variety among combinations of texts in vernacular manuscripts. In this respect the corpus of Latin hagiographic manuscripts differs significantly from the subpopulation surveyed here. Characterizing medieval man as a codifier and a system builder, C. S. Lewis remarks that "there was nothing which medieval people liked better or did better, than sorting out and tidying up." "Of all our modern inventions," he quips, "I suspect that they would most have admired the card index" (Lewis [1964] 1967, 10). A codicological study corroborating Lewis's synthesis appears in *Les légendiers latins et autres manuscrits hagiographiques* by Guy Philippart (1977). Philippart's project began as a study of the textual tradition of the passion of Saint Cyprian. While he cites general studies of legendaries and monographs on particular libraries or manuscripts, his own investigation involves a subpopulation of manuscripts containing his text, which he calls an *échantillon*, or representative sample, added to a list of legendaries. The first chapter of the study, entitled "Définition du genre," proposes a glossary for the classification of manuscripts containing hagiography. More categories emerge in his discussion of the structure and contents of legendaries. Philippart's categories, some of which derive from medieval prefaces and catalogues, include types of collections (legendaries, lectionaries, homilaries, martyrologies, *abbreviationes*, *libelli*, passionaries, and the *Vitae Patrum*), methods of organization (alphabetical, *circulum anni*, or according to types of saints), and types of saints (confessors/martyrs, men/women, apostles, "doctors," monks and hermits, saints of certain orders, local or regional saints, national saints, saints whose relics are collected at a certain place).

Keeping in mind C. S. Lewis's view of the medieval "card-index mentality," we would expect to find similar categories obtaining in the compilation of medieval vernacular collections, or at least a few analogues to the nonliturgical Latin manuscripts. In fact, some Old French *prose* legendaries are direct translations of thirteenth-century

Latin collections. However, the subpopulation I have defined suggests a completely different mental portrait. What can be inferred from the divergence in the codicological evidence?

In "Information, Codification, and Metacommunication," Gregory Bateson has distinguished between two types of decision process that may characterize personalities or cultures (1966). He calls them, respectively, selective and progressional integration. In the selective mode, the individual chooses from a static field of categorized alternatives based on past experience. For example, in selecting an apple, we all draw on our past experience of categories of fruit and of varieties of apples. Progressional integration, on the other hand, is contextual and dynamic. Thus an extemporizing dancer's choice is influenced more by the ongoing sequence of his actions and those of his partner than by any classification of movements.

Although both modes are probably present to some degree in every human decision, generalities can apply on a cultural level. Bateson contrasts the rigid caste system of Balinese culture, where one must know the caste of an individual before engaging in conversation with him, with the relative freedom of interaction in occidental cultures. Conversely, the Balinese may behave as spontaneously as they wish once social categories have been determined, while occidentals seem to observe a "compulsive categorization of the *details* of behavior" (ibid., 423-25).

Bateson's distinction allows us to consider the possibility that despite the appearance of a lack of organization in the combination of Old French texts, decisions could have been made on the basis of a tradition not characterized by categorization, but no less established than that of Latin hagiography. Oral traditional poetry, though it reaches us in fossilized form, reflects in its composition the situation of extemporaneous performance. I would like to suggest that the influence of the performance tradition is felt not only in the text itself, but in the decision process of the scribe combining texts in a given manuscript. Although in the twelfth and thirteenth centuries vernacular verse texts were not only transmitted but composed in writing, they were still intended primarily for oral recitation. At the same time oral traditional poetry continued to flourish as the vernacular written tradition grew. In the process of compilation, the mentality of the living communication situation seems to have prevailed against that of the written medium.[6]

Manuscript collections have been perceived as heterogeneous because of the failure of generic categories, whether medieval or modern, to explain them. Along with Bateson's distinction between selective and progressional integration, Mikhail Bakhtin's

---

[6] Huot's discussion of B.N. f. fr. 375 corroborates this impression. The scribe who composes the table of summaries, in rhymed couplets, imitates the oral presentation of the *jongleur*, using the first-person plural and including short prayers and invocations. Huot remarks: "The scribe assumes a role analogous to the performer: he is an intermediary between the audience and the story, and the book is the space in which his written 'performance' takes place" (1987, 21-27).

concept of the twofold orientation of genre in reality and Hans Robert Jauss's project of a history of reception provide a meaningful context for the analysis of combinations.

The theory of reception history implies a view of the literary system in motion: each audience represents a different coordinate of time and space. In contrast, a system that identifies the genre of each work according to its context of origin, if not specifically to its author's intention, is static. If we suppose that the selection of texts was made not on the basis of a categorization of fixed alternatives (the selective mode) but as part of an ongoing process (the progressional mode), the appearance of generic heterogeneity need not preclude interpretation of the combinations. The failure of the manuscripts of my sample to "fall" into distinct categories implies that each combination reflects its own distinct principles of inclusion. Similarly, in the process of compilation the extemporaneous choice of each text in a given manuscript suggests not a lack of decision, but a decision based on something other than a static literary system.

I now turn to Bakhtin's theory of genre as a frame for the articulation of observations relating the distinct systems of book production and vernacular literature. A work has, on the one hand, an "internal" orientation based on its thematic unity, its point of view toward the world, and its conceptualization of reality (Medvedev and Bakhtin 1978, 133-34). According to its "external" orientation, on the other hand, the work "presupposes a particular audience," "takes a position between people organized in some way," and "occupies a certain place in everyday life" (ibid., 131). For Bakhtin, genre identity and stability reside in the necessary interdependence between the two orientations. The principles of reception theory, however, present the possibility of analyzing a work's "internal" aspects in terms of its context of origin, while interpreting the "external" orientation as polyvalent, a function of its context of reception.

My approach to the analysis of the manuscripts integrates Bakhtin's concept of dual orientation with Jauss's aim of reconstructing a work's horizon of expectations.

> For the specific disposition toward a particular work that the author anticipates from the audience can also be arrived at, even if explicit signals are lacking, through three generally presupposed factors: first, through familiar norms or the immanent poetics of the genre; second, through the implicit relationships to familiar works of the literary-historical surroundings; and third, through the opposition between fiction and reality, between the poetic and the practical function of language, which is always available to the reflective reader during the reading as a possibility of comparison. (Jauss 1982, 24)

Jauss's study emphasizes the "audience's disposition" rather than the "author's anticipation," and the second of the three implicit factors: its companion works in a collection constitute the "literary-historical surroundings" of a given text.

Accordingly, each text is first considered in turn as a version of a particular work, as an example of its genre, and, as far as possible, in terms of its context of origin. This part of the analysis is confined to the "internal" orientation of the text.[7] It may not always be evident how the discussion of the texts' internal orientation pertains to the analysis of textual combination. I believe, nevertheless, that such a comprehensive overview provides essential background to the eventual interpretation of the manuscript's function.

I then take into account the articulation between texts, including, where applicable, page layout, rubrics, paragraphing, incipits and explicits, prologues, and tables of contents. For some manuscripts, these codicological details provide valuable clues to an understanding of the scribe's overall purpose. Such details pertain to the "place in everyday life," the situation of communication, and thus the "external" orientation of the texts.

Maintaining this orientation, a "hermeneutics of question and answer" will then relate each text to its literary-historical context as indicated by the other texts in the manuscript. The sequence of texts is considered, as well as the overall combination.

In some cases we will find clear connections between juxtaposed texts, from which we might plausibly infer that the scribe got the idea of including the second as he copied or read over the first. If he was commissioned to include certain works or had a limited selection of works available to him at the time, he may have decided upon a particular sequence based on such affinities as my analysis reveals. Some sequential links, however, appear weak or superficial. Here I would suggest that the scribe worked from a global conception of the collection's purpose. Sequence may have been less generally motivated than global unity, although numerous examples suggest that scribes intentionally juxtaposed some texts. In the absence of evidence that would explain how scribes were instructed or how they proceeded in their work, I think it most useful to propose that *both* kinds of process may have occurred in the production of any given combination, and to approach the combinations accordingly.

Analyzed in this way, each manuscript provides a synchronic cross section of texts that, regardless of their various origins, were simultaneously available (Jauss 1982, 37). I will aim to interpret the dialogue among texts in terms of each manuscript's function in social life, the function, presumably, that motivated the scribe's selection, and that determined the principles of inclusion he more or less deliberately observed.

The theoretical notions informing this study are meant to facilitate the fullest possible description of examples. A focus on the manuscript as a unity adds a concrete dimension to the study of literature, for, unlike the composition of the texts themselves, the confection of a given codex can be attributed to a finite, if not always clearly identifiable, number of individual purposes. Our perspective on the medieval literary system, blurred

---

[7] A listing of manuscript contents at the end of each chapter includes titles (where available), incipits, explicits, information about language, date, and meter, bibliography, and plot summaries to supplement discussion of the individual texts.

by the *mouvance* of texts and the elusiveness of origins and of authors, will be accordingly sharpened by the elucidation of even a few specific cases. It is not as a microcosm but rather as the vestige of a particular event, a "transient example," in the process of literary production that each manuscript can offer us a glimpse of the system.

The choice of manuscripts for close analysis reflects the variety among combinations of texts and includes some of the most frequently occurring works. I have excluded large miscellanies, which contain so many texts as to obscure the issue of principles of inclusion. Manuscripts containing only one text (the saint's life) also fall outside the scope of this study. Two "religious" and two "secular" manuscripts have been selected.

B.N. f. fr. 2162 begins with a "Bible" and constitutes a kind of catechism on confession and penance. Romance and epic texts with hagiographic tendencies are combined in B.N. f. fr. 1374. UCB 106 opens with the *Vie des Pères*, a collection of pious *fabliau*-like tales, and closes with two branches of the vulgate Grail cycle, among romances the most religious in character. Finally, the life of Saint Francis, a collection of miracles, and a collection of texts with popular eschatological themes are combined in B.N. f. fr. 2094.

2
Confession and Penance
Sincere Observance as a Means of Salvation

TEXTS

Herman de Valenciennes, *Bible*
Gautier de Coinci, "Dou riche et de la veve fame"
Life of Saint Jehan Paulus
"De le nonain ki Deu desiroit a vir"
"D'une none ki fu trop biele"
"Li miracles del capiel de roses"
"D'un clerc cui Nostre Dame delivra de se feme"
Sacristine
Gautier de Coinci, "D'un moigne qui fu ou fleuve"
Dit de l'unicorne et du serpent
Life of Saint Thaïs
Life of Saint Margaret
Silvestres, *Pater Noster*
Life of Saint Alexis
Li ver de Couloigne

    Herman de Valenciennes's *Bible*, the opening text of B.N. f. fr. 2162, offers an especially appropriate departure for the study of medieval hagiographic collections: it is itself a compilation of biblical extracts. Except for references such as "si *com* trovons escrit" (l. 474 Spiele, f. 7r16),[1] which it has in common with other vernacular works claiming veracity, the text is silent concerning its immediate sources. J. Bonnard ([1884] 1967, 110) claims it is based on a Latin compilation, while Friedrich Mehne (1900, 11) posits the poet's direct access to and liberal adaptation of the ultimate sources, Scripture and the church fathers. Suggesting it was somehow based on the liturgical calendar and

---

[1] A line reference to the published text (when available) is followed by an indication of the folio, side, column (where applicable), and line in the manuscript. See p. 3 above for a statement of editorial policy.

the ecclesiastical year, Ina Spiele cites Jean Leclercq's remark that "la source principale de la formation biblique des hommes du moyen âge était la liturgie" (1975, 393 n. 13; Leclercq 1963, 127).

From this brief discussion of the work's possible sources, we turn to a consideration of the assortment of versions found in the various manuscripts, followed by observations concerning its generic identity and a discussion of its context of origin.

In order to make sense of the manuscript tradition, Spiele has broken the work down into its constituent parts to produce a table showing which of them are contained in each of the thirty-three manuscripts. While the contents do provide a system for assembling the manuscripts into "groups," no attempt has ever succeeded in producing a philologically grounded stemma for the entire work. A team of editors at Greifswald gives family groupings for several parts of the work (see Spiele 1975, 158-59);[2] however, these families only partially correspond from section to section. Moreover, the sections on Genesis, the Passion, and the Assumption seem more or less detachable and are often omitted or found independently (Smeets 1970, 88). The complexity of the manuscript tradition contributes enormously to the problems facing any prospective editor of a work represented by such a large number of witnesses. Spiele's study brings it into print for the first time, not as a critical edition or even as a "best manuscript": she gives no special reason for the selection of B.N. f. fr. 20039. (See Spiele 1975, 160-61.)

The foregoing remarks provide some context for the consideration of the text in B.N. f. fr. 2162 as a version of the work. It is normal for medieval vernacular works to reflect a large degree of textual *mouvance*, but often those attributed to authors (as opposed to anonymous texts) have more consistent manuscript traditions. In this case, however, the attribution seems not to be accompanied by a more stable text. Mehne contrasts the text of B.N. f. fr. 2162, which he considers anomalous, with the version in MS 1, 4, 2*, 1 of the Fürstlich Oettingen-Wallersteinschen Bibliothek at Maihingen (Bavaria), now at the castle of Harburg (Donauwörth). He regards the Maihingen manuscript as a representative of the group including B.N. f. fr. 20039 (Spiele's no. 6 and "base" manuscript) along with several other manuscripts (Mehne 1900, 4). Spiele, on the other hand, includes B.N. f. fr. 2162 (no. 4) and the Maihingen manuscript (no. 18) in the same group (1975, 159). A review of some significant divergences between the Maihingen manuscript and B.N. f. fr. 2162, as surveyed by Mehne, will give an indication of the scope of variation to be found in the manuscript tradition as a whole.

First, the version in B.N. f. fr. 2162 contains six passages composed in couplets, ranging in length from 12 to 247 verses. Mehne takes this as evidence of a redactor's work (1900, 6). In addition, this redactor includes allegorical interpretations in his versifications of the marriage feast at Cana, the story of the woman taken in adultery, and the awakening of the dead (the daughter of Jairus, the widow's son at Naim, and

---

[2] The team was made up of O. Moldenhauer, H. Burkowitz, E. Kremers, E. Martin (1914).

Lazarus) and expands the interpretation of the gifts of the three kings. The beginning of the Exodus section is more detailed in this version, and the story of Simeon is added. The Passion, headed by the rubric "li [sic] soufrance Ihesucrist" (f. 65v1) is written entirely in verses assonanced in [e]. If such variations are to be found between versions considered by one editor to belong to the same group, the breadth of variation among less closely related witnesses must be very significant indeed.

In conjunction with the manuscript tradition, the text's formal and stylistic traits evince close affinities with vernacular genres, particularly epic: Bonnard called it a "*chanson de geste* ecclésiastique" ([1884] 1967, 41). The text refers to itself as a "cansons" as well as a "livres" and a "lechon" (f. 1r31, 1, 14). The poet frequently summons his listeners' attention and reminds them of the truth and importance of his subject. He dramatizes important episodes by inventing lively dialogue, which could easily be adapted for theatrical performance. His descriptions often expand on the biblical source, using more vivid and precise vocabulary. Many episodes are shortened or suppressed, while others are exaggerated or enhanced: the strife between Jacob and Esau in Rebecca's womb, for example, is presented as a veritable epic battle (f. 9r-v); poignant monologues express both Jacob's and Rachel's grief at the apparent loss of Joseph (f. 16r-v) (see Mehne 1900, 43-52). The poem is much more than a translation: the biblical material has been virtually reconstructed to compete with the most entertaining secular narrative.

Turning now to the question of author and origin, we will find good reasons to relinquish the notion of a single author (Herman), sitting at his desk in the scriptorium with his sources spread out in front of him and composing the whole work, in favor of a series of poets, perhaps *beginning* with, and certainly *including*, a Herman, each bearing in his memory word for word whole passages of Scripture and liturgy along with the basic chronology of biblical events (see Leclercq 1963; Mehne 1900, 11). Bonnard cites several "corrupt" manuscripts containing the names of what I would regard as some of those who contributed to the work (Hervien, Hernaut, Chermans, Guillaume or Willemme, Thomas) ([1884] 1967, 38-40). Paul Meyer places Herman's birth in 1167 and the poem's composition in 1189.[3] While John Robert Smeets notes that closer study of the genesis and structure of the work is needed for more accurate dating (1970, 87), the nature and extent of variations and accretions persuade us to consider it as more the creative property of an entire community over the course of several decades than the original composition of an individual poet.

Just as the *Bible* of Herman de Valenciennes might appear on the surface to be an integral text, the eight tales that follow it (ff. 77r-104vb), headed by the rubric "Chi commence li miracles de nostre dame," may seem to be excerpted from an established collection. Only the first and last stories come from Gautier de Coinci, however, while

---

[3] For a discussion of the evidence advanced for dates by Bonnard ([1884] 1967, 33-38) and Meyer (1891, 202), among others, see Smeets 1970, 87.

the rest are more or less independent texts. Two are versions of stories also told by Gautier (texts 7 and 8),[4] one of which appears in the *Vie des Pères* as well (text 8).[5] Jean Morawski notes that these two apparently imitate Gautier's style of composing in *rimes riches*, and attributes two of the other tales, for stylistic reasons, to the same author (1935, 172-74).[6] Since the first and last tales are copied from Gautier de Coinci, and since four of the other texts resemble his work, I am tempted to speculate that the compiler wanted to give the impression of an integral copy.[7] After briefly describing the stories, I will take up their generic identities and context of origin as a group.

Each of the "miracles" is announced by a rubric. The first (ff. 77r-80vb) is entitled "D'un priestre, d'un userier et d'une vieillette" (Koenig 1955, 2: 158-80). There is a fourth main character, a "dyakenes" or cleric who, though he is not mentioned in any of the rubrics listed in Frédéric Koenig's apparatus (ibid., 158), experiences miraculous visions.

The second of the eight texts (ff. 81ra-94ra), preceded by the rubric "De saint Jehan Paulus," has no Marian emphasis. It is much longer than the others in this group (2,078 lines) and is composed in two distinct parts: the vision of Saint Basil (an underworld journey) and a biography of Saint Jehan Paulus. Two important studies have been devoted to the development and the various versions of the legend (Williams and Allen 1935; Morawski 1947).

Charles Williams discusses the Western Christian legend in terms of the vast, old tradition of the beast man, one representative of which is the Enkidu episode of *Gilgamesh*. In Williams's view it represents the persistence of a pagan myth in which the king of a barren land sends a courtesan to seduce the god of fertility (Williams and Allen 1935, 9-10). Morawski studies the Romance tradition more closely, tracing the French redaction to a Catalan legend apparently linked to historical realities (1947, 15-17).

Louis Karl's articles on the *Vie de Saint Jehan Paulus* (1913 and 1928) use the text of B.N. f. fr. 2162 as a base; he remarks that it varies little from the other two copies

---

[4] See the list of contents beginning on p. 44.

[5] An anonymous collection represented in at least thirty-eight manuscripts, the *Vie des Pères* includes a wide variety of pious tales in addition to lives of desert fathers. See chapters 4 and 5 for a more detailed description.

[6] This article on Old French miracles in verse contains a section entitled "Interpolation du ms. fr. 2162 de la Bibl. nat." (pp. 168-74) where the author focuses on the texts not attributed to Gautier de Coinci, and reserves comment on the second item, the life of Jehan Paulus, for a later article (see Morawski 1947). He edits the fifth text, "D'un clerc cui Nostre Dame delivra de se feme," in the second part of the earlier article (1935, 326-35).

[7] For a more detailed account of Gautier's work, see chapter 4, pp. 88-90.

(1913, 426-27).[8] There is a version of the legend in prose,[9] as well as a miracle play (Paris and Robert 1880, 5: 89-151). According to Karl, the play gives an important role to the Virgin, focusing on the crime and the miracle while omitting Saint Basil's vision and the biographical details of Jehan's and his mother's lives. In the play, the devil disguises himself as the hermit's valet, "Huet" (Karl 1913, 441- 45).

The two parts of the story are carefully combined by the poet: he reinforces the link with numerous references to Pope Basil, who had special knowledge of Jehan's destiny, and it is near the end of the story that we learn of Jehan's great-grandmother's salvation, foretold by her tormented soul during Basil's journey through hell. Thus merged, the two sections nevertheless reflect distinctly different traditions and belong to separate classes of hagiographic tales.

The first line of the poem claims as its source the *Vitae Patrum*. The Latin collection does contain a life of Saint Basil, but its hero is a bishop, not a pope; he experiences no visions but retires from the world to live as an anchorite. The first part of the poem belongs rather to the popular tradition of otherworld journeys. It imitates Saint Paul's descent into hell, of which there exist seven Old French versions tracing their origins to an eighth-century Latin translation of the lost third-century Greek legend.[10] The second part of the poem, in the form of a biography, has a number of analogues among Old French works. The life of Jehan Paulus's mother resembles that of the Virgin Mary, both in its content and in its function as a link between the two parts of the legend. Mary belongs to the Old Testament as a descendant of David, to the New as the mother of Jesus. The genealogical tie between related stories occurs similarly in epic narrative (see Karl 1913, 437). Jehan's return to his father's house resembles an episode in the life of Saint Alexis (Karl 1913, 438), and his mother's death echoes that of Perceval's mother in the *Conte du Graal*. The hermit's double crime of seduction and murder occurs in a tale in the Old French *Vie des Pères* that is traced by its editor to oriental models (Bornäs 1968, 26-32). Karl also mentions elements analogous to episodes in the lives of Saint Alban and of Saint John Chrysostome (1913, 437-40). The text is generically hybrid (an otherworld journey combined with biography) and of manifold inspiration, though it has a convincing narrative coherence.

The following text (ff. 94ra-96rb) is headed by the rubric "De le nonain ki deu desiroit a vir." Only one other copy of this work is known (B.N. f. fr. 24431), and other versions differ widely in detail. According to Morawski this is the only version

---

[8] Paris, B.N. f. fr. 1553 and Arsenal 3518(2).

[9] Florence, Laurencian Med.-Pal. 141, dated 1399; summary by Paul Meyer (1904, 1-49); published in Williams and Allen 1935, 134-40.

[10] Owen 1958; Jauss 1970, 240-42. See p. 130 below for a discussion of the version of Saint Paul's descent occurring in B.N. f. fr. 2094.

with a nun as the protagonist, and it alone omits the child's explicit announcement that he is the Lord. Though the text mentions a recitation ("Un miracle k'oï l'atrier," l. 7), and a tale in the collection of Caesar of Heisterbach features the apparition of a three-year-old Christ (*Dial. mirac.*, viii, 8), no direct source has been confirmed (Morawski 1935, 169-79). This version lacks any Marian emphasis, though a prose miracle exists in which the Virgin allows a nun to hold her baby.

Another unusual prayer is answered in the next miracle (ff. 96rb-97ra), "D'une none ki fu trop biele." No source is known for this miracle, the shortest text in the manuscript (136 lines), although it corresponds to a tale type in which a girl disfigures herself to avoid marriage and to preserve her chastity (Morawski 1935, 170 n. 2; 197-98).

The protagonist of the next tale "Li miracles del capiel de roses" (ff. 97ra-99vb) is the son of a rich widow. The tale probably derives from one in the collection of Marian miracles in B.N. ms. lat. 18134. There is also a *miracle par personnages* developed from the same source; later versions in Latin and French prose alter many elements (Morawski 1935, 171-72).

The rubric "D'un clerc cui Nostre Dame delivra de se feme" announces the next miracle (ff. 99vb-102ra), which belongs to the cycle of the "Fiancé de la Vierge" (see Morawski 1935, 172; Morawski 1938, 472-73). Gautier de Coinci includes in his collection a version of this story known as the "Clerc de Pise" (Koenig 1955, 4: 340-77).

The next text (ff. 102ra-103vb) is a version of the well-known tale "Sacristine," which appears in almost all French miracle collections (according to Morawski 1935, 172). Like the story of the cleric, it has an analogue among Gautier de Coinci's *Miracles*, "De la nonain" (Koenig 1955, 3: 191-212).

The last in this group of "miracles" (ff. 103vb-104vb), announced by the rubric "D'un moine ki fu noiés," was composed by Gautier de Coinci (Koenig 1955, 3: 165-73).[11]

The texts of this small "miracle" collection come from diverse sources and have traditions of varying breadth. Though the rubricator calls them "li miracles de Nostre Dame," they also have diverse generic identities. A miracle may be described as the narrative of a supernatural event demonstrating, on the one hand, divine approval of certain behaviors or practices, or, on the other hand, a saint's magical power. In the case of miracles of the Virgin, the saint in question is Mary, whose power seems in some texts to eclipse that of God himself.[12] The protagonists of these stories range from the most pious and humble to the most proud and sinful. Mary demonstrates the fullest

---

[11] The copy in B.N. f. fr. 2162 ends at line 214 in Koenig's edition, which has a total of 642 lines.

[12] Spangenberg [1980]; Ebel 1965, 13-18. Though the genre definition of the Marian miracle remains problematic, a description such as this is helpful in making comparisons between texts.

extent of her power when she rewards the devotion toward her demonstrated by the greatest sinners.

In a broad sense the eight stories do belong to such a category. Not all of them, however, feature the Virgin as a magical helper. She miraculously *appears* in the first tale (text 2 of the manuscript), without performing any supernatural feats. She is absent from texts 4 and 5, and unnamed (though there is little doubt of her identity) in text 6. Moreover, the story of Jehan Paulus, while it does recount miracles, is better described as a combination of vision and saint's life than as a miracle or even a *conte*.

The context of origin of the collection, which appears to be the scribe's own work, consists in all likelihood in the confection of this manuscript. In other words, the texts designated as "li miracles de Nostre Dame" by the rubricator were *not* copied together from another manuscript. No explicit signals the end of the group, unless one appeared on a hypothetical missing folio.[13] The miracles of Gautier de Coinci that open and close the section lend an effect of symmetry, which may or may not have impressed the contemporary audience, and could have been used to deceive a client who had requested a copy of Gautier's *Miracles de Nostre Dame*.

The tenth text of the manuscript (ff. 105ra-107ra), like the collection of miracles, is written in octosyllabic rhymed couplets. The title has been supplied by a later hand: "De licorne et del serpent." The poem exists in more than a dozen copies, including B.N. f. fr. 2094, also treated in this study (see Långfors 1917, 227). An extract from *Barlaam et Josaphat*, its origins can be traced to India (Le Clerc [1856] 1895, 257). Though it has been referred to as a *dit*, the genre designation of this text remains unclear.

The life of Saint Thaïs occurring in B.N. f. fr. 2162 (text 11, ff. 107ra-115ra) is an extract from the *Poème moral*.[14] Two other extant versifications belong to the Old French *Vie des Pères* and to the works of Henri d'Arci, respectively (Meyer 1906a, 375). The *Poème moral* is represented by twelve manuscripts, none of which contain the entire text, and some of which have only the *Thaïs* section (Bayot [1929], x-xxiv). Latin treatises on confession and penance may have inspired the poet, though none have been confirmed as sources.[15] Like the other two versions, this biography can be traced to the Latin *Vitae Patrum* (Bayot [1929], clxxix-clxxxii). It is distinguished by long

---

[13] My discussion of codicological details raises this possibility. See pp. 20-21 below.

[14] A thirteenth-century didactic work composed in alexandrines, the *Poème moral* favors confronting and overcoming sin rather than withdrawal from the world. It begins with a discourse on the vanity of pleasure and contains an account of the conversion of "Saint Moses" as well as a life of Saint Thaïs.

[15] *De vera et falsa poenitentia* (*PL* 40, 1114-30), Gratien's *Decretum* (*PL* 187), and the *Quatuor libri sententiarum* of Peter Lombard (*PL* 192, 519-962) are mentioned by Bayot ([1929], clxxxiii-iv).

sections of didactic dialogue and by its verse form, monorhymed quatrains of alexandrines. The reformed prostitute is a popular subject for hagiography.

Another female saint is commemorated in the following story (ff. 155rb-119ra). Twelve verse versions of the life of Saint Margaret survive, including one by the Anglo-Norman poet Wace. Most of these are represented by unique manuscripts, and all but two are in octosyllables (Francis 1932, ix-xi). The version in B.N. f. fr. 2162, however, exists in over a hundred copies, many in books of hours. It follows the same Latin text that Wace translated,[16] but omits certain details of Margaret's torture and amplifies description by means of conventional courtly motifs (ibid., xi).

The next text in B.N. f. fr. 2162 (ff. 119ra-125vb) is an Old French versification of the *Pater Noster*, in a version attributed to Silvestres and represented in three other manuscripts as well (Långfors 1917, 28). Arthur Långfors classifies five of the extant versions as translations and seven as paraphrases (1912). Extending to over a thousand lines, this text is more aptly characterized as a discursive gloss. No edition or major study has undertaken the question of the poem's origin. Preliminary research has not uncovered any Latin source, though Augustine's influence is evident.[17]

The abundant scholarship devoted to the versions and sources of the legend of Saint Alexis, whose biography follows the *Pater Noster* gloss in this manuscript (ff. 125vb-133va), will not be reviewed here. The ultimate source of the story is believed to be a Byzantine or Syrian legend of the fifth century; its immediate source is a Latin prose *vita* of the tenth.[18] In addition to versifications based on the Latin life, there is a tradition of vernacular poems, headed by the celebrated Hildesheim version in Old French, which reflect many features of oral composition and transmission; these share the erroneous place-name Alsis, where Alexis is supposed to have gone when he left his bride. The Latin text and versions derived from it send him to Edessa, referred to in some cases, including that of B.N. f. fr. 2162, as Rohais (Elliott 1983, 13-15). The Alexis legend yields an unusual number of versions *not* in octosyllabic couplets, the verse form favored by the majority of hagiographers writing in Old French. The version in question here, like the *Bible* of Herman de Valenciennes, is in monorhymed laisses of alexandrines.

The last text in the manuscript (ff. 133vb-136vb) is a confession and complaint addressed directly to God. Composed around the middle of the thirteenth century, it

---

[16] Wace's Latin source is represented in Francis's edition by a tenth-century manuscript, B.N. f. lat. 17002.

[17] Augustine is mentioned in the text (f. 124a), and the threefold meaning of "daily bread" comes from his commentary on the Sermon on the Mount (*CCSL* 35, 1967, 104-30). See *Dictionnaire de spiritualité chrétien*, s.v. "Pater Noster."

[18] See Elliott 1983; Stebbins 1974, 1978; Uitti 1967.

survives in two manuscripts (see Kleineidam 1968, 8-9).[19] Although the poem is written in quatrains of monorhymed alexandrines, this version begins with an octosyllabic prologue advising the listeners to read it fervently and in private if they sincerely want to repent. This admonition constitutes a witness to the way books were used in the thirteenth century: it shows that vernacular, as well as Latin, texts might provide subjects for private meditation.

CODICOLOGICAL ARTICULATIONS

While the manuscript on the whole has a homogeneous appearance, a number of codicological details mark the human element in its construction. Eight changes of hand can be distinguished. Folio 66 has been glued onto a stub and coincides with a passage near the beginning of a text of the Passion (part of the *Bible* of Herman de Valenciennes) assonanced almost entirely in [e]. This text opens with the rubric "Li soufrance Ihesucrist" at the top of 65v and proceeds in couplets up to a point eight lines from the bottom of 66r. The scribe, if he is the person responsible for the interpolated passages in couplets, perhaps decided to revise what he had composed on the original folio 66r.

Another break in the manuscript's relatively even pattern occurs in the section containing the eight "miracles." The first six gatherings, senions with uniform signatures and, except for the first gathering, with no catchwords, contain the first text of the manuscript, which ends on the fifth folio of the seventh gathering. The miracle section begins on that same folio and is completed in gatherings 8 and 9, two more senions. Beginning with the tenth gathering, quaternions with catchwords and without Roman numeral signatures make up the remainder of the manuscript. Gathering 9, the last senion, breaks off in the middle of a text: some 428 lines of the miracle of the drowned monk (Koenig 1955, 3: 165-90) are missing. The tenth gathering begins a new text without a rubric (the title was added later) and in a different hand. The fact that the tenth text is the only one in the collection without a rubricated title supports a hypothesis of lost folios: an explicit or rubricated title would have ended the missing section. Though it is unusual for a title to appear at the end of a folio for a text beginning on the next one, this scribe made at least one such articulation: a rubric introducing the text beginning on the verso of folio 77 occurs at the bottom of column 77b.

The juncture of the two sections of the manuscript dominated by senions and by quaternions, respectively, occurs just at this point, and the signatures "x" and modern "11" appear in the *middle* of the tenth gathering, reflecting confusion on the part of the person(s) adding the signatures. Indeed, the section of the manuscript containing the miracles has more variations in inks and handwriting than either the preceding or the

---

[19] The copy in B.N. f. fr. 2162 breaks off midway through the poem. B.N. f. fr. 12471 contains the complete text.

following part. In contrast, gathering 11, for example, begins two new texts (at 115b, 119a) without any significant changes in appearance. The incomplete text, the missing title, and the change in organization together indicate missing folios, or perhaps an entire missing gathering, including the two to three folios needed to conclude the "miracle," together with at least one other text.

It is also possible that the compiler had available to him only limited selections of Gautier de Coinci. This might explain why he interpolated tales from other sources between the two extracts from the *Miracles de Nostre Dame*. If his model lacked a conclusion for the story of the drowning monk, perhaps he thought the unicorn parable would give it a suitable sermonizing finish.

On the other hand, the compiler may have deliberately omitted the ending of Gautier's story (text 9), wishing to begin the next text at the beginning of a new gathering. The miracle breaks off in the midst of a digression on the powers of the Virgin, which could blend almost imperceptibly into the sermonizing text of the *Licorne*, except for the use of an ornamental initial at the beginning of the latter. The lack of narrative closure (what finally happens to the drowned monk?) might have gone unnoticed in this miracle,[20] just as it does in the seventh text (what happens at the wedding banquet after the cleric disappears? how is the miracle revealed?).

Of course it would be more prudent to posit a missing gathering than to attribute specific motives to scribes. We should bear in mind, however, that their intelligence lies behind the compilation, and their possible motives should in any case be considered. Whatever the reason for the missing lines, the rubricator may have simply neglected to give a title to the unicorn parable.

Finally, it is striking that almost exactly half of the *Ver de Couloigne*, by comparison with the other extant copy of that work, is included in B.N. f. fr. 2162. Adding to this the observation that the scribe begins using two lines for each alexandrine verse on folio 134, I am led to believe he may have run out of parchment. Had he used a single line for each verse, as in the *Alexis* text, the complete *Ver* would have exactly filled the gathering. This suggests that someone chose the texts ahead of time to fit a certain amount of parchment, and his calculations were forgotten or ignored when the copies were executed.

ANALYSIS AND INTERPRETATION

Having advanced some speculations concerning the construction of the manuscript, I now turn to textual analysis. Items will first be considered in sequence, as though the scribes made each selection on the basis of the previous text. Finally, I will describe the combination globally.

---

[20] In other copies, the Virgin wins another chance for the monk, and he returns to life.

Was the compiler's selection process sequential, or did he work from a plan or list of texts he wished to include? To begin with, Herman's *Bible* consists of a series of episodes that are generally in chronological order, but to which the poet takes care to give narrative continuity as well (Mehne 1900, 47-48). The selection of episodes emphasizes miraculous revelation of divine power,[21] and the text concludes with the greatest of these, the Resurrection. The poet lingers over the discovery of Christ's empty grave (ff. 75v-76r) and describes how he appears to various people, even eating "corporelment" in the company of 500 brothers (eight lines at the bottom of 76v).[22]

The emphasis on miracles in this text responds to the implied questions of who is favored by God, in the Old Testament section, and whether or not Jesus is the true Son of God, in the section based on the Gospels. Despite their diversity, the eight miracles that follow all respond similarly to the desire for revelation of God's power and of his favor. In addition, each is linked to the next by an interplay of question and response.

The first miracle (text 2 of the manuscript) narrates a cleric's miraculous vision demonstrating the Virgin's favor toward a sincerely devout beggar woman, on the one hand, and her neglect of a rich but unrepentant sinner, on the other. When he arrives at her hovel bringing Holy Communion, the young cleric sees the Virgin and "xii. puceles/Si avenans *et* si tres biele" (ll. 221-22, f. 78vb23-24), at her bedside. Thrilled by the vision, he returns to his *seigneur*, the priest, at the deathbed of the usurer, where he is privileged to witness the torture of the dying man by a hundred or a thousand frightful cats "plus noirs *que* sas a carboniers" (l.302, f. 79rb24). These, of course, represent raging devils anxious to snatch away the dying man's soul. The cleric's implied question, whether or not the old woman and the rich man will receive their respective just deserts, is answered by the glimpses he is allowed of the woman's heavenly reward and of the usurer's eternal punishment.

This preview having whetted the audience's curiosity about the afterlife, the next text, a life of Saint Jehan Paulus, recounts in detail Saint Basil's tour of hell. He witnesses the various torments assigned to different kinds of sinners, ranging from usurers, drunks, and loose women to renegades and sodomites. The narrative is vivid and animated, punctuated by Basil's inquiry and the angel's explanation, as though by a refrain, at each stop. While some of the punishments correspond to the particular weaknesses of the damned (perjurers, for example, are hung from the wheel of torture by their tongues, adulterers by their "membres bas"), the poet does not insist on any hierarchy of sins. The view of paradise sketched toward the end of Jehan Paulus's biography, when he

---

[21] This is true in both Old Testament and New Testament sections. Moses, for example, worries a great deal about how he will convince the people to follow him (see ff. 27v and 28r).

[22] This laisse occurs neither in B.N. f. fr. 20039 nor in the Maihingen manuscript and may have been added by the scribe of B.N. f. fr. 2162, setting the scene in a "convent." The biblical source (1 Cor. 15:6) does not mention the meal, which would prove Christ had returned "in the flesh."

restores to life the princess he had murdered, is only a vignette, but no author before Dante gives full treatment to the celestial landscape.

The roles of magical children link the third and fourth texts of the manuscript. The sanctity of Jehan Paulus is revealed by a baby, miraculously gifted with full powers of speech for the purpose. Living as a hermit, the young Jehan, tempted by the devil, murders the princess of Toulouse. He confesses his crimes to God and, as penance, lives in the forest for ten years as a wild animal. When a hunting party captures him and brings him to the court of Toulouse, the infant reports that Jehan has accomplished his penance and earned the pardon of Christ. The miracle of the nun who wanted to see God depicts a three-year-old Christ child frolicking on her lap: his identity is revealed enticingly by his remark that he has known his *Pater* for a long time, by the sweet odor of his breath, and by his disappearance into the ciborium (f. 96rb-va).

This tale raises a spiritual issue that is addressed in turn by the one following it. The nun's passion and her confession to the abbess, a lengthy dialogue, imply that strong desire is in itself sinful. Although the abbess reassures her, and God ultimately answers her prayer, the text suggests that desire for him is the exception to the rule. The next miracle (text 5) responds to this suggestion by demonstrating that souls might indeed be lost through even unaccomplished carnal lust. When the nun prays to lose her beauty, it is not her own soul she fears for, but those of the men attracted to her (f. 96va). When God miraculously restores her beauty near the end of her earthly life, the audience learns that her disfiguring illness has been the answer to her prayer, and that she had, in fact, had cause to worry about souls lost out of desire for her.

The Virgin returns to the stage in the miracle of the "Capiel de roses," which begins a short series of Marian stories all copied by one scribe. The link between the fifth and sixth texts of the manuscript derives not from a spiritual problematic, but rather from the repetition of a literary convention. The "too beautiful" nun has all the traits of a romance heroine:

> Tant *par* estoit blance *et* vrumelle,
> *Que* cou estoit une miervelle.
> Mu*lt* estoit bien fait a devis:
> Blonc ot le cief *et* cler le vis,
> Traitie *et* coulourés de sanc,
> *Que* bien couvint desour le blans
> *Et* [sic] trop estoit bele a desmesure.
> Toute s'etente mist nature
> A fourmer ses bras *et* ses mains.
> (f. 96rb19-27)

Such descriptions do occur elsewhere in pious literature, but not so frequently that coincidence would necessarily account for the matching portrait in a contiguous text. Several aspects of the story have analogues with other texts of the manuscript, but its description of the "lady of the mule," unidentified by the ill-intentioned witnesses but easily recognized by the audience, echoes the conventional terms of the passage just cited:

> Plus blance que n'est flours de lis,
> De li veoir iert grans delis.
> Tant par estoit blance et vermelle
> Que ce sanbloit une meruelle
> Qu'ele estoit trop bele a devis.
> Doucs [sic] de bouche, de nes, de vis
> De front, de mençon, et de face:
> Ne sai quatre parolle en face.
> Mais tant vos di: onques nature
> Ne fist si bele criature.
> (f. 98vb14-23)

If the audience has been dazzled by the too beautiful nun, the vision experienced by the three "mordriers," who were instantly converted, demonstrates the superior power of the Virgin's celestial beauty. The juxtaposition of the two texts enhances the contrast between the earthly and the divine.

The seventh text, like the tale of the "Capiel de roses," has as its protagonist a rich young cleric devoted to the Virgin Mary. His relatives, concerned lest he "enpire son affaire" (l. 105, f. 100rb39), persuade him to marry. Both texts address the problem of how a devout man may maintain his customs of worship in challenging circumstances brought about by his station in life.

The last four tales of the miracle collection (texts 6 to 9 of the manuscript) all have protagonists who have made their personal devotion to the Virgin Mary part of a daily observance. The opening lines of the seventh and eighth texts run parallel in their presentations of the main characters' special qualities (pious erudition in the case of the cleric; virtuous beauty for the nun) and habits of worship. The contrasting plots of the two stories underscore the social positions of the rich young man and the *sacristine*: since she is a nun, her sexuality makes her an outlaw, and eventually she lives on the margin of society as a prostitute. The cleric's sexuality, on the other hand, is not only sanctioned, but also celebrated in the marriage ceremony. Both are ultimately restored to chastity by virtue of the Virgin's power.

This nun and cleric may be viewed as paired opposites; three other protagonist doublets also occur in the sequence: nuns in texts 4 and 5, rich heirs in 6 and 7, and convent treasurers in 8 and 9.[23] The tales of the *sacristine* and the sacristan have in

---

[23] Although the protagonist of text 9 is not referred to as sacristan, these lines attest to his role in the community: "Signor et maistre fait l'avoient/ Et del tresor et de l'eglise,/ Car molt estoit de boin service" (f. 104ra1-3).

common as well the predicament of characters whose very goodness motivates the devil to tempt them. In each case, the Virgin's power comes to the rescue of a devotee who has fallen from the highest virtue to the greatest depths of sin.

The unicorn parable (text 10) represents in generalized terms the temptations to which the *sacristine* and the drowned monk have fallen. It responds to the implied question of how a good Christian can so easily be taken in by *faus delit*. The concluding sermon evokes the appearance of earthly beauty such as that which might have tempted the monk:

> Cascune tout son poour met
> En lui acesmer cointement,
> N'est pas pour Dieu, mas pour la gent.
> Quant elles sont apareillies,
> Estroit viestues *et* caucies,
> Si vont devant lor huis sëoir,
> Pour cou c'on les puist miex vëoir.
> (f. 106vb4-10)

The legend of Thaïs reverses the problem and answers those who would wonder about the soul of the temptress herself. Thaïs has no history of pious devotion to redeem her and no virtuous position from which to stray. Paphnuntius is a doublet of the drowned sacristan, but instead of falling under the lady's influence, he tames and converts her.

Thaïs and Margaret (text 12) form an opposing pair: the converted prostitute endures imprisonment as her penance, while the virgin martyr is imprisoned to be subjected to temptation. Margaret is as proud of her virtue as Thaïs is humbled by her sin; prison constitutes the foyer of heaven for both.

This 600-line version of the life of Saint Margaret contains more than 100 lines of prayer. Upon entering her prison, Margaret prays for the Lord's pardon (ll. 261-74, f. 116va1-14).[24] When she has overcome both the devil and the little black man (another manifestation of the devil), she invokes the Creator with a long description of Nature and begs to be excused from the world (ll. 383-425, f. 117ra33-b30). Finally, at the chopping block, she gives thanks and prays for divine favor toward anyone who writes her biography or any pregnant woman who serves her, in addition to inhabitants of any dwelling possessing a copy of her life (ll. 517-74, ff. 117vb39-118rb23). Each prayer is longer than the previous one.

Prayer becomes the focus of the thirteenth text, a line-by-line explication of the *Pater Noster*. In stark contrast to the fabulous narrative preceding it, this text has a sober

---

[24] In the text of B.N. f. fr. 1555, printed by Joly, Margaret prays that she might meet her tormenter: "Que celui voie face à face" (l. 270). Cf. the corresponding line in B.N. f. fr. 2162, "De ses pechies pardon me faces," which is much less appropriate for the context, since the devil confronts her in the passage that follows.

didactic tone. The belief in magical power so colorfully reflected in Margaret's story, however, is not totally absent. Verses such as "amen recede sathanas" (f. 125va5) and the assurance that recitation of the *Pater* will help to protect the petitioner from temptation parallel Margaret's use of her cross to dispatch the dragon. Though the similarity of outlook lies for the most part beneath the surface, the conclusion of the *Margaret* text raises an important question subsequently addressed in the gloss of the *Pater*. Margaret's life offers no practical model for imitation, and her final prayer implies that all Christians need do to obtain heavenly favor is acknowledge her power. But how should they conduct their lives?

The last three texts of the manuscript share an explicit didactic intention. The speaker of the *Pater Noster* gloss prefaces his lesson with a prayer to the Holy Spirit for illumination:

> Au saint espir *con*manç m'entente,
> Ki a b*ie*n dire me consente,
> Enluminer puist mon corage,
> Ke cil ki m'oront, fol *et* sage,
> Ne puissent rep*re*ndre mesfais.
> (f. 119ra6-10)

The *Alexis* poet presents the saint's life as an example, comparing it with a lamp showing the way to heaven: the oil in the lamp represents Alexis's good works (ll. 14-21, f. 125vb20-27). The lyric "I" of the *Ver de Couloigne* ends with a prayer to the Holy Spirit for visual confirmation of his faith:

> Fai la grasce descendre del Saint Espir en moi
> Que mon cuer faice esprendre de la douçour de toi!
> Si me maint, si m'aprenge c'avenir puisse a toi!
> Et a mes oels me fai veïr çou que jou croi!
> (ll. 473-76)[25]

The prologue of the *Ver*, unique to this manuscript, calls attention to the text's usefulness for anyone sincerely wishing to repent. It responds to the implied problem of how to recognize sincerity in one's doubts, a problem raised by the references to mechanical recitation of prayer in the *Pater Noster* gloss.

This sequential review uncovers only a few of the elements that could have inspired a scribe to follow a given text with another that came to mind in the process of copying. While some of the items may have entered the manuscript in this way, I believe the person responsible for the manuscript was nevertheless guided by a concept. As his

---

[25] Although B.N. f. fr. 2162 lacks this conclusion, the catchword suggests it originally contained at least one other gathering, or should have (see p. 21).

ultimate purpose is nowhere explicit, I will discuss several indications of what might constitute the foundation of the combination.

I would like to suggest that this manuscript, though it includes some instances of sinners redeemed solely through their devotion to Mary (texts 8 and 9), favors instead the alternatives of avoiding temptation on the one hand (texts 3, 5, 7, 10, 12, and 14), and of sincere confession and penance on the other (texts 3, 4, 11, 13, and 15). The closing lines of Herman's *Bible*, including three unique to this manuscript (shown here in italics), support this view:

> Signor *par* tel maniere nos vint Dex racater:
> Non pas por no deserte, mais *par* sa carité.
> Del servage al diauble nos a il tous jetés,
> Se par no *gra*nt folie ni volons retorner.
> Se vos faites pechiés ne vos en desperés:
> *A vostre mere eglise isnelement alés.*
> *Si proies Deu merchi et si vos confessés;*
> *Se merchit i querrés, alluec le troverés.*
> *Co*nnissiés vo*s*t*r*e coupe, penitance prendés,
> Puis aiés esperance *et* foi *et* caritet:
> Par ices .iii. v*os* t*os* porés a Deu aler,
> *et* en la g*ra*nde gloire ki dure sans finer.
> Ja nos parmaint li sires ki fu de v*ir*gene nes.
> (f. 77r24-36.)[26]

The lines added by this scribe provide significant evidence as to the function he intended the compilation to fulfill.

Moreover, the story of the drowned monk breaks off in the midst of a frivolous passage on Mary's power:

> S'elle disoit li pie est noire,
> Et l'iage tourble est toute clere,
> Se diroit il: "Voir dist ma mere."
> Otrians est, tout li otroie.
> S'elle faisoit d'un afin troie,
> Se dirout il q*u'*elle a bien trait.
> Sovent nous mesciet *et* mestrait;
> Sovent nous fait d'anbes atierne,
> De .ii. *et* das [*sic*] quines *et* tiernes.
> (ending of text, f. 104vb32-40)

Rather than confirming the implication that the Virgin can save a sinner under any circumstances, the manuscript responds in the *Dit de l'unicorne* with the admonition to

---

[26] See Mehne 1900, 36.

avoid worldly pleasure in the first place. We do not learn what happens to the monk's soul, but we understand that he would have been much better off staying on his own side of the river.[27]

The concluding text, even unfinished, makes an eloquent appeal to the audience's sense of responsibility, echoing the admonition that closes the first one. The problem raised in the *Pater Noster* gloss concerning the sixth part of the prayer (*Et ne nos inducas in tentationem*) has been a thorny one for exegetes and theologians. The *Ver de Couloigne* focuses on the sinner's inner struggle with temptation but reaffirms the necessity to be guided by models such as Saint Thaïs, even in a world where Margaret and Alexis may not have succeeded in living sinless lives.

It might be argued that medieval spiritual life was fundamentally concerned with models for imitation, and that these observations could be made of any collection of pious texts. In the Middle Ages, however, Christian belief had both an ethical and a magical aspect. The magical power of saints and of the Virgin Mary was taken for granted, as reflected in many miracle narratives and in texts such as the life of Saint Margaret.

In *Maria ist immer und überall* Peter-Michael Spangenberg suggests a correlation between the rise of Marianism and the social conditions of the twelfth and thirteenth centuries, which call into question the possibility of saintly behavior. The magical aspect prevails, he argues, when city life, unstable social structures, thriving heresies, and factions within the Church blur the distinctions between good and evil. In such conditions, the miracle would seem to function as escapist literature, and partly as a model for devotion to the Virgin. Any sinner could achieve salvation if he piously served the Queen of Heaven (1987, 109-45).

That the Virgin can wield a powerful influence over her son the Judge even in cases of monstrous sin is amply illustrated in UCB 106, analyzed in chapter 4 of this study. However, none of the stories in this miracle collection depicts her as the sinner's advocate against damnation. In text 2 the miracle consists of a vision of the Virgin honoring the pious widow and the sacrament of Holy Communion. The third text has nothing to do with Mary at all, and the nun in the fourth text conceives her desire at Candlemas, when she imagines she sees the infant Jesus as he is presented at the temple. The story thus focuses on the christological aspect of this feast rather than on the Purification of the Virgin. In the fifth text she magically makes a beautiful nun ugly to save the souls of men desiring her, who may or may not have performed special Marian devotions. Her miraculous appearance frightens and then converts thieves who were

---

[27] The codicological articulation between these two texts is discussed above, pp. 20-21. Though it is by no means certain that the scribe deliberately omitted the ending of the story as it appears in other manuscripts, where the monk is restored to life because of his nightly devotions to the Virgin, such an omission would be consistent with other choices he seems to have made in compiling this collection.

threatening the life of a devout monk in the sixth text, and in the following miracle she preserves the chastity of a young man about to marry. In text 8 the Virgin serves as a stand-in for a devout nun suffering a temporary fall from virtue. Only in the last text of the group of miracles is she given the role of advocate for the sinner against devils who justifiably claim his soul, and the judgment and its outcome are missing from the manuscript. While the Virgin does play a major role in several of the miracles, then, none of them represents a model of Marian devotion as the antidote for an otherwise sinful life.

Only six texts in the manuscript emphasize Mary's role, and four of these were copied by a single scribe (6-9). In addition, other works in the compilation seem to play down her importance. The *Bible* of Herman de Valenciennes has been described as having a "Marian character" (Smeets 1970, 88), yet the Assumption is not included in this manuscript. The life of Alexis used in the manuscript sends the saint to Edessa where there is an image of Christ in Majesty, not of the Virgin Mary, as in some versions.[28] The other saints' lives in the manuscript do not happen to be among those that feature her prominently.

The selection of texts, then, reflects a *specific* didactic function. The story of the usurer and the old woman (text 2 of the manuscript) serves as a key to its message, presenting four models of behavior. The rich man's way of life is clearly undeserving of heavenly reward: he not only enjoys worldly luxuries, but also dies unrepentant. The old woman is a paragon of both piety and poverty. If Spangenberg's view of the spiritual contradictions of urban life is accurate, then she, like Alexis and Margaret, exceeds the level of perfection the audience would be likely to attempt. He maintains that the lady's poverty is a neutral quality, and that Gautier does not intend her as a model for imitation ([1982], 9-13). The real villain and hero of the story are the avaricious priest and the young cleric; the issue is the importance of sincere confession and repentance. However we may sympathize with the rich sinner suffering hell's torments, the hypocritical priest arouses no pity. The "dyakenes," closer to the audience, provides the narrative point of view: through his visions, we behold both heaven and hell. His role in the story is to hear the lady's confession and give her absolution as the Virgin and her court of angels attend, honoring by their presence not only the deserving soul, but the sacrament itself.

If the manuscript on the whole advocates the sincere observance of the Church's sacraments, are we to conclude that it was made at the behest of some clerical authority? A brief review of the sources and traditions of these texts would seem to oppose such a position. I will take up the question again at the conclusion of this study.

---

[28] "La trova une ymage de grant atorité/ Del fil Dieu Jhesu Crist qui siet en maiesté" (ll. 331-32, f. 127vb25-26). Note, however, that the image that speaks to the sacristan, commanding him to seek out the "saint home," is "El non saint Marie et faite et figuree" (l. 519, f. 129ra23).

MATERIAL DESCRIPTION: B.N. f. fr. 2162

Generalities

Bound with cardboard covered in smooth red leather, much worn at the corners and on the spine, this manuscript bears arms embossed in gold on both the front and back covers.[29] The coat of arms, which the description at the Institut de Recherche et d'Histoire des Textes identifies as the "imperial crown," includes the fleur-de-lis, a crown, and the monogram "H"; the title "Bible en vers" is stamped on the spine. There are three parchment guard sheets in front and one in back, with another possibly glued under the paper end sheet added at the time of binding. The manuscript is foliated correctly in ink in a modern hand, upper right recto, to 137 (not counting the front guard sheets). The leaves measure between 313 and 315 by 148 to 150 mm. The parchment is consistently dark and rather coarse, in full sheets. On the whole the manuscript appears homogeneous in style and quality.

Eight primitive gothic and gothic bookhands can be distinguished.[30] The first (ff. 1-12; see figure 1) has a stiff, uneven appearance, with letters well separated. The *a* has an open, abbreviated top loop; *s* and *r* take the upright form. The horizontal bar of *t* is uncrossed, and *i* is marked only occasionally by a hair stroke. *V* is used sometimes in initial position, but *u* predominates. These traits are characteristic of the first quarter of the thirteenth century.

The second hand (ff. 13r-80vb; see figure 2), in contrast, is smooth and rounded, using a thick quill. Adjacent curves are unjoined, the upper loop of *a* is open, round *r* is absent, and *s* is predominantly upright. Round final *s* occurs occasionally, especially at line ends; *i* is not systematically marked. No phonetic distinction is made between *u* and *v*, which appears only in initial position. Like the first, this hand has features typical of the early part of the century.

The third hand (ff. 81ra-88vb; see figure 3) appears slightly later than the rest. The letters are of uneven size, angular and compressed in appearance, with some joined curves. The upper loop of *a* is sometimes closed. Ascenders are tall: round *s* appears in final position about one-third of the time. The upright of *t* does not protrude above the bar. Round *r* is used occasionally in final position after *o*, *a*, and *u*. This hand suggests a *terminus ante quem* of about 1250 for the manuscript.

---

[29] A table outlining the organization of the volume precedes the list of contents for each manuscript analyzed in this study. See table 2 for B.N. f. fr. 2162, discussed in this chapter.

[30] For paleographic vocabulary and dating characteristics I have relied principally on Denholm-Young (1954) and Walpole (1976).

The fourth hand (ff. 89ra-94ra; see figure 4), with characteristics of the first quarter of the thirteenth century, gives a homely, austere, straightforward impression. The thickness of the quill is uneven, and the interlinear space undulates. Vertical strokes are simple, sometimes slightly heavier at the bottom. Minims curve to the right, resembling elephants' trunks; ascenders are kept short. The *t* is uncrossed, the top of *a* consists of a short leftward curve of the shaft, and *s* is consistently upright, even in final position. Round *r* does not appear; adjacent curves are detached.

The fifth hand copies the fourth and fifth texts (94a-97a; see figure 5). It uses a very large round *s* at word ends about half the time. The crossbar of *t* has a bump on top where it joins the upright, and *a* has an open upper loop. The curves of *d* and *e* sometimes blend, but other letters stand separate. Angles and curls reflect twists of the scribe's quill at the end of his strokes. This hand's traits date it to the second quarter of the thirteenth century.

Texts six through nine, with protagonists devoted to the Virgin Mary, are all copied by the sixth scribe (ff. 97ra-104vb; see figure 6). The hand has a cramped, squat appearance and favors round *s* to the upright form in final position about four to one. This trait, combined with the otherwise primitive appearance of the hand, suggests a date approaching 1250. The round *r* occurs rarely, and in various positions: initial, following *u* and after uncial *d*, for example, but not generally after *o*. A fine, flat stroke occasionally marks *i*; the tall, straight upright of *a* is topped with a hook to the left. With the exception of *de*, adjacent curves are not usually joined.

The hand that copies the unicorn parable (ff. 105ra-107ra; see figure 7) is disciplined, regular, and clear. It favors round *s* over the upright form in final position about three to one. Miniscule *g*, *c*, upright *r*, and *t* are ligatured to the letter following, but round letters, other than *de*, are not blended. The upright of *t* does not cross the horizontal bar, and no hair stroke marks *i*. The potbellied *a* has an open upper loop. Together, these traits indicate a date of the mid-thirteenth century.

The eighth hand (ff. 107ra-136vb; see figure 8) appears balanced, even, and square. Like the previous one, it dates to around 1250. It occasionally uses round *s* in final position, and *a* has an open top loop. Adjacent round letters are not usually joined, except sometimes *de*, and the round *r* with following *o*, *p*, or *d*. The bar of *t* extends to the right, uncrossed by the upright stroke. Ascenders are kept low, and *i* in final position extends slightly below the line. A backward swing of the quill on the downward stroke distinguishes this scribe's tall *s*, *m*, and *h*, and an upward twist finishes straight *r* at line ends. These traits are recognizable even when the hand adjusts its size in changing between eight- and twelve-syllable lines.

Paleographic evidence thus indicates a date for the manuscript of not later than the middle of the thirteenth century. The ink varies between dark brown and black; decoration consists of ornamental red initials and highlighted line initials, with small, faint indications for the rubricator either in the margin or under the letter to be added or decorated.

Particularities

The inside front cover bears a pasted label reading "FR 2162," which is repeated in blue crayon on the recto of the front end sheet. Folio 1 has two old shelf marks at the top, "s. 24" and "7986"; the bottom is stamped "bibliothecae regi[ae]." Traces of fifteenth-century cursive appear on the recto of the paper end sheet, glued to the first guard sheet; the verso lists the contents, also in fifteenth-century cursive; the recto of the second guard sheet has faded traces of an early cursive hand. A modern hand lists the contents, with the title "poesies du XIII siecle," on the verso of the third guard sheet. This table is signed with the initials "G.D.L.R.," which I have not been able to identify.

Folios 4 and 5 each have erasures of several lines, written over. A large drop of ink was spilled between 23v and 24. Folio 66 has been glued onto a stub, visible on the recto; a fifteenth-century hand copies the last lines of 66v and 67 at the bottom of each folio. Folio 85 has two lines crossed out and corrections in red at the top. Errors are crossed out in red on folios 125 and 130v; nine lines appear either erased or faded on 130v.

A hole in the bottom of folio 7 has been written around on both sides; folio 81 has a long vertical tear, repaired before writing. Folios 116 and 117 are repaired at the bottom in the gutter; holes occur on folios 118 and 123.

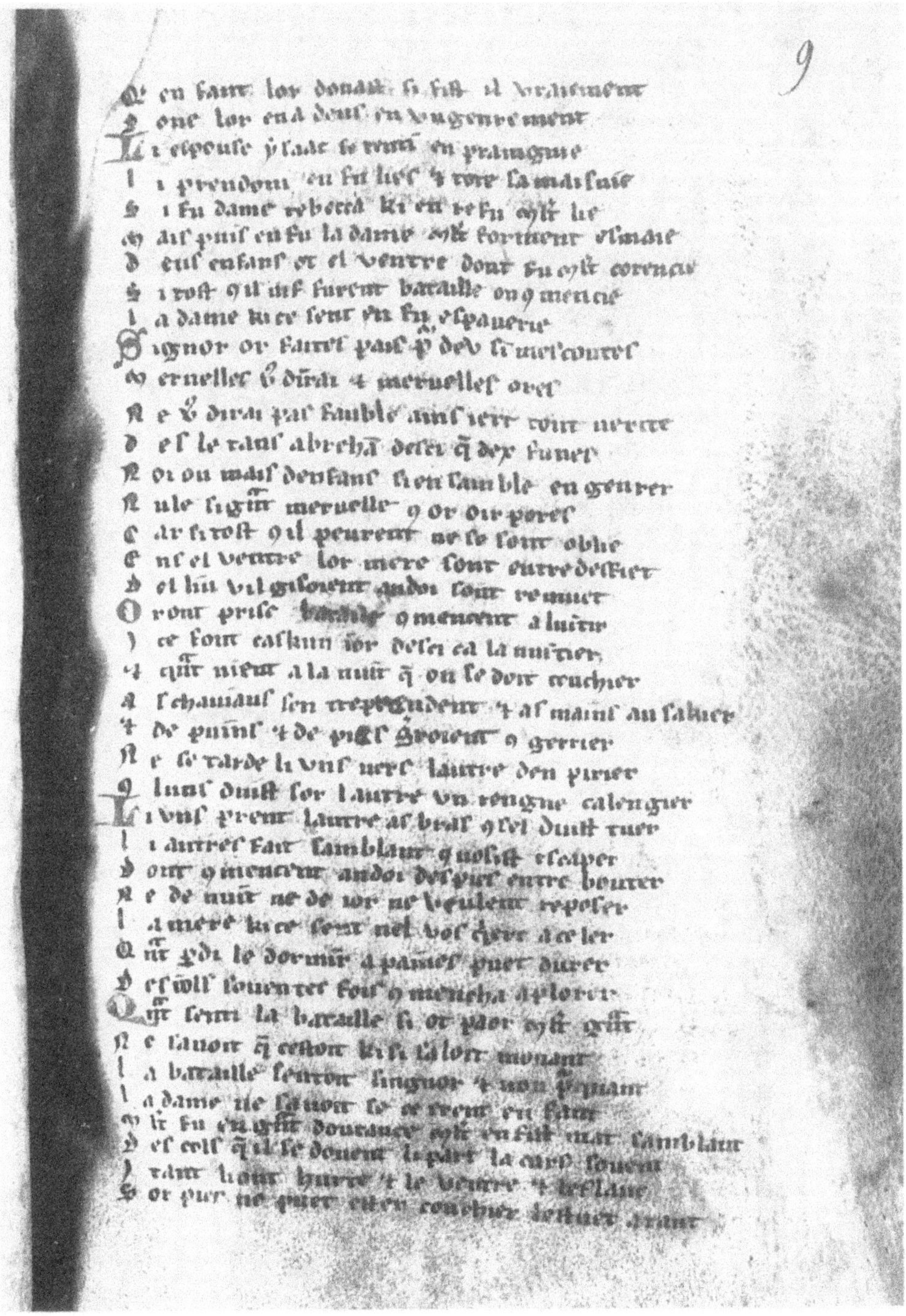

Q en faire lor donast si fist il vraiement
One lor ena doel en ourgenrement
Li espouse ysaac se remut en pranagme
I a prendom en fu lies 7 toit sa maisnie
E t sa dame rebecca ki en receu oist lie
A prus en fu la dame molt fortment sindie
D eus enfans ot el ventre dont su oist corenais
S i tost qil iurs furent bataille ont mencie
L a dame ki ce sent en fu espaourie
S ignor or saires pais p deu si nus escontes
M erueilles v dirai 7 merueilles oies
N e v dirai pas saunble ainsi iert voit neuere
D es le tans abrehā dela q deus fumes
N oi ou mais denfans si on saunble engenrer
N ule sigūr merueille q or oir pores
C ar si tost qil peurent nese sont oblie
E ns el ventre lor mere sont entredesfies
D et lui vil gisoient andoi sont remuer
O ront prise bataille o menoent a luiter
I se sont caskun ior dels en la nuitier
E quit nient a la nuit q on se doit coucher
A s chamaus sen rependent 7 as mains au sablier
7 de puins 7 de pies sentendent o gerier
N e se tarde li uns uers lautre den pirer
I lnust duist sor lautre un congne calongier
L i uns prent lautre as bras qel duist tuer
L i autres fait samblant quosist escaper
D oit q menoent andoi desques entre bouter
N e de nuit ne de ior ne veulent reposer
L a mere ki ce sent nel vot cheu aceler
A nt fort le dormir a painnes puet durer
D essoilt souentes fois q mencha a plorer
Q ut sent la bataille si or paor ouste gsir
N e sauoit q ceton tut li oiert manant
L a bataille sentron singnor 7 non gnant
L a dame ne sauoit ce ce venir en sant
M lt su en grast douraunce molt en fut mal samblant
D es cols qil se douent li part la cars souent
T ant lour hurte 7 le ventre 7 le laine
S or puet ne quier ellen couchier deshues trant

Fig. 1. Paris, B.N. f. fr. 2162: f. 9r (hand 1)
Phot. Bibl. Nat. Paris

Si 9 dist lescripture il vit del ciel lentree
Vit a valer les angles & vit la remontree
De la celeste gent tant bele & honoree
Fit li sambla peine icele reposee
Dout les uilla iacob car bel avoit dormit
E garda deriere soi un angle ester vit
Prist la entre ses bras que il lot bie choisit
A dont par la li angeles & oste biel li dist
Laime tost mes biaus freres p coi mal tu sauhr
Non seras par ma foit si maras benert
Iacob lai moi ester p ma foi nel ferai
De ta beneicon dec̄ sausi serai
Iacob ce respont langeles ie te corecerai
Tu de coi amis ie te mehaīgnerai
La soi lie doi dev p ce ne te lirai
Ensi q de ta bouce beneicon aurai
Oh est il de la cuille que il li estouta
Que se sent mehaīgnit iacob a lui parla
Very ares de moi car tos li iors sen va
Dout le laissa li sers kuit est li mostra
E il li en alpies a pres si la ora
Or se va dans iacob ola beneicon
Son oncle vait qrant icel santisnes hom
En ara ia est entres en une region
Son oncle a demande trouue la en maison
Ille salua biel ses noma p son non
Laban ie sui tes nies iacob mapele on
Fius sui de ta seror biaus nies bie le sauons
Ment le sai tes peres mors est voir li preudons
Tes freres estant meçacha del pais
Celli respont laban nel sai bie biaus amis
Por la beneicon esau ̄ fuis
Ce me fait maniere p foi tu messesis
Mais ie te reterrai garderas mes brebis
E te donrai soldees bones ie te plevis
Avec auec ient li nermes costume est del pais
Ce li respont iacob biaus oncles volenters
Vit ie te servirai p ma foi vol̄ en tiers
E it seront aoph q pres soit nes loiers
Ne saudrai pas a rerme ne remenrai nient

Fig. 3. Paris, B.N. f. fr. 2162: f. 83r (hand 3)
Phot. Bibl. Nat. Paris

p or coi vos estes trauilies   d el fil ⁊ del s. esperit
d ont est caskuns agenoilies   q' ni metes plus de respit
M ont par lor grant plorison   l aissies le puch sans nul sojor
⁊ jehans de fin cuer ⁊ bon   S i venes tost cha fors a nour
d e iours pleure del cuer sospire   C ar nos ⳨ nous grant talent
D edens le puch souent remire   T antost se drece amont la gent
S i gs. esp̃rs li en saingne   P la main tout fors del puch mise
Y lieue sa main si se sainne   D e la sanblance ⁊ de la guise
⁊ sorison a dite briene   Q' li sachans li a porta
E n qtre mont son chief re heue   Q uant de la cambre le iera
O nt doucement le roi apiele   D e ses menbres ne cangierent
9 ment ot non la damoisele   N e si vestement nen pirierent
P or ton ie sui en discipline   V remelle ert grose nomele
b iaus sire ele ot a non sabine   Q uant la mere le voit sibile
T an tost qu roit lor nomee   E n plorant le baise ⁊ acole
I ⁊ li mares la apielee   P trois as ses barons parolle
K i cuidoit estre pris au piege   A ues veu le biel miracle
M ns deu loi de son haut siege   Et dex a fait par le signacle
K i bien entent ⳍ caskuns oueure   d el s. home ⳍ nos sabaismes
G rant honor li fist a cele oueure   Q uant a toulouse leu portasmes
L a damoisele respondi   E n la sanblance dune bieste
S i q̃ li rois bien lentendi   M out en doit on faire grant feste
⁊ la roine ⁊ li haut home   S ui a lever ⁊ en saucher
b a ki est ce dex kime nomme   Q' mont laime dex ⁊ cuer chier
C est al cui s. espirs q fort   B ien ba hui sa mor moustree
K i laiens te re ta tort   Q uant ceh a resusitee
S ouent en ai triste le cuer   K i en tost puch a giu pls. ans
S ire le triste ie rer puer   Q ue ni souferi mal ne abans
S i loes deu le creatour   L   l i rois en rent deus guerendon
K i me sostient par soie amour   S ire b dires bien raison
Q' il nest riens ka moi soffraigne   T out sa genoillent ioinctes mains
J ou di ci mont biele qpaigne   S i fist trois tout premerains
A ngeles ai o moi tout a dies   M er chit li criere doucement
M artirs ⁊ viergenes ⁊ q fies   I llor par done bonement
E n si grant ioie sui rondis   D enies les a ⁊ atour
9 se ie fuise en paradis   b ien li a dex son loier souls
P or vos me vient ore qfors   A cheual fisent a prester
D amoisiele venes cha fors   S us le voururent faire monter
M ont vos de sire vre mere   I l dist qu ens ol bos de morrois
J e vos q sir de par le pere   S a penance parferoit

a nus mlt bien dire me loist
k'ami vous estes trop repus
a mis viers moi estes trop durs
c epuise bien dire pour voir
c omment puecut un oel neur
k i si sout dont plain de pire
k e iai si longement este
e n tel pour ke uous saues bien
a sire ksaie dit cest vout uous
f aites domout a uo plaisir
q ie uiel avour obeir
q souhet caukes q uores faire
q li dous sires de bonaires
k i bien conuistout le pensee
q ki l'auoit bien esprouuee
q onissoit son desirier
l en volt en cel iour apaisier
q acomplir se volere
v oies dieu de grant amiste
q destroite amour amans
J lle mait en tourne deiluit
D e tours iij ans + deniers plus
q se stoit tout sermdaus vestus
a une cotelete a se point
a le noumain vout sia point
k elle estoit a liue en son lis
q lien fes li va sipres
e elle vere les aulins pour prendre
q cil ki bien se sot defendre
s e trair deli un pau en sus
b iaus fius bien sores uous uenues
D ist li damfuenes anni
q en disaut ses bras ouurir
q ili court sans demoree
e le preut aa coler
q en straude guire son pis
q les garda enmi le vis
q li sauia ki remanlour
e dui nsi son neur pensour
s en eut acuer ioie mlt grant

b iaus fius dit la dame alenfant
v ous estes mlt biaus + mout dous
a ramours en fius estes uous
D ame iesus li fius monpere
q sai mlt boine dame amere
k mdaut des 9 fors et 9 fars
l nomme ki estour de uose
l eure damours mar lot parler
i bien q ni set camen der
s i kelle en ert toute en bahie
q li en fes par mainte fie
I rerdout de ses mains les ieus
q li nomme libist biaus fius
s aues nous mere uo paresnoistre
q ais dame saues uous le nostre
D ist li en ses grant pieca lesai
o r le dires + ulordi
b iaus fius foi ke mi deues
v olon tiers dame son uoles
o il biaus dous fius 9 mon cuer
l i redoise ou me lines
e di sour si tre doucemput
e ale nomain tout uidement
s au blou bien q dies li desist
c ar une douceurs de lui ist
p ar le bouce dout il parlout
i ke sour pau no de salour
i norme de le grant douceur
l le estoit a la ke sour leur
s e croire kil estoit verais dies
a ut li tres dous inoceus preus
s e uolor en uiers li conuert
q ut il or dit tout par loisir
e elle parenostre tre douce
D e celle prisieuse bouce
v our li saint prudent delir
D ame fait il aisse bien dit
k e nous samble le sane bien
b ien biaus dous fius aius nur si bien
e le sene tretes ce mest uis

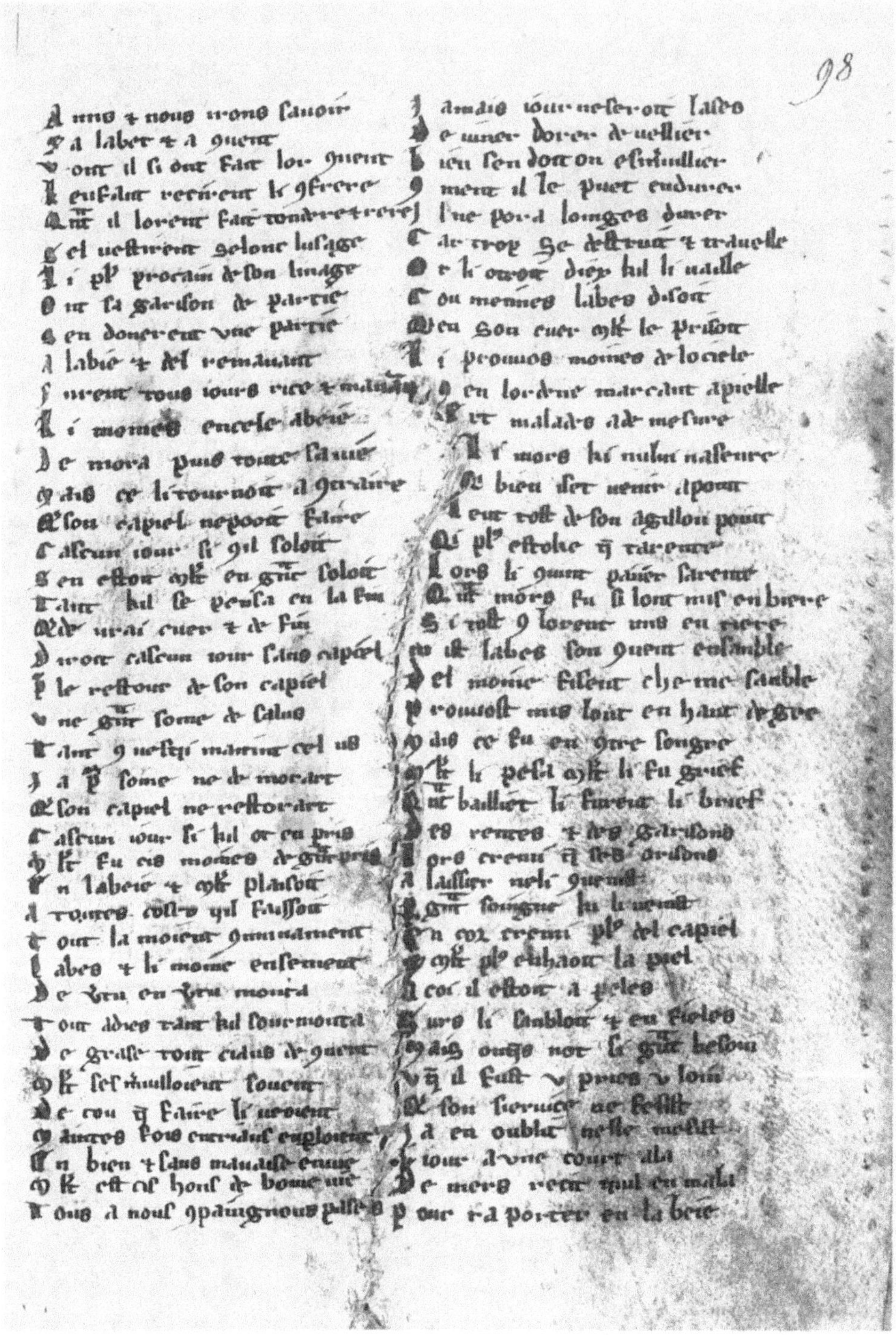

Fig. 6. Paris, B.N. f. fr. 2162: f. 98r (hand 6)
Phot. Bibl. Nat. Paris

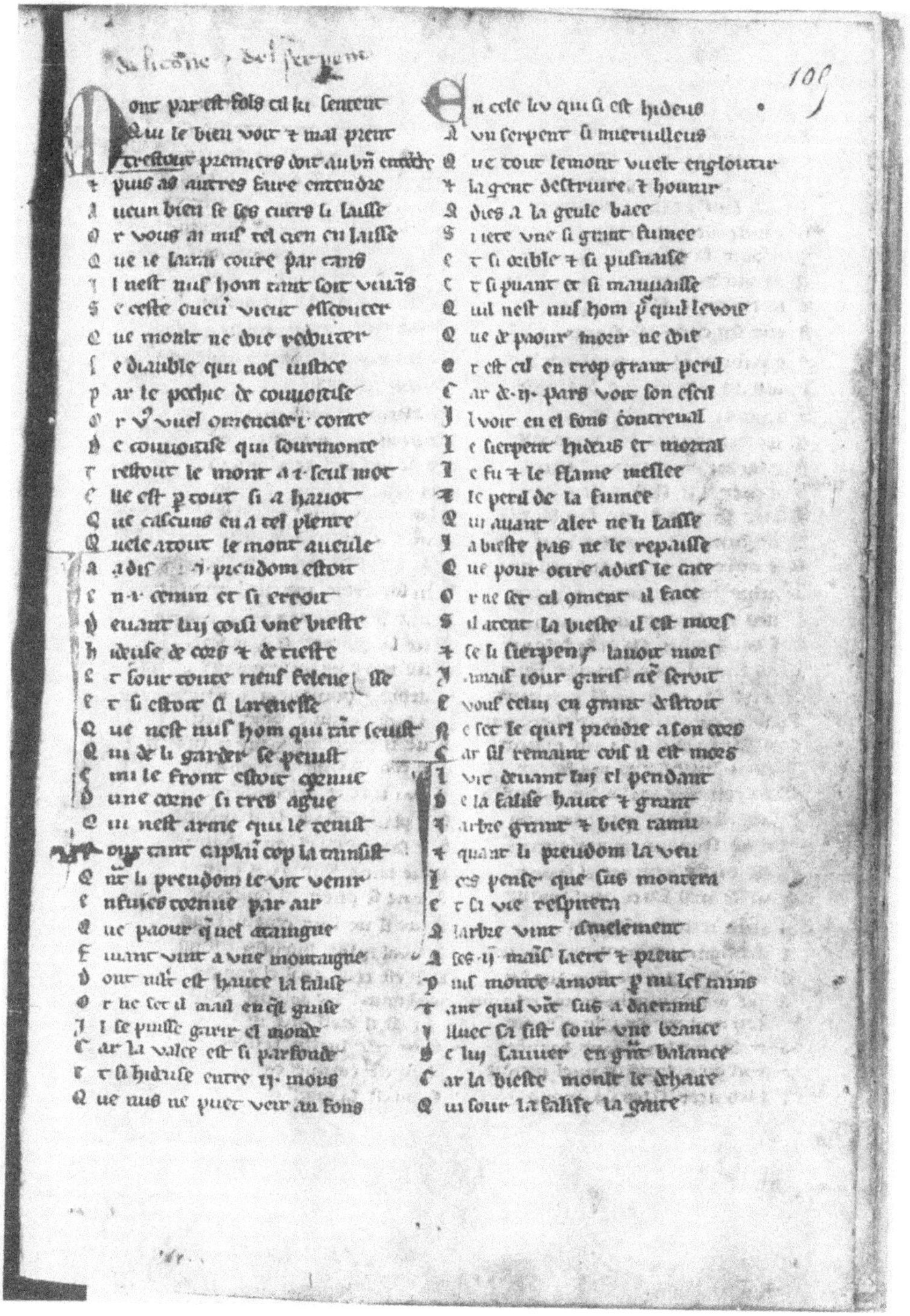

de licorne & del serpent

Mout par est fols cil ki lentent
Qui le bien voit & mal prent
Trestout premiers doit au bien entendre
& puis as autres faire entendre
Aucun bien se ses cuers li laisse
Or vous ai mis tel cien en laisse
Que ne larrai courre par tans
Il n'est nul hom tant soit veulz
Se ceste oueil vieut escouter
Que moult ne doie redouter
Le diauble qui nos iustice
Par le pechie de couuoitise
Or s'vueil ormentart conte
De couuoitise qui sourmonte
Trestout le mont a i seul mot
Ele est p tout si a haut
Que cascuns en a tel plente
Quele atout le mont auculle
Iadis i .i. preudom estoit
En .i. cemin et si erroit
Deuant luy cousi une bieste
hideuse de cors & de tieste
Et sour toutes rieuf felenese ele
Et si estoit si lareness
Que n'est nul hom qui rire seust
Qui de li garder se peüst
Mi le front estoit cornue
D'une corne si tres ague
Qui nest arme qui le tenist
Puis tant c'uphii cop la tensist
Que li preudom le vit venir
Enfuies vouuir par air
Que paour quel ataingue
Fuiant vint a une montaigne
Dont molt est haute la falise
Or se set il mal en est guise
Il se puisse garir el monde
Car la valee est si parfonde
Et si hidüse entre ij mons
Que nus ne puet veir au fons

En cele leu qui si est hideus
A un serpent si mervilleus
Que tout lemont vuele engloutir
& la gent destruire & hounir
Dies a la geule baee
Siiere une si grant fumee
Et si ocible & si puluouse
Et si puant & si mauuaisse
Qui nest nul hom p qui le voie
Que de paour moeir ne doit
Et est cil en trop grant peril
Car d' ij pars voit son escil
Ivoir en el fons contreual
Le serpent hideus et mortal
Le fu & le flame meslee
Et le peril de la fumee
Qui auant aler ne li laisse
A biste pas ne le repaisse
Que pour ocire ades le tace
O r ue ser cel orment il face
S'arent la bieste il est mors
Se li serpens l'auoir mors
Iamais iour garis ne seroit
Et vous celuy en grant destroit
Ne set le quel prendre a son cors
Car s'il remaint cois il est mors
I vit deuant lui el pendant
De la falise haute & grant
J arbre grant & bien ramu
& quant li preudom l'a veu
I es pense que sus montera
Et si vie respitera
A larbre vint durement
A ses ij mais lieue & pleue
p uis monte amont p mi les rains
T ant quil vit sus a daremsil
Illuec si fist tour une beance
Et luy sauuer en grant balance
Car la bieste moult le dekaure
Qui sour la falise la gaure

Fig. 7. Paris, B.N. f. fr. 2162: f. 105r (hand 7)
Phot. Bibl. Nat. Paris

D dune grant cope deuis
Quar li prestres a cante
Cel haut sacrement fine
Il emprent priueremenc
E puis le depart alagent
T el costume ont en la ocree
Qais li nre est pl' acesmee
Il le prendent corporelment
E nos espirituelment
Si endeuons sacle estre
Car no pasteur la sont li pstre
Cel sacrement sont dune dulce
K i nest nus ne grant ne tee
E dun poi deum ensemb
Car nus ne le doit gloenir
Preid ne super fluue
E pruee le sent ou tant plenre
Qais al saint pains e sacres
L i uns e en sic mues
I pstres nos en fait envoi
R nt en pais beusons t en toi
I uns latine t en piere
Si somes euryons
E ale resurrexion
Corporelment le receuon
Pruee qi li charz resuscitz
Que ihesus en dū aporta
E caskuns en lui resusite
Si receuons gnt t peru
Q uit de mort auons peur
R nos pl' en nous senti
Ne poz diable faire mie
Ei us mit auons esseu
Des perses quandss fait lones
Si receuons corporelment
Le signor lu saluor nos don
Car qnt li diables couvoit
Ses a tel duel t tel rozmir
Et sen puant cuer li dolent

Que nus ne li savoit deseure
Son grant duel ne son gnt martire
Hodie unum i presenti uita
Ce est li pains de caskun ior
Que demandes vo creator
Lui co est en uue preteure
Q' il auoir le nos osente
Mais saches se net receuons
Erement q faire deuons
A s armes prendons uigement
Car si paut dies ensement
Que en la main iudas mua
Il pains qui ihc li paui
Ason ua li cors pele t clere
Uient corrumpue a son pe
Nol ql cose i receues
Le morsel dont damne serons
Ores troit cus aies
Let curuusions queutendes
A dont gnt panem urm dires
Saces que pis ne se peutes
Qais al lu haut siet t lot uoir
Cel glorios pain nos en uoir
Honor od sain eyen
Squauoir l puillons si bn
Q nos latine pain nen perdes
Dont longement nuure dues
C ns entensions vores croit
Le nos otroit li soureuns roir
Qui uit t regne t regnera
In seculoz secula
Puis quor la quarte nos d'aue
La qute nos sere deseriere
Et dimitte nobis debita nra
Le nos deter nos fai pdon
Ceres nule requres grant don
Qnt co dires al tornai voi
Qais de regart caskuns en soi
Et co est que uos requres

Organization of the Page

Prickings consist of diamond-shaped holes at the bottom and outside edges. Many have been trimmed off. In some parts of the manuscript the prickings coincide through several folios. Ruling is barely visible, apparently in plummet.

Folio dimensions: 313-15 x 148-50 mm

Fig. 9. Page layout, long lines (ff. 1-77)

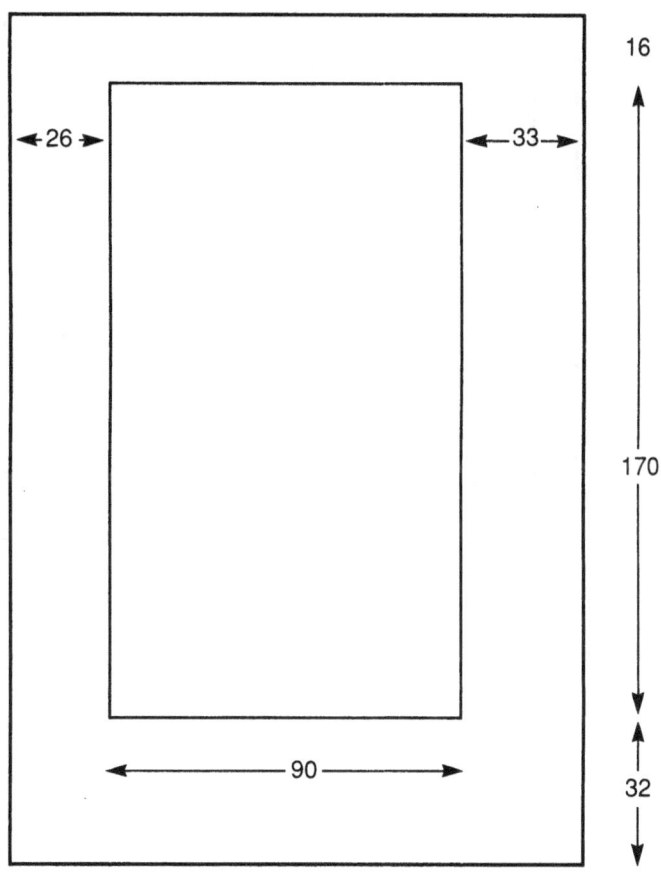

Justification:
40 lines, 165-70 x 85-90 mm

Fig. 10. Page layout, 2 columns (ff. 77v-136v)

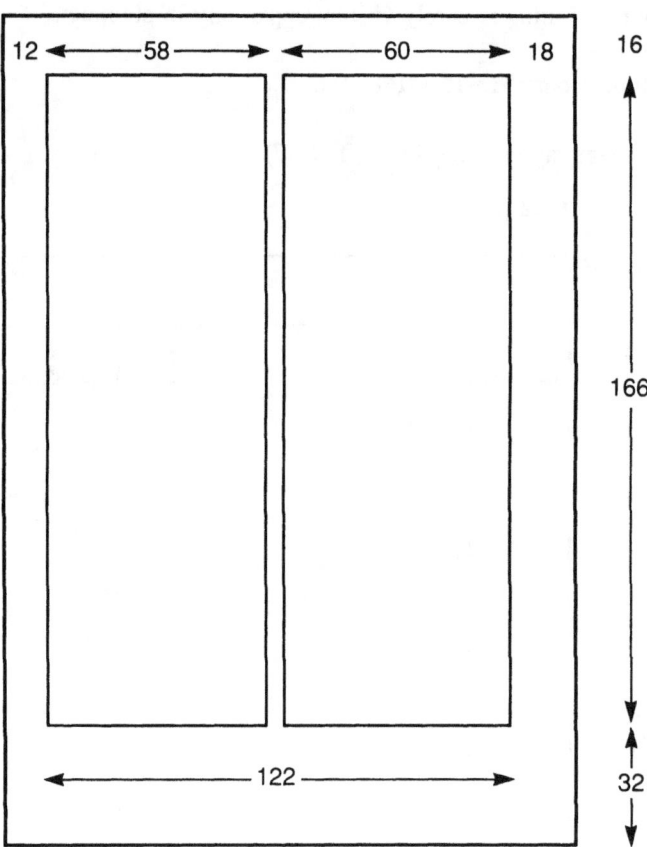

Justification:
39-41 lines, 158-70 x 105-28 mm

Table 2

Organization of the Volume

Gathering	Type	Catchword	Signatures	Remarks	Texts
1 (1-12)	6/6	yes	2, LLR f. 1, pencil; contemporary I, LCV f. 12	hand 1	Herman de Valenciennes, *Bible*, f. 1r
2 (13-24)	6/6	no	3, f. 13r; ii, f. 24v	hand 2, f. 13r	
3 (25-36)	6/6	no	4, f. 25r; iii, f. 36v		
4 (37-48)	6/6	no	5, f. 37r; iiii, f. 48v		
5 (49-60)	6/6	no	6, f. 49r; v, f. 60v	couplets, ff. 54-55, 58-59v	
6 (61-72)	6/6	no	7, f. 61r; vi, f. 72v	f. 65v, rubric; f. 66 glued onto stub *Li Souffrance Jhesucrist*, interpolation? couplets, ff. 62-66; assonance in [e], ff. 66-77	
7 (73-80)	4/4	no	8, f. 73r; vii, f. 80v		Gautier de Coinci, "Dou riche et de la veve fame," f. 77r
8 (81-92)	6/6	yes	9, f. 81r	change in ink, ff. 81ra, 89ra, 89va, 90va, 91ra; hand 3, f. 81ra; hand 4, f. 89ra	Life of Saint Jehan Paulus, f. 81ra
9 (93-104)	6/6	no	10, f. 93r	hand 5, f. 94ra; hand 6, f. 97ra	"De le nonain ki Deu desiroit a vir," f. 94ra; "D'une none ki fu trop biele," f. 96rb; "Li miracles del capiel de roses," f. 97ra; "D'un clerc cui Nostre Dame delivra de se feme," f. 99vb; *Sacristine*, f. 102ra; Gautier de Coinci, "D'un moigne qui fu ou fleuve," f. 103vb
10 (105-12)	4/4	yes	11, f. 109r; x, f. 108v	hand 7, f. 105ra; hand 8, f. 107ra	*Dit de l'unicorne et du serpent*, f. 105ra; Life of Saint Thaïs, f. 107ra
11 (113-20)	4/4	yes	12, f. 113r		Life of Saint Margaret, f. 115rb; Silvestre, *Pater Noster*, f. 119ra
12 (121-28)	4/4	yes	13, f. 121r		Life of Saint Alexis, f. 125vb
13 (129-36)	4/4	yes	14, f. 129r; xiii f. 137r (guard sheet)	begins using 2 lines for each verse, f. 134ra	*Li ver de Couloigne*, f. 133vb

CONTENTS

(1) ff. 1r-77r: [Herman de Valenciennes, *Bible*],[31] northwest France, twelfth century (Smeets 1970, 87), laisses of assonanced alexandrines
   Title: li livres de le bible [rubr.]
   Incipit: Qui chou quil set de bien ensaigne volentiers
   Explicit: Ja nos par maint li sires ki fu de virgene nes
   Edition: Spiele 1975
   See also Bonnard [1884] 1967, 11-41; Gröber 1902, 21, 655; Smeets 1968, 51ff, 57; Smeets 1970, 86-89; Mehne 1900.
   Summary: The narrative opens with the Creation, including that of the angels and archangels, followed swiftly by the fall of the rebel angels and subsequently of Adam. The stories of Noah, Abraham, Isaac, and Jacob lead to a long section on Joseph (ff. 15r17-25v15), who was probably known to cleric and layman alike as a total prefiguration of Christ (Spiele 1975, 29-37). Moses and David play extensive roles; episodes concerning Samuel, Saul, and Solomon are also included. The poet emphasizes the genealogical continuity of the narrative and links the Old and New Testament sections by tracing, in the Tree of Jesse, Mary's ancestors back to David.

   While the collation of Old Testament themes with passages in the poem follows more or less the order of the biblical narrative, citations from the four Gospels are interspersed throughout the section on the life of Christ. In B.N. f. fr. 2162 the narrative ends at Pentecost, though other versions conclude with the Assumption of the Virgin.

(2) ff. 77r-80vb: [Gautier de Coinci, "Dou riche et de la veve fame"], "langue qui caractérise l'Ile-de-France" (Cazelles 1978, 2), 1218-36 (Koenig 1955, 1: xxv-xxx), octosyllabic couplets
   Title: Chi commence li miracles de nostre dame
      D'un Priestre, d'un userier, et d'unme vieille [rubr., bottom f. 77r]
   Incipit: Tot li miracle nostre dame [f. 77v]
   Explicit: La mors mordans tous les puist mordre
   Edition: Koenig 1955, 2: 158-80
   See also Ducrot-Granderye 1932; Gröber 1902, 651-53.
   Summary: The tale describes the deaths on the same day of a poor beggar woman devoted to the Virgin and a rich man, "Useriers, fors, avers *et* cices" (l. 18 Koenig, f. 77va18). The greedy priest, against the advice of his "dyakenes,"

---

[31] A conventional title for each work is cited in brackets if different from that appearing in the manuscript under consideration.

elects to succor the wealthy sinner and his family, while the young cleric brings Holy Communion to the poor woman. The lady's welcome into heaven is described, as are the punishments awaiting the rich man in hell. The tale ends with an interpretation of the miracle as a warning to the faithful.

(3) ff. 81ra-94ra: [Life of Saint Jehan Paulus], northern Francien or Picard, mid-thirteenth century (Cazelles 1982, 24 n. 34; 25-26), octosyllabic couplets
Title: De saint jehan paulus [rubr.]
Incipit: En vitas patrum un haut livre
Explicit: Ce nos otroit Dex Jhesucris. Amen.
Edition: Williams and Allen 1935
See also Karl 1913, 1928; Morawski 1947; Cazelles 1982.
Summary: The first part of the verse legend describes a tour of hell that Pope Basil experiences while praying, guided by the angel Saint Michael. Basil is astonished to see a soul laughing amidst tormenting flames. Saint Michael commands the devils to grant them an interview with the lady, who explains that although she was guilty of pride during her life, she joyfully anticipates the birth of a sainted great-grandson, Jehan Paulus, who will earn her release from hell. Her daughter, currently residing in Rome, is in fact pregnant with the saint's mother.

This prophecy introduces the second part of the legend, while the life of Jehan Paulus's mother provides narrative continuity. The child Jehan distinguishes himself as a *puer senex* among his schoolmates, and, learning of his destiny from his grandmother, takes up the life of a hermit.[32] The devil tempts him with the daughter of the king of Toulouse, whom Jehan ravishes and then, ashamed and angry, throws down a well. He abandons his saintly life, until a view of the sun's rays and a prayer to God and to the Virgin bring about his deliverance from ill intention. When he travels to Rome to confess to the pope, he is refused absolution, and when he accidentally winds up at his father's doorstep, he is turned away unrecognized.

Finally, Jehan makes his confession to God himself and as penance lives in the forest for ten years as a wild animal: he goes on all fours, eats plants, and speaks only to pray. One Easter, he is captured by a hunting party and brought to the court of Toulouse as a curiosity. A small baby miraculously reports that Jehan has accomplished his penance, and an angel appears to assure Jehan that the soul of his great-grandmother has been delivered from hell. He amazes the crowd by rising up on two feet and singing out. Clothed through the king's charity, Jehan uses his newly restored power of speech to make a public

---

[32] Saints are often characterized in childhood as *pueri* or *puellae senes*. See Elliott 1987, 78.

confession of the sin for which he has already been pardoned. He returns with the king and all the court to the site, and they experience a vision of the princess happy among the angels and martyrs. Her contentment notwithstanding, Jehan's prayer restores her to life, whereupon the king persuades him to return to the city to continue his good works. Having been made bishop, he performs other miracles and composes saints' lives.

(4) ff. 94ra-96rb: De le nonain ki Deu disiroit a vir [rubr.], Picard traits (Morawski 1935, 174), octosyllabic couplets
   Incipit: Moult volentiers se ie savoie
   Explicit: Sans jamais faire de partie
   Edition: ?
   See Morawski 1935, 169-70.
   Summary: This tale describes the experience of a nun who, while praying one Candlemas, visualizes in her thoughts the baby Jesus being offered at the temple by his mother.[33] She is suddenly seized by a burning desire to see God in the flesh ("corporenment," f. 94a). After a year, a three-year-old child appears to the nun. In the course of an affectionate conversation, when he demonstrates at the nun's request that he knows his *Pater Noster*, she all but faints when she realizes who he is. After the child returns to the ciborium, a voice informs the nun that she will be in heaven within a month. She recounts her marvelous experience to the abbess, who tells her story to the community after she dies.

(5) ff. 96rb-97ra: D'une none ki fu trop biele [rubr.], Picard traits (Morawski 1935, 174), octosyllabic couplets
   Incipit: Or mentendes *et* clerc *et* lai
   Explicit: Q'iert ades sans finement
   Edition: ?
   See Morawski 1935, 170.
   Summary: A beautiful nun, feeling sorry that so many men's souls are lost for desire of her, prays to God and the Virgin that her appearance be changed in such a way that no one will wish to see her face again. She becomes so ill that her skin turns yellow as wax and she nearly dies, coming so close to hell that her nose is half burned off by its fires. Confession and communion effect a

---

[33] Concluding the Christmas cycle, the feast of Candlemas is both christological and Marian. The Purification of the Virgin coincides with the Presentation of Christ in the Temple forty days after Epiphany (2 February). The tradition of blessing candles for sacred uses on this day dates to the eleventh century (*Catholic Encyclopedia*, 1908 ed., s.v. "Candlemas").

miraculous cure, but she remains disfigured and lives a pure life to old age. As she approaches death, her beauty returns.

(6) ff. 97ra-99vb: Li miracles del capiel de roses [rubr.], Picard traits (Morawski 1935, 174), octosyllabic couplets
Incipit: Iadis si *comme* iou ai apris
Explicit: *Et* Diex le nous doinst de siervir
Edition: ?
See Morawski 1935, 170-72.
Summary: In his childhood he had been in the habit of gathering the best roses to bedeck the image of the Virgin in the private chapel where he worshiped. His covetous relatives consider this a wasteful practice, and when his mother dies they persuade him to become a monk. Although he can no longer collect roses, he continues to serve the Virgin by reciting many *Ave Maria*s to her each day. Once while performing an errand for the monastery, he stops in the woods to say his *capiel*, unaware of the presence of two thieves who are about to ambush him. The thieves witness a miraculous vision: a very beautiful lady riding a mule gathers roses from the monk's mouth as he prays. Instead of robbing him, they approach and relate what they have seen. They beg his forgiveness and return with him to the monastery, living the rest of their lives honestly.

(7) ff. 99vb-102ra: D'un clerc cui Nostre Dame delivra de se feme [rubr.], Picard traits (Morawski 1935, 174), octosyllabic couplets
Incipit: Encor veul mon sens esprouver
Explicit: Cis miracles trait ci a fin
Edition: Morawski 1935, 326-35
See also Morawski 1935, 172.
Summary: A rich young cleric devoutly serves Notre Dame by reciting a special office in her honor every day before eating anything. In addition, he makes a point of remaining chaste for her sake. When his relatives persuade him to marry, however, he finds himself seated at the wedding feast before it occurs to him that he has almost neglected his customary service to the Virgin. He excuses himself to perform the ritual, intending to return at once. The Virgin appears to him, extremely beautiful, but angry. When she complains that he was about to renounce his chastity, he vows he will give up everything if she will pardon him. The Virgin suggests that this is unnecessary, but, finding him firm in his resolution, she transports him miraculously to a strange place where he happily lives out his days serving her, having escaped from his wedding banquet.

(8) ff. 102ra-103vb: [*Sacristine*], Picard traits (Morawski 1935, 174), octosyllabic couplets

Title: D'une nonain ki issi de son abbeie [rubr.]
Incipit: Un miracle miervelles gent
Explicit: A li siervir del tout se misent
Edition: Guiette 1953
See also Guiette 1927, Morawski 1935, 172-74.

Summary: Gautier's nun wishes to leave the convent and join her lover, but the Virgin prevents her escape by barring the exits to the chapel where the nun, being especially devoted to the Virgin, stops to pray on her way out.[34] Instead of thwarting her purpose in this tale, probably based directly or indirectly on the Latin prose version of Caesar of Heisterbach (*Dial. mirac.*, vii, 34),[35] the Virgin takes on the nun's appearance and performs her tasks as *sacristine* during a fifteen-year absence. When the nun returns, having thoroughly abused her vows, she learns of the miracle, repents, and confesses to the community.

(9) ff. 103vb-104vb: [Gautier de Coinci, "D'un moigne qui fu ou fleuve"], "langue qui caractérise l'Ile-de-France" (Cazelles 1978, 2), 1218-36 (Koenig 1955, 1: xxv-xxx), octosyllabic couplets

Title: D'un moine ki fu noies [rubr.]
Incipit: Celle en cui prist humanité
Explicit: De .ii. & das quines & tiernes
Edition: Koenig 1955, 3: 165-73
See also Cazelles 1978.

Summary: The devil assails the most devout monk in the convent until he begins a liaison with a lady who lives across the river. Each night upon his return, he says matins to the Virgin. During a storm, the devil plunges his boat into the river as he prays. An argument ensues between the angels and the devils for possession of his soul. This text breaks off as the speaker praises the Virgin's influence over the ultimate Judge. In other copies, the story goes on to describe how the monk, who, like the protagonist of the previous text, has charge of the convent's treasure, is missed and discovered drowned by his brothers. They then witness his miraculous return to life, and he lives out his days in perfect chastity. The story concludes with a sermon on lechery among the clergy.

---

[34] Guiette (1927) refers to the Virgin's imprisoning the nun in the chapel as the "secondary theme," while the version appearing in B.N. f. fr. 2162 belongs to a group of "primary" versions.

[35] See Morawski 1935, 173; Guiette 1953, 11-12. Guiette believes the tale may belong to the work of Gautier de Coinci. His 1953 article includes an edition.

(10) ff. 105ra-107ra: [*Dit de l'unicorne et du serpent*], Francien, thirteenth century (Jauss 1970, 204), octosyllabic couplets
   Title: De licorne *et* del serpent [later hand]
   Incipit: Mout par est fols cil ki s'entent
   Explicit: *et* duinst vraie confession
   Edition: Jubinal 1839-42, 2: 113-23
   See also Långfors 1917, 227; Jauss 1968, 160, 165; 1970, 204.
   Summary: The unicorn (death) chases a man (everyman) into a valley where he encounters a serpent (hell). When he climbs a tree (life) to escape, two little animals, one black and one white (night and day), gnaw on the roots. Believing he is doomed, the man distracts himself by enjoying the drops of honey running along the branches of the tree (false pleasures of earthly life). The text explains the allegory and concludes with an exhortation against *faus delit*.

(11) ff. 107ra-115ra: [Life of Saint Thaïs, extract from the *Poème moral*], Wallon, end of twelfth century? (Segre 1970, 108), monorhymed quatrains of alexandrines
   Title: De sainte Taïs [rubr.]
   Incipit: Cui diex done droit cens certes moult puet hair
   Explicit: ke tote male tache de *vos* puist lestre *cons*tee
      Explicit vita Sainte Taisses [decorated in red]
   Edition: Bayot [1929]
   See also Gröber 1902, 30, 698; Meyer 1906a, 375.
   Summary: The story is prefaced by a sermon, addressed particularly to the ladies, on the devil's use of beauty to win souls. The desert father Paphnutius, disguised as a client, visits the courtesan Thaïs, whose beauty has caused the loss of many souls. Converted by him, she suffers in solitary confinement for four years, after being thoroughly instructed concerning confession and repentance. Paphnutius's severity toward her occasions a digression on civil justice. A miraculous revelation of her place in heaven finally convinces him to release her.

(12) ff. 115rb-119ra: [Life of Saint Margaret], octosyllabic couplets
   Title: De *sainte* margerite [rubr.]
   Incipit: Après la sainte Passion
   Explicit: Dites amen, que Dieux l'otroit
      Explicit vita beate Margarete [decorated in red]
   Edition: Joly 1879
   See also Meyer 1906a, 362-63; Francis 1932.
   Summary: Born of pagan parents, Margaret converts to Christianity through the influence of her nurse. Left an orphan at an early age, she tends her nurse's

sheep. Olymbrius, "sires du pais," takes a fancy to her. When she rejects Olymbrius's offer of marriage and scorns his threats in the most insulting terms, she is stripped naked, beaten, and thrown into a dungeon, where she triumphs in two violent confrontations with devils. Her prayer for death is answered by an earthquake and a miraculous vision, which converts the crowd outside her cell. When it comes time for Margaret to meet her death, the executioner experiences a vision and as a result wants to spare her life. She insists on dying, asking only a brief delay to pray for her devotees, especially anyone having anything to do with her biography and pregnant women. All who participate in her funeral suffer martyrdom.

(13) ff. 119ra-125vb: [Silvestres, *Pater noster*], Picard, late twelfth century (Brayer 1970, 24), octosyllabic couplets
    Title: li pa*ter* n*os*te*r* [rubr.]
    Incipit: Au saint espir *con*manc m'entente
    Explicit: En cel non di pa*ter* noster
        Ex----pli----cit
    Edition: ?
    See Bonnard [1884] 1967, 144-46; Gröber 1902, 690; Långfors 1912; Långfors 1917, 28; Brayer 1970, 24-25.
    Summary: The poet, "Selviestres," names himself (in the third person) in line 8 of the text (f. 119ra14). His work is not a "lai, conte, fauble, ne aventure," but rather a prayer, which he will explain so that listeners who *think* they know it will not simply repeat it like magpies. He prefaces the gloss by explaining that the prayer has seven parts, and alerts the listener as he proceeds from one to the next:

> Signor .ii. en avés eues:
> Gardés q*ue*s aiés entendues
> Encore en devés .v. avoir
> (f. 121ra24-26)

Our filial duties to God are reflected in the word *Pater*, while *Noster* implies, in addition, our fraternity with all mankind. *In caelis* evokes both everlasting life and the corrupt life here below. The sacrament of baptism is explained in connection with *sanctificetur nomen tuum*. *Adveniat regnum tuum* entails a comparison of divine with earthly rule, naming "Karles, Rollans, Cesar," with a warning against pride and a reminder of Lucifer's fall. *Panem nostrum quotidianum* (the only Latin verse omitted from the text) has three meanings: it is our earthly sustenance, the word of God, and the divine sacrament. When we ask that our debts be forgiven, God knows whether or not we sincerely repent. The poet validates his own undertaking by echoing the words of the prologue:

> Mais Diex tres bien entent et ot:
> Tot ot, tot entent, et tot voit;
> Pruec saciés bien que cil mescroit
> Ki seulement des levres prie.
> (f. 123ra38-b2)

Sicut et nos dimittimus debitoribus nostris provokes a lengthy sermon concerning man's peaceful conduct on earth, in which the poet exhorts:

> Plus devons nos le roi doter
> Ki tos rois a a governer
> Que les autres rois teriens.
> (f. 123va32-34)

A digression on confession and penance includes the example of Mary Magdalene. Two meanings are ascribed to *et ne nos inducas in temptationem*: active and passive. In the case of passive temptation, the devil's influence may be averted by reciting the *Pater Noster*. The last verse, claims the poet, hardly needs a gloss:

> Jo ne vos i fai plus gloser;
> A dieu dites apertement:
> De mal nos delivre et defent.
> (f. 125va20-22)

The closing lines dedicate the work to the daughter of a count "Mahui" of "Boloigne."[36]

(14) ff. 125vb-133va: [Life of Saint Alexis], Picard, thirteenth century (Stebbins 1974, 20), laisses of monorhymed alexandrines
  Title: De saint alexit [rubr.]
  Incipit: Plaist vos a escoter d'un saint home la geste
  Explicit: Or est dite la vie d'un glorieus signour
  Edition: Stebbins 1974
  See also Meyer 1906a, 337-38; Stebbins 1978; Uitti 1967; Elliott 1983.
  Summary: The prologue states that the story will serve as an example to the faithful. Alexis's parents, rich, powerful, and devout Roman Christians, are childless until his mother, like the biblical Sarah and Elizabeth, conceives him in old age. Having dedicated his life to Christ as a child, on his wedding day

---

[36] Bonnard identifies the lady as Ide, daughter of Matthieu d'Alsace, and accordingly dates the poem between 1175 and 1180 ([1884] 1967, 146). Edith Brayer finds his argument "douteux" (1970, 24).

Alexis flees to Rohais, sells his treasure, and gives everything away for charity. His bride and his parents grieve and search for him, but because of his changed appearance, they never succeed in finding him. He leads a saintly life for seventeen years, until an image of the Virgin magically speaks, asking a sacristan to seek him out. Alexis, wishing to avoid the temptations inherent in notoriety, returns to Rome, and lives incognito on the charity of his own family. After another seventeen years of fasts and vigils, Alexis requests pen and parchment to write the secrets of his life. His identity is not discovered until the pope and the two emperors, along with a vast crowd, are magically summoned to the palace of Alexis's father to honor the saint's remains and hear his autobiography read. The story closes with his funeral and an account of miracles performed at his tomb.

(15) ff. 133vb-136vb: [*Li ver de Couloigne*], Picard or Wallon, mid-thirteenth century (Kleineidam 1968, 31-33), quatrains of monorhymed alexandrines
  Title: Li vier de couloigne [rubr.]
  Incipit: Cil vier n'ont nul mestier [prologue]
        Glorious Sire Pere qui le mont racatas [text]
  Explicit: Que denes un seul vise viers cui i seconba
  Edition: Kleineidam 1968
  See also Långfors 1917, 70; Gröber 1902, 747-48, 985.
  Summary: Acknowledging his fear of God's justice, the speaker enumerates the sins that master him, with special attention to pride. He complains of the conflict between the heart attracted to sins and the will to avoid them:

> Mais ce sui ge meïsme
>   qui a moi me *com*bat,
> Je sui cil qui deffent,
>   je sui cis ki assalt,
> Je sui cis qui trebut,
>   je sui cis ki abat;
> Dieu, merchi cis estors!
>   s'auques fui c'or n'en a.
> (ll. 109-12 Kleineidam, f. 135rb9-16)

He recognizes his responsibility for his own sins but prays for strength against the devil. It would not be right to blame God for one's sin, as did Adam and Eve: those who admit their faults deserve God's mercy. God has given man enough force, virtue, and sense to combat and overcome any vice. The text in B.N. f. fr. 2162 stops here, at the end of a gathering. In the other manuscript, the poem goes on to lament that the sinner, voluntarily in the devil's service, fails to respond even when God, out of pity, calls him back. The speaker complains of his sinful life but affirms his Christian belief in spite of his actions. Remembering the Crucifixion, he calls on Christ's mercy, praying for tears of remorse. The examples of Mary Magdalene, Saint Peter, David, and Mary the Egyptian are mentioned. Finally he begs for the gifts of good works, moderation, charity, humility, wisdom, the power to avoid worldly pleasures, and the grace of the Holy Spirit to find his way to God: "Et a mes oels me foi veïr çou que je croi" (l. 476).

The poem is much more passionate and complex than this brief summary would indicate. It can be considered as constituting the personal aspect of the sacrament of repentance: no mention is made of confession to a priest or of absolution.

3
"Literature in the True Sense"
Aristocratic Virtues and Textual Travels

TEXTS

Parise la duchesse
Chrétien de Troyes, *Cligès*
Life of Saint Eustace
La venjance Nostre Seigneur
Bertrand de Bar-sur-Aube, *Girart de Vienne*
Gerbert de Montreuil, *Roman de la violette*
Aimon de Varennes, *Florimont*

Textual critics who have been obliged to deal with B.N. f. fr. 1374 unanimously condemn the scribe. G. F. de Martonne, the first editor of *Parise la duchesse*, inveighs:

> L'incorrection de cette copie ne pouvait être réparée par la confrontation avec aucune autre du même temps. Le scribe, qui semble n'avoir que médiocrement entendu ce qu'il copiait, a peut-être créé des mots dont nous avons vainement cherché à donner l'explication. Il en est de même de son orthographie, que, si nous ne craignions le reproche de pédantisme, nous qualifierions plus volontiers d'*hétérographie*.
>
> Ce que nous devons regretter le plus, c'est qu'il ait tronqué des vers et des passages entiers, comme un examen attentif a pu nous en convaincre. ([1834] 1969, xxiii)

In his 1912 edition of the Old French version of the life of Saint Eustace, Andreas C. Ott remarks: "Der Schreiber ist Südfranzose, hat manches nicht verstanden und ist überdies nachlässig und flüchtig" (482). Douglas Buffum, editor of the *Roman de la violette*, recognizes the possible advantage of an inferior scribe: "Le copiste était négligent et souvent il ne comprenait pas l'original . . . mais il tâchait de le copier sans y rien ajouter; malgré ses nombreuses erreurs, il nous apporte donc un témoignage qui n'est pas sans valeur" (1928, vii-viii).

Alexandre Micha, who prefers to trust the more intelligent Guiot for the base text of his *Cligès* edition, expatiates on the scribe's shortcomings:

> Le ms. omet des vers absolument indispensables pour la construction et pour le sens. . . . Il faudrait que le scribe fût entièrement dépourvu du sens de la construction pour supprimer ces vers nécessaires. . . . D'esprit lent, de main lent aussi . . . il s'égare, débordé par la dictée. . . . Distrait, peut-être un peu sourd, . . . le scribe manque de finesse et abime des passages où la pensée était délicate. . . . Ce copiste très négligent a peut-être de mauvais yeux. . . . Inintelligent et maladroit, il a assez de mal à ne pas oublier ses mots, à ne pas manger de lettre, pour ne pas se mêler encore de réfections! ([1939] 1966, 223-25)

Loyal Gryting observes that "scholars who have studied these other works all agree on the poor reputation which the copyist has and deserves. The many gaps, verses omitted, verses repeated, not to mention mutilated words, attest his carelessness and perhaps ignorance" (1952, 23). Wolfgang van Emden concurs in more restrained terms: "C'est un homme qui a fait beaucoup de fautes d'inattention" (1977, xlviii).

Such a consensus of disparagement goes far beyond the editorial topos of the simpleminded scribe: taken together, the criticisms imply a particularly vivid characterization, without, however, necessitating too many speculations about the scribe's situation. In fact, the manuscript was written not by one careless individual, but by six different ones. I shall return to this problem after surveying the manuscript's contents and analyzing relationships among the texts.

Medieval poets, as well as scribes, sometimes suffer the disapproval of modern critics. The nineteenth-century editors of the first text in the manuscript, *Parise la duchesse*, disdainfully characterize it as a *chanson de geste* of inferior rank.[1] Martonne would have it that the prologue mentions Charlemagne, who has little to do with the story, only to add dignity to a "simple et modeste tableau de malheurs domestiques" ([1834] 1969, ix). According to F. Guessard and L. Larchey, the heroic tale of Parise's misfortunes and ultimate triumph is supported by elements that in themselves form "les fondements d'un mélodrame bien plus que les bases d'un monument épique" (1860, v). In her literary study of *Parise*, its recent editor May Plouzeau evaluates it in generic terms, concluding that the author "paraît gêné, plutôt que servi" by the exigencies of epic form (1986, 1: 117-22). She characterizes the poem as an adventure story, a simple romance cast in the epic mold to make it accessible to the vast public of the *jongleur* (ibid., 159-61).

The poem belongs genealogically to the Mayence-Nanteuil cycle of Old French epic, Parise being the daughter of Garnier de Nanteuil (ll. 35-36, f. 10vb). However, the fact that other poems of the cycle are frequently found together in manuscripts without *Parise*

---

[1] Until it was recently edited by May Plouzeau (1986), it had been treated only in passing by modern critics (see Riquer [1957], 278). An exception was Alfred Adler (1974), who used it as an example of "epic speculation," showing how questions raised in *Parise* concerning the duties of a sovereign and his warriors are addressed in the later poem *Tristan de Nanteuil*. Another new edition of this text has been announced by Dorothy Schrader and Richard Hartman (*Olifant* 8:2 [1980]: 219).

implies that it is relatively independent of the *geste* (Hartman and Shrader 1982, 178-79). *Beuve de Hantone* was once considered a source for *Parise*; Plouzeau explains their affinity by suggesting the author of *Parise* may have borrowed themes from an early version of *Beuve*, while later versions of *Beuve* in their turn cited *Parise* (1986, 132-35). The editor also considers possible borrowings from *Macaire*, *Doon de la Roche*, *Renaut de Montauban*, *Gui de Bourgogne*, and *Gaydon* (ibid., 129-50). Among fourteenth-century epics the poem's influence can be easily recognized in *Lion de Bourges* and in *Tristan de Nanteuil* (ibid., 150-59). No other versions of the story have been discovered, and B.N. f. fr. 1374 contains the only extant copy.

Parise features a great many familiar motifs, including the unjustly accused woman banished and eventually reunited with her husband, the exiled rightful heir returning to claim his fief, the wellborn hero ignorant of his true identity, the poisoned apple, the pilgrim disguise, the judicial duel, the kidnapping of a newborn baby, the noble birthmark, the chess game, and the single combat in which the father fails to recognize his son.[2]

Just as *Parise* has been considered marginal in its genre by some critics of the *chanson de geste*, the tradition of Chrétien scholarship has given *Cligès* (ff. 21va-64vb) the "reputation as being a mosaic of sources, an abortive structural experiment, and a curious anomaly in Chrétien's repertory" (Maddox 1973, 745). It derives from Greco-oriental rather than Celtic material (Frappier 1968a, 104), and its structure is bipartite rather than tripartite (Lacy 1970, 307). While its relationship to the Tristan legend has been a central concern in interpreting the work, the *Roman d'Enéas*, Wace's *Brut*, and Ovid have also been regarded as sources. It has been suggested that contemporary Byzantine history is reflected in the plot. On the basis of these influences, as well as of the chronology of Chrétien's work, Micha (1957) posits 1176 as the poem's date of composition. Having established *S* as an authority closer to the original than *A* (sigla assigned by Wendelin Foerster to B.N. f.fr. 1374 and 794 [1884]), Guido Favati (1967) rereads line 22 from the manuscript (it had been silently "corrected" by Foerster): "De la fu cist livres estraiz." He takes this to mean Chrétien used a book that had been saved from a fire known to have taken place at Saint-Pierre de Beauvais in 1180, and accordingly proposes this date as the *terminus a quo*. Passages in the *Chevalier de la charette* and the *Conte du Graal* dedicating them to Marie de Champagne and Philippe d'Alsace, respectively, added to the courtly ambiance depicted in the romances themselves, suggest that Chrétien wrote for an aristocratic public. A discussion of the

---

[2] See also Plouzeau 1986, 1: 125-28.

generic traits of *Cligès* would approach tautology, since studies of medieval romance often take Chrétien's work as the principal reference point.³

A text of some 6,700 lines, *Cligès* comes down to us in nine manuscripts: six contain more than one work by Chrétien (five of these include other texts as well), and one has *Cligès* alone. Only two, including B.N. f. fr. 1374 (Foerster's *S*), single out *Cligès* for combination with works not by Chrétien. No critical edition, strictly speaking, has been made of *Cligès* (or of any of Chrétien's works). The text has been published by Foerster using B.N. f. fr. 1374 as a base, and by Micha using the Guiot manuscript (B.N. f. fr. 794, Foerster's *A*). Neither gives a complete explanation of his method of selection or of establishing the text. Though *S* appears both contaminated and flawed by scribal negligence (see Micha 1957, xx), Favati (1967) argues for the relative authenticity of *S* over the more consistent *A*.

Text 3 of B.N. f. fr. 1374 (ff. 65ra-75rb) is the unique copy of the only Old French verse version of the life of Saint Eustace that has an opening line in the epic style: "Seignor et dames, entendez tuit a moi" (f. 65ra).⁴ All the surviving Old French versions (eleven in verse and thirteen in prose) derive from one of two Latin translations of the earliest of three Greek texts, dating to the eighth century or earlier (Petersen 1924, 53-54, 58-59). Holger Petersen postulates a Greek-speaking monk, perhaps in Syria, as the creator of the legend (1925, 86). The praise of the soul ripe for conversion but not yet Christian and the appearance of Christ in animal form have analogues in Buddhist tradition; the kidnapping of children by animals occurs in Greek romances but may derive from Indian legend through Syrian intermediaries (ibid., 66-84). Chapter 3 of the Book of Daniel and the legend of Phalaris are probable sources for the particular style of martyrdom suffered by Eustace and his family (ibid., 84-86). The poem's appeal to an aristocratic public, its emphasis on the hero's individual goals rather than on his success as a Roman general, its portrayal of Eustace's internal motivation, and its use of *aventure* in motivating the plot are traits that make it similar to the romance in character.

The *Venjance Nostre Seigneur* (the fourth text in our manuscript, ff. 75rb-90vb) is the Old French epic version of a legend combining the avenging of the Crucifixion, the curing of Tiberius with the vernicle, and the capture of Jerusalem by Titus. The legend replaces Tiberius with Vespasian and joins the story of Pilate's arrest to that of the capture of Jerusalem. It occurs in all medieval Christian cultures and in a variety of literary forms (Gryting 1952, 1-2). The Old French epic version survives in five redactions preserved in nine manuscripts, the oldest of which is B.N. f. fr. 1374. On

---

³ For surveys of the most prominent issues relating to this romance, see Frappier 1968a (especially 104-21) and Maddox 1973.

⁴ See Petersen 1924, 67-68 and Meyer 1906a, 348-49. Versions 1 and 9 are fragments and lack first lines.

the basis of his language study, Gryting, the editor, dates the composition of this redaction to the end of the twelfth century (ibid., 31).

Composed in laisses of monorhymed alexandrines, the text is formally and stylistically a *chanson de geste*. The siege of Jerusalem constitutes the principal event of the poem, giving it a military emphasis that overshadows the hagiographic episodes. Uncommon for epic, however, the multiplicity of fully developed characters precludes the representation of any single heroic model. Titus would seem the obvious candidate, but his role is matched by those of several others, including Jacob, father of Mary Magdalene, Gai, the emperor's seneschal, and Veronica.

In the next text in B.N. f. fr. 1374, *Girart de Vienne* (ff. 91ra-132vb), Bertrand de Bar-sur-Aube, one of the first poets to name himself as the author of a *chanson de geste*, delineates the three Old French epic cycles of King Charles, Doon de Mayence, and Garin de Monglane. *Girart* belongs in some sense to all three: it relates the beginning of the legendary friendship between Roland and Oliver, central to the story of King Charles's war against the Saracens; its hero defies his lord, as do members of the lineage of Doon; and he is the great-grandfather of Guillaume d'Orange, descendant of Garin de Monglane. According to its most recent editor, Wolfgang van Emden, Bertrand attaches Girart to Guillaume's lineage in order to keep him out of the family of the rebellious vassals and thus render him sympathetic (1977, xxv). The political climate of Philippe-Auguste's reign would make such a characterization appropriate, corroborating the hypothetical date of 1180 that Van Emden derives by comparing the genealogical details of several songs (ibid., xxx-xxxiv). Analogues to Girart's character occur in the *Chanson d'Aspremont* (Girart de Fraite) and in *Girart de Rousillon* (ibid., xxiii-xxiv). By inventing the family of Garin de Monglane, Bertrand not only legitimizes Girart's rebellion, but elaborates the ancestry of Guillaume d'Orange. Four of the five manuscripts known to contain *Girart de Vienne* preserve it in the context of the cycle of Garin de Monglane: in three of these it is followed by *Aymeri de Narbonne*, believed by some scholars also to have been composed by Bertrand (ibid., xxv-xxxvii).

B.N. f. fr. 1374 is the only noncyclical manuscript in the tradition of *Girart de Vienne*. Van Emden is obliged to propose two stemmata based on different sections of the song, since the scribe of *S* seems to have used two different models, and renounces the Lachmannian method in establishing his text (ibid., lv-lxv).

According to its editor, Buffum, Gerbert de Montreuil's *Roman de la violette*, the sixth text in B.N. f.fr. 1374 (ff. 133ra-172vb, 183r), derives from the *Roman de la rose*, also called the *Roman de Guillaume de Dole*, by Jean Renart, and the anonymous *Comte de Poitiers*, edited by Koenig in 1937 (1928, xl). Like them, it belongs to the *Cycle de la gageure*, in which a challenger tests a lady's chastity: her weakness is "proved" by trickery, and the restoration of her rightful honor completes the story.[5] Like the *Roman de la rose*, the *Roman de la violette* contains passages of lyric (and one extract from an epic), where various characters are depicted singing. Buffum has shown analogues to a number of other contemporary works (ibid., xlv-lv), and has researched possible references to historical figures, including Marie, countess of Ponthieu, to whom the poem is dedicated (ibid., lv-lxxiii). On the basis of these references, he dates the poem's composition at 1227-29. B.N. f.fr. 1374 contains the oldest of the four surviving copies.

B.N. f. fr. 1374 contains only 2,042 lines of *Florimont* (ff. 173ra-182vb), a romance that extends to more than 13,000 lines. The poet, Aimon de Varennes, names himself several times in the course of the poem and says he wrote it at Châtillon in the year 1188. Because he uses Greek expressions and apologizes for his substandard French, Paulin Paris believed Aimon to have been born a Greek (1840, 11-12); it is much more likely that he spoke a Lotharingian (Hilka 1933, liii) or Lyonnais dialect and owed his knowledge of Greek and of geography to experience from a pilgrimage (Fourrier 1960, 472-85). He may also have acquired certain details of the plot from oriental popular sources (see Gröber 1902, 589-90).[6] A variation of the Psyche myth, the story of Florimont's relationship with the *Dame de l'Ile Selee* is probably borrowed from *Partonopeus de Blois* (see Fourrier 1960, 447-60); other important sources include Ovid, Wace, *Piramus*, the *Roman d'Enéas*, the *Roman d'Alexandre*, Chrétien de Troyes, Marie de France, and *Floire et Blancheflor* (Hilka 1933, cxiii). Aimon emphasizes the virtue of *largesse* and enjoys expounding etymologies and fabricating acronyms as well as displaying his knowledge of Greek. The Golden Age motif opens the poem with reference to *largesse* and returns to bemoan the decline of *fine amors*. Fortune's wheel is a prominent device introducing new episodes, and the progressive interpretation of Florimont's father's prophetic dream lends continuity to the narrative.

CODICOLOGICAL ARTICULATIONS

In conjunction with the foregoing survey of the manuscript's contents, scrutiny of several codicological anomalies will provide background for an analysis of the collection. Further codicological details are described at the end of the chapter, accompanied by table 3, which outlines the organization of the volume.

---

[5] See Gaston Paris 1903. There are some forty versions in the cycle, including Boccaccio's *Decameron* II, 9.

[6] Fourrier claims to have identified the author in a charter signed by both Ayminus de Varennes and Bernardus de Castellione in 1197. The Juliana to whom the poem is dedicated could have been Bernard's sister (Fourrier 1960, 467-71).

First, *Cligès*, the second text, remains unfinished by about one folio. The interruption of the text corresponds with the end of gathering 8. Gatherings 8 and 9 are both complete, and no lines are missing from the beginning of the next text. The *Roman de la violette*, the sixth text, also suffers an interruption just before the end. In this case the next text begins on the recto of the *last* folio of gathering 20, and the missing ending is supplied on folio 183 (gathering 21).[7] The manuscript's third unfinished text, *Florimont*, lacks more than 11,000 of a total of some 13,000 lines. It stops abruptly in the middle of a grammatical construction (on the second to last folio of gathering 21), and there is no reason to suppose the collection was not meant to include the entire work. While a missing gathering could explain the truncation of *Cligès*, the relationship between the other two texts resists interpretation. The circumstance of traveling models could account for the states of all three: the scribe was perhaps obliged to pass on his model before completing his own copy. In the case of *Violette*, he was able to consult the model again before it left the vicinity; *Florimont*'s scribe failed to allot enough time for it.

Although the editors cited above give uniformly depreciatory views of "the scribe," a number of factors disrupting the pattern of the manuscript's organization confirm the work of several scribes, six to be exact. The third gathering, for example, has the only surviving catchword of the first eighteen. A different hand using different ink appears suddenly in the middle of gathering 9: it copies folios 66-71v, all but the outside bifolia. A third scribe, very similar to the first, copies folios 72-132v (the last folio of gathering 9 through gathering 16), and another begins gathering 17 (f. 133) with text 6 (the *Roman de la violette*). He uses lowercase rather than capitals for initials of lines. At this point the gathering size becomes irregular, and the number of lines per column changes from a regular thirty-eight to between forty and forty-three, with a corresponding enlargement of the text page. In gathering 17, another new hand begins at folio 135a, and a supply of blacker ink becomes evident at folio 138. A sixth scribe copies the *Florimont* fragment (gatherings 20 and 21)(see Van Emden 1977, xlix).

Van Emden has pointed out that gatherings 17-21 might represent a separate unit (ibid., xliv). Micha's observation that the scribe of *Cligès* seems to be working from dictation, together with the manuscript traditions of the first five works of the collection, suggests an orally transmitted series. *Parise la duchesse* and the life of Saint Eustace are unique copies; the stemma proposed by Favati for *Cligès* sets *S* quite apart from the other witnesses (1967, 402). This manuscript has the oldest surviving copy of the *Venjance Nostre Seigneur* (for which the editor has provided no stemma), and *Girart de Vienne*

---

[7] Van Emden suggests that a gathering containing the beginning of *Florimont* (ff. 174-82) has been inserted between the last two folios of *Violette*, implying that gathering 20 is a quinion lacking one folio, and that folio 183 would complete it (1977, xlix). However, a stub in the middle of that gathering accounts for the missing folio, and the text of *Florimont* begins one folio *before* the supposed insertion.

appears to be contaminated (see above p. 58). Text 6 is the oldest surviving copy of *Violette*, but since it is copied by a different hand and its articulation with the fragment of *Florimont* is so peculiar, I would hesitate to extend the claim of oral transmission beyond the sixteenth gathering. Still, it is not unlikely that some of the "traveling models" posited above were transported by means of human memory. Such a position is supported by the observation that the changes of hands occur at mid-gathering and mid-text, which would seem more consistent with a performance situation than with a controlled professional or monastic scriptorium setting.

Despite the division of labor among scribes, the manuscript's consistent absence of decoration confirms the collection's integrity: similar spaces have been left by all the scribes for ornamental initials at the texts' incipits. Whatever their working situation, the scribes must have received instructions from a single source. An examination of affinities apparent in sequential groups of texts as well as in the collection as a whole will help to characterize this source and the audience it served.

ANALYSIS AND INTERPRETATION

Parise, *Cligès*, and the life of Saint Eustace all raise questions concerning the feudal obligations of a virtuous vassal to an unworthy lord. In *Parise*, Clarembaut does not hesitate to defend his lady's honor, even against her husband; when he is in a position to overpower him, however, he prefers to seek peaceful terms:

> Et respont Clarembaus: "Par mon chief, non ferez;
> Li dus est pere Hugon, que de voir le savez,
> Et, se il se voloit anvers nos acorder,
> Nos le devrions bien servir et anorer."
> (ll. 2502-5 Plouzeau, f. 17rb33-36)

The passage implies that though Raymond has forfeited his right to Clarembaut's support, the old man's loyalty to the family motivates him to treat the duke generously.

Cligès has long been viewed as a kind of analogue to the Tristan legend: an "anti-Tristan," a "hyper-Tristan," or a "neo-Tristan" (see Frappier 1968a, 106, 111-14). The parallel obtains not only for the illicit love between the husband's nephew and the wife, but for the nephew's betrayal of his uncle and liege lord. In the case of *Cligès*, it is not the inevitability of their passion that inspires our sympathy for the lovers, but rather the dishonorable conduct of the husband toward his vassal: Cligès seems to have a right to Fenice based on Alis's contract with his father, added to the fact that he has won her in battle against the Saxons on his uncle's behalf.

The story of Eustace demonstrates how strong the saint's virtue is when tested first by his family ties and then by his loyalty to the emperor, whom he serves as seneschal.

He has given up his worldly position and his family to serve God, but returns to the emperor's service when he feels it is in God's best interest to do so:

> La n'irai pas por gré d'empereor,
> Ne p*or* richece d'avoir ne por anor,
> Ne p*or* mostrer mon sen ne ma valor,
> Mais por desfandre mon natival seignor.
> (ll. 761-64 Ott, f. 70ra3-6)

When faced with a choice between God and Caesar, however, he goes so far as to insult the emperor's golden gods in the name of Christianity: he would sell them or melt them down to buy food for the poor:

> Je ne leiroie p*or* crime de seignor,
> Ne por loier ne por losengeor,
> Q *u*'a povres gens ne fussent del meillor.
> (ll. 1337-39, f. 73va36-38)

Thus for various reasons Clarembaut, Cligès, and Eustace all have legitimate complaints against their respective lords, two of whom are emperors.

Like *Cligès* and the life of Saint Eustace, the *Venjance Nostre Seigneur*, which follows the life of Saint Eustace in B.N. f. fr. 1374, is concerned with the rule of an emperor, and it echoes the hagiographic theme of the saint's life. Though it has no martyr as its hero, a Christian miracle motivates the principal event of the poem, the siege of Jerusalem. The magical healing power of the vernicle is identical with that which enables Saint Eustace and his family to sing as they are being incinerated within the bronze bull. The power of Christian virtue is also reflected in the contrast between the two emperors: the emperor Trangïens's holdings become greatly reduced in the absence of his worthy Christian seneschal Placidas, while Vespasian's vow to embrace Christianity makes him invincible against God's enemies.

The next text returns to the problem of the righteous defiance of one's liege lord. *Girart de Vienne* may have been designed specifically to legitimize the role of the rebellious vassal (see p. 58 above). It makes an appropriate sequel to the *Venjance Nostre Seigneur*, however, in other ways. Both depict sieges of important cities, for example. An even more striking connection appears in laisse 135 of *Girart*, describing the armor worn by Oliver for his battle against Roland:

> Si *com* armer se dut li gentius
> Atant ez v*os* .i. juïf, Johachin;
> Blanche ot la barbe ainsi *com* flors de lis.
> Puis cele hore q*ue* Pilatre fu pris,
> Per cui Jhe*s*u ot esté en crois mis,
> —mais plus en prist venjence, ce m'est vis,

> Vaspasïens, l'emperere gentis;
> Car il fist pandre, si *com* dist li escriz
> [Toz les Jus qui erent a ceu dis][8]
> En Jhru*s*al*a*m, la cité seignoriz,
> Defors la vile furent trestot ocis—
> Tres icele ore, que je v*os* devis,
> Fuia*n*t Vïanne cil Jus, Johachi*n*s.
> (ll. 4880-92 Van Emden, f. 121rb19-31)

While coincidence might account for the presence of these two texts in the manuscript, their juxtaposition suggests a deliberate selection by someone who knew both works in enough detail to remember this small passage. It intimates a connection between the cities of Vienne and Jerusalem and makes of the *Venjance Nostre Seigneur* a "historical" antecedent to *Girart*. This seems appropriate in view of the fact that the epic ends with an exhortation to rout the infidel.

Codicological evidence indicates a possible division of the manuscript between *Girart de Vienne* and the *Roman de la violette* (see pp. 60-61 above) at the break between gatherings 16 and 17. Although the literary analysis supports the *inclusion* of the last two texts in the collection, it is not immediately obvious why *Girart* and the *Roman de la violette* are juxtaposed. There is, however, a coincidence between the heroes' names (*Gerart* de Nevers being the protagonist of the romance), and a similarly limited geographical area is represented in both poems. All the *other* texts in the manuscript narrate ventures into central Europe and the Middle East, while *Girart de Vienne* and the *Roman de la violette* concern themselves exclusively with French-speaking territories. Although the king of a *chanson de geste* differs fundamentally from the king of a romance,[9] and an epic royal assembly has a distinctly masculine ambiance compared with the plenary courts held by romance sovereigns, these two texts nevertheless offer a contrast between a king who properly executes his duties and one who, through ill will or weakness, continually provokes his men.

Violette and *Florimont* (assuming that the whole of *Florimont* originally belonged in the collection), both romances, have a great many traits in common. In *Violette*, Gerart's wager and his subsequent foolishness cost him his land and separate him from Euriaut, though she continues to love him. Florimont, as yet unlanded, squanders what wealth he does possess in an effort to mitigate his sorrow when his lady unjustly accuses and rejects him. Like Gerart and Euriaut, he assumes the identity of a lower station to achieve intermediate goals: he visits Romadanaple disguised as a tailor, concealing his

---

[8] This important line is missing from B.N. f. fr. 1374. See Van Emden 1977, 217.

[9] "One puts a princess in a fairy tale next to a princess in a novella, and one notices the difference" (Jolles 1956, 196, quoted in Jauss 1982, 82).

face with a bolt of cloth. Gerart entertains the wicked Lisiart as a *jongleur*, and Euriaut avoids marrying the duke of Metz by posing as a prostitute. Both heroes, through a series of loosely connected adventures embellished by courtly diversions and digressions, eventually triumph in possession of both lady and land.

While the sequence of texts reveals affinities that link them one to the next, groups of texts considered out of sequence raise still more common issues. A marked resemblance in plot unites the epic *Parise* with the romance *Violette*. The characters and predicaments of the heroines as well as the devious treachery of the villains motivate the action in both. The theme of the unjustly accused woman is doubled in the case of Euriaut: first separated from her lover by an accusation of infidelity, she is alienated from her new protector, the duke of Metz, by an accusation of murder. Even more striking, while Parise is framed for killing her husband's brother, Euriaut's supposed victim is the duke's sister. In both stories, the lady spends her exile at the court of a German nobleman.

In addition to these parallels of detail, *Parise* and *Violette*, along with *Cligès*, the life of Saint Eustace, and *Florimont*, have similar plot structures resembling that of *Apollonii regis Tyri*, principal example of a subgenre derived from Greek romance (see Perry 1967, app. 2). Michel Zink identifies the tradition of the "Mediterranean romance":

> Toute une série de romans . . . promènent leur héros tout autour du bassin méditerranéen, combinent les réminiscences de l'Antiquité classique et du monde byzantin, les modèles narratifs nés à l'époque alexandrine—aventures sentimentales, rapts, séparations, voyages—, la fascination de l'Orient mêlée à l'esprit des croisades. (1987, 27-28)

I will return to the question of geographical settings; Zink's characterization of the typical Mediterranean romance plot would describe most of the texts in B.N. f. fr. 1374.

Connections such as these offer a glimpse of the collector at work, but a clearer notion of his purpose takes shape when we analyze elements common to all the texts. The implication of an aristocratic audience and the predominance of a kind of geographic realism, combined with extratextual considerations, suggest a particular function.

Each of the texts in B.N. f. fr. 1374 addresses itself in some way to the concerns of the noble class. Even the saint's life has a hero distinguished by noble traits and military prowess, and chivalric values dominate the characters' motivations. Many of the texts dwell on details of a young nobleman's education, including his eventually being dubbed a knight. The innate nobility of Eustace's sons prevails over their humble upbringing, and their right to bear arms is unquestioned. Similarly, at the court of the king of Hungary Parise's son Hugh must prove he has noble blood in a test of character, corresponding to the assumption that noblemen are by birth morally superior to others. Conversely, in the same poem, the behavior of the bourgeois of Vauvenice to the duke's traitor wife, though they side with the sympathetic faction, shows their innate meanness.

The narrators of *Cligès* and *Florimont* emphasize the aristocratic virtue of *largesse*. When Alexander departs for Arthur's court, his father makes it the keynote of his farewell speech; Aimon returns to it again and again in the course of his story and goes so far as to speculate about the danger of an excess of this virtue when he makes Florimont destitute because of his own foolishness. *Largesse* takes on a slightly different significance in the story of Eustace, whose generosity is colored more by charity than by chivalry.

As another aspect of *largesse*, the noble host's concern with the quality of courtly entertainment is reflected in the texts' portrayal of deficient, as well as magnificent, examples. In *Girart de Vienne*, the abbot of Cluny and a bourgeois of Vienne both exceed the hospitality of Charlemagne toward Girart and Renier. The opening scene of the *Roman de la violette* recreates an Easter feast of King Louis: one beautiful lady after another contributes her grace and charm to the agreeable ambiance of leisure.

Economic concerns of the noble class also appear in the characterization of impoverished fathers, particularly those with several sons. Parise's old friend Clarembaut has fourteen; *Girart de Vienne* opens with the exploits of the four sons of Garin de Monglane in the process of recuperating his losses from the Saracens. Florimont's father, the duke of Albania, has lost his wealth to a giant, whom Florimont is obliged to dispatch.

In addition to the implication of a noble audience, the seven texts have in common an unusual degree of realism in geographic detail. In all but two, settings include locations in Hungary, Greece, or the Levant. Arthur's court appears only once, in the least Arthurian of Chrétien's romances. Place-names repeatedly beckon the reader to a map of central Europe and the Mediterranean. Parise travels through the forest of Hungary and eventually arrives in Cologne. Fenice is the daughter of the German emperor, whose court is at Cologne, and the primary setting of *Cligès* is imperial Greece. The "pilgrims" seeking Eustace on the emperor's behalf travel through Lombardy, Germany, France, Spain, Greece, and Hungary before they find him (f. 69a), and Eustace reconquers the emperor's territory in Greece. The action centers on Rome and Jerusalem, homes of the new and the old faiths, in the *Venjance Nostre Seigneur*; Vespasian takes Haifa in a preliminary siege, and Pilate is taken to Vienne for punishment. Albania, Cairo, Adrianople, Antioch, Bulgaria, Hungary, Carthage, Damietta, the Danube, Philippopolis, Gallipoli, Macedonia, Persia, Russia, Syria, Cyprus, and Turkey are among the places mentioned in *Florimont*.[10]

Many romances reflect a fascination with exotic, far-off lands unfamiliar to the listeners. In this case, however, the combination of *several* texts focusing on *realistic* geographic details and cataloguing specific place-names would seem to imply an audience

---

[10] Fourrier has shown that Aimon must have been personally familiar with many of these places, including itineraries such as the Via Egnatia, a route well known to pilgrims and Crusaders (1960, 172-82).

of travelers, or of people who are otherwise familiar with places in which the narratives are set. The aristocratic emphasis of the texts suggests Crusaders or colonists, rather than pilgrims or merchants. The question of feudal obligations raised in several of them addresses the concerns of the warlike noble class, troubled by territorial disputes and dynastic struggles, which had diverted its violent tendencies toward the infidel when such measures as the Truce of God and the Peace of God had proved insufficient to quell fighting (Prawer 1972a, 6-10). In *Girart de Vienne*, in fact, it is an angel of God who interrupts the combat between Roland and Oliver to recommend they make peace between them and turn their energies against the Saracens (ll. 5898-905 Van Emden, f. 127va13-19).

The thirteenth century was an active period for Western involvement in the eastern Mediterranean area. The First, Second, and Third Crusades, which had traveled both by sea and overland through German territory and the kingdom of Hungary, had established holdings in Edessa, Antioch, Tripoli, and Jerusalem (Prawer 1972b, 68-69). The leaders of the Fourth Crusade, in debt to the city of Venice for passage to the Holy Land, assisted the Venetians in recapturing Dalmatia from the king of Hungary before attacking Constantinople (McNeal and Wolff 1969, 167-69). The military religious orders—Templars, Hospitallers, and others—played an important role in defending Frankish territories against both Byzantines and Muslims. Throughout this period, southern France, particularly the town of Saint-Gilles, was a vital station for communication and travel to the Middle East (Baratier et al. 1969, 130-31, 143).[11] In this light it is significant that four editors have discerned southern traits in the scribes' language (Plouzeau 1986, 1: 85; Gryting 1952, 23; Ott 1912, 482; and Foerster 1884). The use of yellow-brown ink also points to a southern origin, as does the possibility that the manuscript once belonged to a Dauphinois (see p. 70 below).

Among the first Western houses of the Hospitaller knights, later the Order of Malta, was the priory at Saint-Gilles. The founder of the order, the Blessed Gerard, may have been Provençal by birth (King 1931, 20-21, 24). Text 1 of the manuscript concerns the family of a Raymond of Saint-Gilles; many counts of Toulouse in the twelfth and thirteenth centuries went by this name and were involved in the Crusades.[12] Note also that texts 5 and 6 have "Girart" and "Gerart" as heroes. Does this coincidence of names and places point to an audience of Hospitaller knights? A rule prohibiting Hospitallers from playing chess, eating forbidden foods, and reading *romans* when confined to the

---

[11] B.N. f. fr. 1374 bears witness to its importance in the text of the *Roman de la violette*: "Or oez dou mal traiteur/ Con pelerin feit son ateur. /Ausi *com* alast a *Saint* . Gile /Melez s'est de malvaise guile" (ll. 305-8 Buffum, f. 134vb19-22).

[12] Raymond I led the southern Frankish contingent on the First Crusade beginning in 1096. He claimed the county of Tripoli, which was ruled by his descendants for several generations (Prawer 1972b, 68-69).

infirmary supports the proposition that literature ordinarily provided entertainment for the religious, as well as the lay, military establishment.[13]

To approach the question of the manuscript's creation from another angle, an investigation of its provenance might be useful: the Maltese cross in the arms of Colbert embossed on the cover appears pregnant with possibility. However, although Colbert's librarian, Baluze, tells us how much he paid for the acquisition of twenty-one manuscripts on 14 August 1674 ("moyennant 72 livres") and gives a list of the items purchased (see Delisle 1868, 451; Meyer 1905, 445n), his record of the transaction has not been published, and he was, we are told, in the habit of erasing the *ex libris* from all books in his care (M.-T. d'Alverny, personal communication, 1981). If the table pasted inside the front cover of the manuscript is in Baluze's hand rather than Chorier's (see p. 70 below), then "S[ieur] Coustelier" may be the previous owner. François Coustelier was a book dealer (d. 1694 according to the *Dictionnaire de biographie française*) not necessarily associated with the Order of Malta, and the some 8,000 manuscripts the Bibliothèque Royale acquired from Colbert's descendants in 1732 included all kinds of collections (Delisle 1868, 451).

While the evidence for the manuscript's southern origin appears admissible, its previous ownership by a military religious order is far from being established. However, the possibility of an orally transmitted series (see pp. 60-61 above) would support a hypothesis that it was intended for the entertainment of Crusaders, veterans, or colonists in the Levant.[14] Travelers' stations like Saint-Gilles must have attracted many talented *jongleurs*, providing ample opportunities for collectors of texts. While the texts' emphasis on aristocratic concerns would seem to call for a richer material quality, the manuscript's humble appearance suggests one possible intended use: fighting men on campaign could hardly be expected to coddle a precious artifact.

Finally, although two of the texts can be described as hagiographic, there is little possibility that any of them functioned other than as literature in the "true sense":[15] recognized as "literature," the works in this manuscript, which is unique among the

---

[13] "Item il est establli as freres, qui sont en l'enfermarie et jueuront as eschaes ou liront romans, ou mangeront viandes defendues, qui li freres ne leur doine riens de l'enfermerie d'en que en avant, et autre peine n'en doivent avoir" (Article 39, Statuts promulgués par le chapitre général de l'ordre sous le magistère d'Hugues Revel, 19 septembre 1262, Acre [Delaville 1894: 51-52]). There are fourteenth-century witnesses in both French and Latin for the statutes.

[14] Eudes, count of Nevers, was such a one. When he died in Acre in 1265, an inventory of his belongings included a *chansonnier*, a *romanz des Loheranz*, and a *romanz de la terre d'outre mer* as well as a missal and a breviary (Folda 1976, 16).

[15] There has been a prevailing assumption that hagiographic texts "are probably of more importance as historical, linguistic, and sociological documents than as literature in the true sense" (Aston 1970, xxvii). See pp. 164-65 below.

collections chosen for this study, have all been published in modern editions. Surely it is such "romances" as these that Hugh Revel deemed inappropriate for convalescing brethren in his statute concerning the administration of the hospital's infirmary.

MATERIAL DESCRIPTION: B.N. F. FR. 1374

Generalities

The arms of Colbert decorate the front and back of this volume, embossed in gold and framed by a triple gold line. The binding is smooth red leather, and the parchment edges are dappled with red. A fleur-de-lis watermark appears on a front end sheet. The two front paper end sheets are labeled "A" and "B"; two parchment guard sheets in the front, two in the back, and two paper folios following the latter are unnumbered. Otherwise, a modern hand foliates the manuscript 1-183 in black ink, upper right recto. The parchment is of consistently ordinary to good quality, and the decoration and justification give the manuscript a homogeneous appearance. Alternating red and very faded blue initials constitute the decoration; some unfilled blanks are left (notably at the beginnings of texts). The ink, badly worn in some places, varies from pale yellow-brown to black. There are no contemporary rubricated titles, but lyric and epic passages embedded in the *Roman de la violette* (text 6) are written in red.

Six gothic bookhands can be distinguished; only the first and fifth begin new gatherings. All the hands share characteristics of the third quarter of the thirteenth century; the fifth, with its double-looped *a*, perhaps dates to the end of that period, suggesting a date of not earlier than 1275 for the manuscript's confection.

The first (ff. 1r-65v; see figure 11) has a cramped, sober, upright appearance. It uses the tall *s* and *a* has an open loop topping a vertical shaft. Ascenders are kept low. Adjacent curves are blended, and round *r* is used after *d*, *p*, and *o*. The upright of *t* protrudes as a knob above the crossbar, which extends to the right, giving the letter an unbalanced look. There is an occasional hair stroke marking *i* and *j*; periods punctuate some line ends. No phonetic discrimination is made between *u* and *v*.

The second hand copies all but the outside bifolia of gathering 9 (ff. 66r-71v; see figure 12). It uses a broad quill and has a solid, rounded appearance. Ascenders are low and sometimes clubbed. The bottoms of downstrokes curl up as the pen lifts, and diagonal hair strokes finish *e*, mark *i*, and make the tail of *z*. The curves and diagonals add fluidity to the heavy ductus. The *a* has a vertical shaft begun with a tiny hook to the left; *s* is almost always upright. The crossbar of *t* has a small bump where it joins the upright, which ends with a broad curve at the bottom. Round *r* is used after *o*.

The third hand (ff. 72r-132v; see figure 13) is very similar in appearance to the first, but incorporates the round *s* in final position about one-third of the time.

The fourth hand copies only two folios, 133 and 134 (see figure 14). It appears stiff and compressed, with relatively few curves. Upright strokes are thicker at the top than the bottom. Final *s* is mostly in the tall form; the upper loop of *a* is open. No hair strokes mark *i* or *j*. The upright of *t* has a very small hook at the bottom; its meeting with the crossbar appears as a hump at the far left end. Adjacent curves are joined.

The fifth hand copies the remainder of text 6 (the *Roman de la violette*, ff. 135r-172v; see figure 15). It resembles the heavy, round, rhythmical appearance of the second hand, but traits of individual letters distinguish the two. This one favors round final *s* over the upright form by a small margin; *a* has sometimes a small hook, sometimes a complete upper loop. Adjacent curves are blended; round *r* follows *o*, *p*, and *j*. The upright of *t* protrudes slightly above the bar.

The scribe who copies *Florimont* (ff. 173r-183r; see figure 16) uses a round final *s* about half the time, slightly larger than the other miniscule forms, as though he has adapted a capital letter. Ascenders are short and clubbed or topped with spurs; adjacent curves are joined. The upright of *t* has a small bottom loop balanced by a restrained horizontal bar, barely crossed. A potbellied shape distinguishes the *a*, which has an open top hook. The hand has a rounded, controlled appearance.

Particularities

The old shelf mark "7498 3" appears under a pasted label "FR. 1374" on the inside front cover. Folio 1r is marked in black at the top "Codex Colbert 3031" and, over erasures, "Regius 7498.3." The same page is stamped "bibliotecae regiae" on the bottom left corner. Lists of contents appear on end sheets A and B. The first is on the recto of a half-size sheet pasted onto the inside front cover, folded in such a way that part of the verso can be read: four lines from the prologue of *Florimont* appear, identifying "Aymes" as the author of the "Romans . . . de Philipon de Macedoine." These notes are in a hand of the seventeenth or eighteenth century, in brown ink. The historian Fauchet is mentioned (1529-1601) as well as the library of the chancellor Séguier (1588-1672). These dates corroborate a conjecture that the list was made either by Nicolas Chorier, who used this manuscript in preparing his *Recherches . . . sur les antiquités de la ville de Vienne*, published in 1659 (see Van Emden 1977, xlix-l), or by Colbert's librarian Baluze (see Martonne [1834] 1969, xix).

The list on end sheet B, entitled "ancienne poesie," is written in a more formal and later hand in black ink. Another contributor lists the number of verses for each poem and totals them (28,000, approximately correct) on the inside front cover. Martonne identifies these hands as those of the marquis de Cangé [sic] and Paulin Paris, respectively (ibid., xx). Since Charles du Fresne, seigneur du Cange (1610-88) was a historian of Byzantium and the Latin states in the East (Larousse), and Paulin Paris wrote a notice of this manuscript (unpublished: B.N. nouv. acq. fr. 10243, ff. 181r-183v), the identification seems likely.

Brief notes in late medieval cursive hands occur on folios 2r, 7r ("Ci orres du fil"), 15r, 21r, 41r, 62r, 73r ("libera me d*omine*..."), 101r, 156r, and 183r (in blank column) and 183v. Titles are added in the hand and ink of the first table of contents: "Le Roman de Paris la Duchesse" (f. 1r), "Le Roman d'Alixander [*sic*]" (f. 21v, crossed out and corrected in pencil: "d'Erec [*sic*] et Cliges"), "Le Roman de G[i]rard de Vienne" (f. 91r), "Le Roman de Philippies de Macedoine" (f. 173r). A modern hand, in dark ink, remarks, "(lacune d'un feuillet)" (f. 64vb), "(8 vers passé [*sic*])" (f. 141rb), "La suite de cecy est au dernier feuillet" (f. 172vb), "(il y a ici une lacune d'un feuillet)" (f.178vb), "(lacune)" (f. 181vb). A cryptogram and its mirror image occur at the bottom of 90v and 91r (see figure 13), and pointing hands are drawn on 100r and 100v. A passage of five lines is boxed and marked "nul" on folio 121v. Two knights on horseback, one with a fleur-de-lis on his shield, are sketched in ink above the column beginning the single combat between Roland and Oliver in *Girart de Vienne* (f. 123v; see figure 17). Paragraph marks appear in the left margins of 66r and 73r; the laisses of *Girart de Vienne* are numbered 49-100 in Arabic numerals, then CI-CXL in Roman. Passages are marked throughout this text, presumably by Chorier; the passage in *Florimont* naming the author "Aymes" (f. 173r) is underlined in ink similar to Chorier's. A correction over an erasure of six lines occurs on 134v; a black decorated initial "Q" and the beginnings of an "L" have been added on 149ra. The manuscript has several pen trials and indistinct marginalia in ink: folios 5r, 47r, 99v, 101r, and 103r.

Wormholes are evident on folios 1, 164, 165, and 166; other holes in the parchment occur on 10, 29, 44, 54, and 157. Folios 52, 138, 149, and 178 have been repaired with stitching *before* being used; folio 65 was stitched *after* the writing was done. Folios were torn out, leaving stubs, between 169 and 170 and between 181 and 182.

The manuscript was acquired by Colbert along with twenty others, which I have not been able to identify, in 1674. If the hand of table A is that of Baluze, the seller may have been a "S[ieur] Coustelier," whose name appears at the top of the list of contents (see p. 67 above). Meyer notes that the acquisition included the original of Aymar de Rivail's work on the Dauphiné, and believes the collection of manuscripts could have been assembled by a native of this region (1905, 445). The Bibliothèque Royale purchased Colbert's collection of printed and manuscript books from his descendants in 1732.

Fig. 11. Paris, B.N. f. fr. 1374: f. 38v (hand 1)
Phot. Bibl. Nat. Paris

Fig. 12. Paris, B.N. f. fr. 1374: f. 69r (hand 2)
Phot. Bibl. Nat. Paris

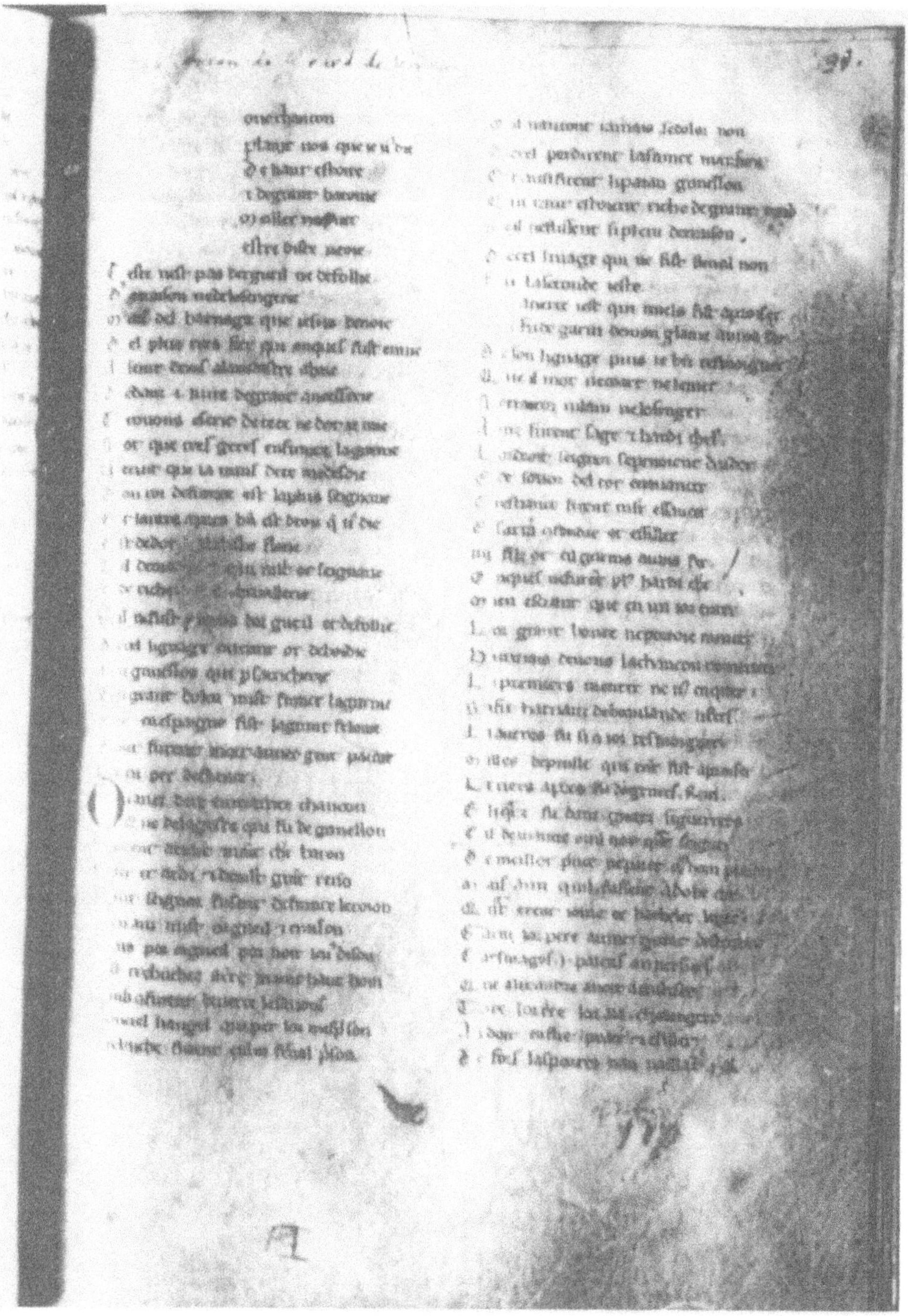

Fig. 13. Paris, B.N. f. fr. 1374: f. 91r (hand 3; cryptogram)
Phot. Bibl. Nat. Paris

Fig. 14. Paris, B.N. f. fr. 1374: f. 134v (hand 4)
Phot. Bibl. Nat. Paris

v aſſal feit il tout aſ ale   q naſiſtreſ granſ couſ ſentredonēt
ſ reſpont p̄ ſaine cluſẽ   e r tant au ferir t'abandonent
e il ne dit mie vor q̄ neut   h lan meſ eſcuſ h̄ feudart
q nant ce vendra au departir   m out p̄ ſe loneſte e dure
l egnerement poreʒ per   l abitaille deſ vj. vaſſlauſ
p oſtre graaig ſe nouſ de ſi   e urel manere vij. aſſauſ
O ʒ a garder ſe nouſ deſi   ʒ e rendirent q̄ ne ſauoit
   Tant tranſ nerſ lautre broiche   ⁊ dire quil e p̄ſ auoit
   ⁊ a cellui qui nient broiche   ıſıarʒ qui miſt ſue ner
d enant en chief de ſon cheual   A ure le cuer ⁊ leſ eux
f il baiſſerent g̃nnal   q ne mar la peſla ou en cort
l eſ lances qua̅t ſe aprocherent   t out maintenant ſere le coit
t es coupſ ſe donent quil peerent   v n coup li done a lentre deus
L es eſcuſ come y. ſaintʒ   q uar miſt fu plainſ dire ⁊ de deuſ
r es p̄ miles hauber ont auſ   l aume tranche ⁊ la coiſe blanch
o ſſert leſ aleʒ le coſte   l i coupſ deſcent p̄ tel ſemblance
m ur a ſi lautre harte   A reſ res areſ de la face
d eſcueſ del cheual ⁊ del pꝛ   a eſ na peor q̄ mal liſace
q ne il ont leſ cheuanʒ guerpiʒ   q n ar get i. pou li guench
⁊ li cheual ſachant ounerent   c e leſ aua la dieu mera
⁊ ı y aſſal ſi fort ſe ſtonerent   l iſıarʒ i. petit ſarreſte
q nil norent ne ueuoient gote   A get dit ſe nouſ ap̄ſte
c haſcune deſ gardes eſconte   o re vauſſanſ i. tel chaſtel
p il nauent ne peu ne point   d ont v ıbureu uit cembel
   ont enſi giſent en tel point   m ieuſ il ne uiſt ſe dieuſ me ſaut
q uil ne remenent main ne pie   A mec uſe amie ozant
A inʒ ſembleʒ biẽ que leur eſpie   A ler p̄ le puſ errant
o ient p̄ nii leſ corʒ paſſeʒ   e t de uiſle en uiſle querant
⁊ eſ aſſeʒ toſt ſont r̄ paſſeʒ   o u nouſ rendre la poulieʒ
l e uaſſal de le ſtonement   L ar grant auoir emiſſieʒ
p uil ſaillent ſuſ uiuellement   ſ loi mot ne ſona
A ⁊ eſpees ont leſ mains miſes   i cop regrete mout ſe haſta
J i furent pas grant a demiſes   A liſiart ſi h cort ſave
e haſ tantoſt la ſoe trait   d eſſouʒ eſme puiſ fiert deſſen̄
i en ſembers lautre ſeſh   i mout granc cop p̄ mile chief
⁹ i ſe fierent fierſ granʒ couſ   m eſ diable p̄ g̃nt meſchief
p̄ tellet et p̄ in couſ   o u fant le cop toꝛner deſoꝛs
o ur eſpaules ⁊ ſur poitrines   ſ fu ne recruſ et ſorʒ
e donent ſi cruels eſcrimes   i cop regrete mout ſe h̄ile
q nap̄ʒ leſ copſ li ſan ſen ſant   q ne del braon une grant haſte
⁹ ont ſe rendent cruel aſſaut   l ı a oſtee de la cuiſſe

Fig. 15. Paris, B.N. f. fr. 1374: f. 171v (hand 5)
Phot. Bibl. Nat. Paris

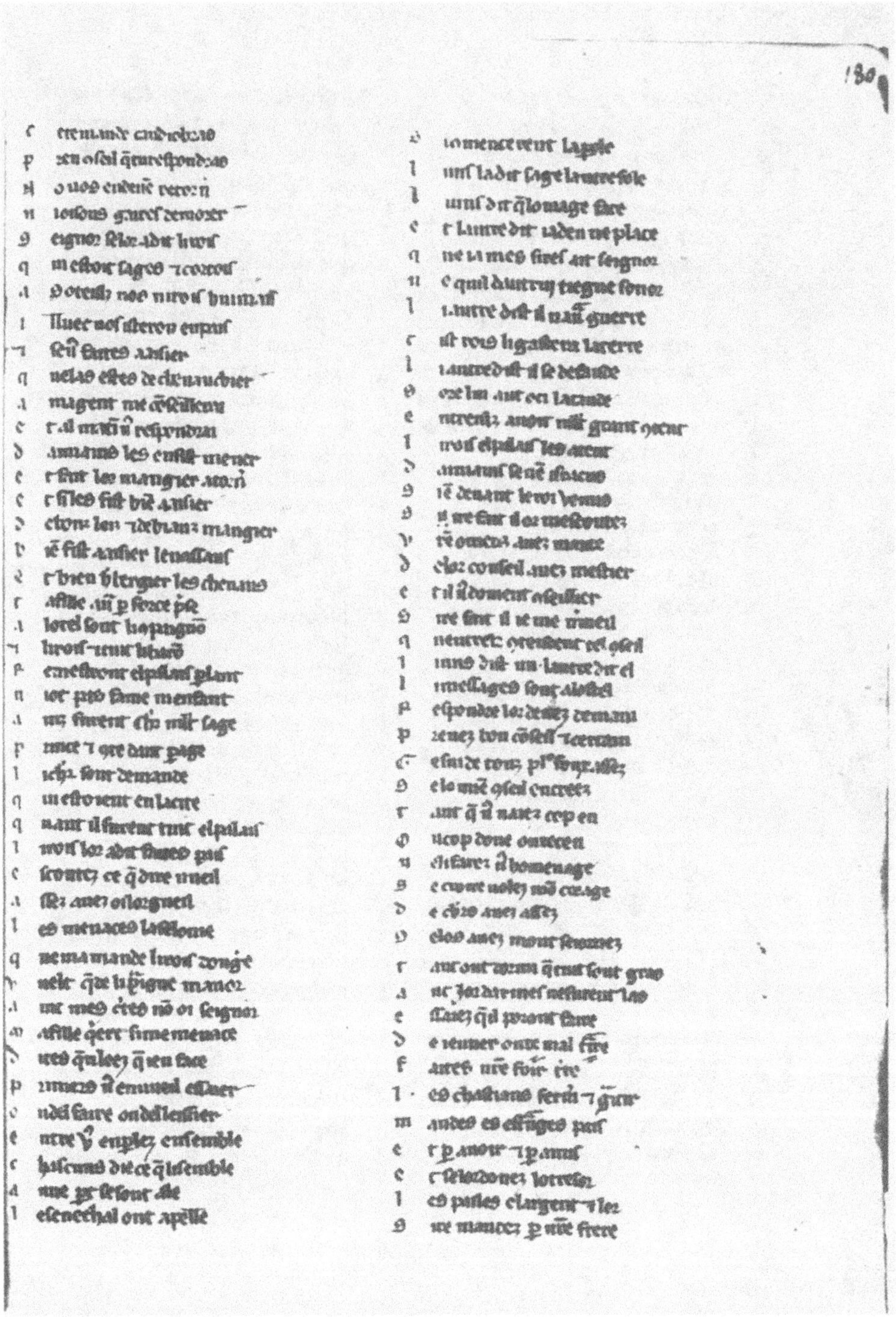

Fig. 16. Paris, B.N. f. fr. 1374: f. 180r (hand 6)
Phot. Bibl. Nat. Paris

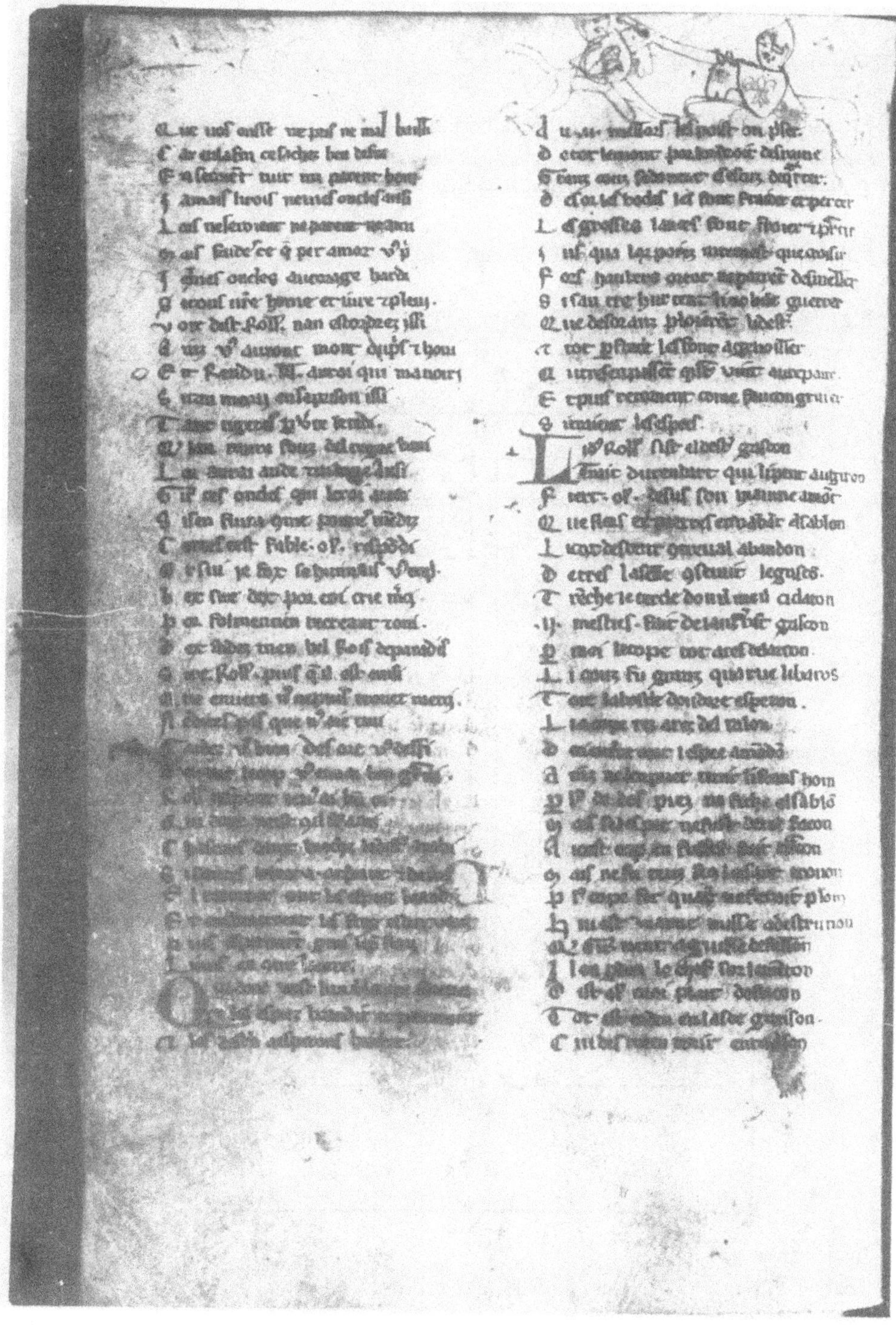

Fig. 17. Paris, B.N. f. fr. 1374: f. 123v (single combat between Roland and Oliver). Phot. Bibl. Nat. Paris

Organization of the Page

Prickings have been made by the gathering, eight across the bottom, and a vertical row close to the gutter, not well aligned. They are especially pronounced in gathering 3. Both plummet and dry point have been used for ruling.

Folio dimensions: 251-53 x 170-73 mm

Fig. 18. Page layout (ff. 1-183, texts 1-5)

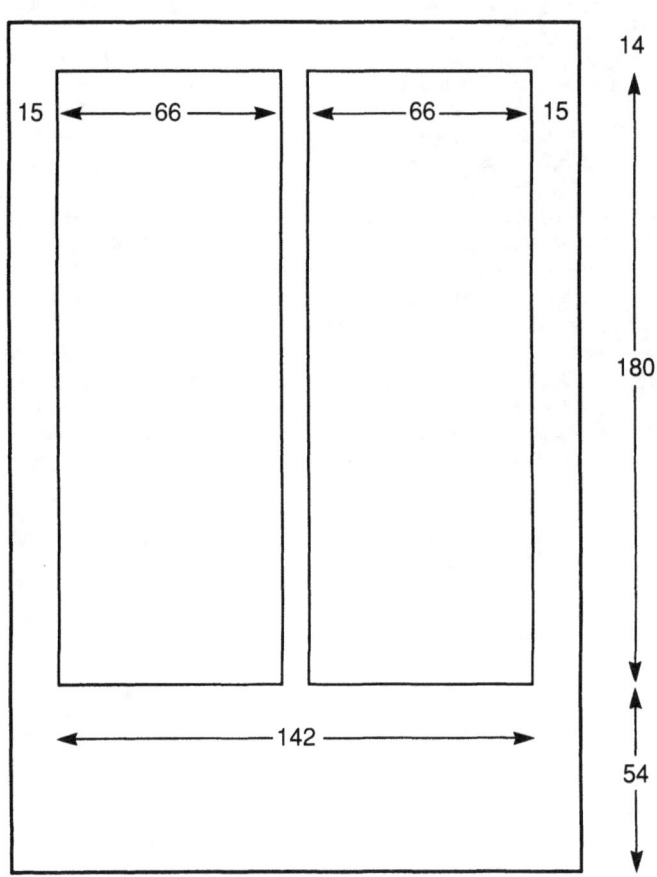

Justification:
Texts 1 through 5, 38 lines, 173-83 mm x 125-45 mm
Text 6, 40 lines, 190 x 135 mm
Text 7, 43 lines, 195 x 125 mm

Table 3

Organization of the Volume

Gathering	Type	Catchword	Signature	Remarks	Texts
1 (1-8)	4/4	no	no		*Parise la duchesse*, f. 1ra
2 (9-16)	4/4	no	no		
3 (17-24)	4/4	yes	no	prickings especially pronounced	text 1 ends 8 lines from the bottom of f. 21rb; Chrétien de Troyes, *Cligès*, f. 21va
4 (25-32)	4/4	no	no		
5 (33-40)	4/4	no	no		
6 (41-48)	4/4	no	no		
7 (49-56)	4/4	no	no		
8 (57-64)	4/4	no	no		text 2 left unfinished by about 1 folio
9 (65-72)	4/4	no	no	hand 2, f. 66ra; hand 3, f. 72ra	Life of Saint Eustace, f. 65ra
10 (73-84)	6/6	no	no		*La venjance Nostre Seigneur*, f. 75rb
11 (85-92)	4/4	no	no		text 4 ends 14 lines from the bottom of f. 90vb; Bertrand de Bar-sur-Aube, *Girart de Vienne*, f. 91ra
12 (93-100)	4/4	no	no		
13 (101-8)	4/4	no	no		
14 (109-16)	4/4	no	no		
15 (117-24)	4/4	no	no		
16 (125-32)	4/4	no	no		
17 (133-46)	7/7	no	no	hand 4, f. 133ra; hand 5, f. 135ra; blacker ink, ff. 138ra-172vb	Gerbert de Montreuil, *Roman de la violette*, f. 133ra
18 (147-54)	4/4	no	no		
19 (155-64)	5/5	yes	no		
20 (165-73)	5/(5)4	yes	no	hand 6, f. 173ra; stub between ff. 169 and 170	Aimon de Varennes, *Florimont*, f. 173ra
21 (174-83)	(6?)5/(6)5	yes	no	lacuna of one folio between ff. 178 and 179; stub between ff. 181 and 182	f. 183ra, end of text 6

CONTENTS

(1) ff. 1ra-21rb: [*Parise la duchesse*], east or northeast, 1225-50 (Plouzeau 1986, 1: 163-64), laisses of assonanced alexandrines

    Incipit: Seignor, plait vos oir gloriose chancon
    Explicit: Ci faut li romanz de Parise la duchece
    Editions: Martonne [1834] 1969; Guessard and Larchey 1860; Plouzeau 1986
    See also Gröber 1902, 77, 551; Paris 1852, 659-67; Adler 1974.
    Summary: The poem begins with the twelve evil peers plotting to poison Parise and marry one of their daughters to her widowed husband. Instead of falling victim to the plan herself, the duchess offers one of the poisoned apples to Duke Raymond's brother and is subsequently accused of murder. Her "defender," one of the traitors, intentionally loses the judicial duel, and she is banished, rather than executed, because she is pregnant with the duke's child. She goes into exile, accompanied by the sons of Clarembaut, an impoverished old family retainer, and bears her son in the wilderness of Hungary. Three noble thieves make off with the baby, mistaking it for treasure. The bereaved duchess travels on to become wet nurse to the son of Count Thierri of Cologne, while her son is taken in and christened Hugh by the king of Hungary.

    After fifteen years, Hugh's native virtue arouses the jealousy of the traitor barons in Hungary: the king plans to make him his son-in-law and heir. When the traitors plot to murder him, he kills them all, with a chessboard as his only weapon. He leaves to escape reprisals and to seek his natural parents. Finding his mother at the court of Count Thierri, he determines to avenge her.

    Together with the count's son, Antoine, Hugh joins forces with Clarembaut, who has been waging war on Parise's behalf against Duke Raymond and the traitor faction back in Vauvenice. Finally in a position of power, the loyal Clarembaut proposes peace to Raymond, persuading him to relinquish his new traitor wife and beg forgiveness of Parise. The king of Hungary arrives in search of Hugh, whose marriage and ascension to the throne of Hungary conclude the narrative.

(2) ff. 21va-64vb: [Chrétien de Troyes, *Cligès*], Champenois, 1176 (Micha 1957, viii), octosyllabic couplets

    Incipit: Cil qui fist d'Erec et d'Enide
    Explicit: Que de chose, qui ne fust voire [about one folio short of the ending, according to other manuscripts]
    Editions: Foerster 1884; Micha 1957
    See also Frappier 1968a; Kelly 1976; Maddox 1973.

Summary: The first part of the story relates the exploits of Alexander, the eldest son of the emperor of Constantinople, at the court of Arthur in Britain. He falls in love with Gawain's daughter, Soredamor, and the queen arranges their marriage. Soredamor bears a son to Alexander, Cligès. Meanwhile, Alexander's brother, Alis, usurps the throne upon their father's death. Alexander agrees to let him keep the title in exchange for a promise never to marry, so that Cligès will inherit the empire.

When Alexander and Soredamor have died, the unscrupulous Alis woos Fénice, the daughter of the German emperor. Although Fénice and Cligès fall in love, she marries the emperor, preserving her innocence by means of a magic potion that makes Alis believe he is enjoying her, when in fact he is asleep. Cligès, like his father before him, journeys to Arthur's court to distinguish himself in deeds of chivalry until his love for Fénice draws him back to Constantinople.

With the help of two loyal servants, Fénice pretends to die. After an extravagant funeral she is exhumed and sequestered in a special tower some distance from the city, where the lovers enjoy each other for several months. Eventually discovered by accident, Cligès and Fénice flee the emperor's wrath and plan to seek Arthur's aid. The text of B.N. f. fr. 1374 ends at this point. In other manuscripts Alis dies of frustration when his men are unable to overtake the fugitives, and they return to Constantinople in triumph.

(3) ff. 65ra-75rb: [Life of Saint Eustace], Picard/Champenois, early thirteenth century (Ott 1912, 515), quatrains of monorhymed decasyllables
   Incipit: Seignor et dames, entendez tuit a moi
   Explicit: Ci est l'estoire de Utachi faillie
         Dex nos otroit, li filz Sainte Marie,
         Part en la gloire q ue il a deservie.
   Edition: Ott 1912
   See also Petersen 1924, 1925; Meyer 1906a, 348-49.
   Summary: Placidas and his wife are characterized as noble pagans assailed by the devil because of their spiritual worthiness. While out hunting one day, Placidas experiences a vision: a cross on the forehead of a buck he pursues, accompanied by brilliant light and the Lord's voice commanding him to be baptized. Taking Eustace as his Christian name, Placidas abandons his wealth and position to seek spiritual blessedness.

   Separated from his family in the course of his travels, Eustace lives as a guardian of the fields for twelve years, while his sons are brought up by peasants and his wife lives virtuously in "another country." Eventually found by agents of the emperor, Eustace is reinstated as seneschal and undertakes to win back the territory lost during his absence. By chance, his two sons are drafted into his service, and the family is reunited when his troops are lodged near a garden kept by his wife.

Meanwhile, the devil has convinced the emperor that Eustace has betrayed him, and the family's refusal to attend pagan rites seems to confirm their treason. Eustace reveals he is Christian, and the family suffers martyrdom by being incinerated in a metal bull. They feel no pain, the earth trembles, the sky splits open, and shadows darken the city even at noon. Angels escort their souls to heaven as they pray for those who will honor their feast day.

(4) ff. 75rb-90vb: [*La venjance Nostre Seigneur*], east or northeast, around 1200 (Gryting 1952, 30-31), laisses of monorhymed alexandrines
   Incipit: [Or] m'entendez baron, chevaliers et serjant
   Explicit: Explicit li romanz de la price de Jherusalem
   Edition: Gryting 1952
   See also Paris 1852, 412-16; Suchier 1901; Gröber 1902, 658.
   Summary: The emperor Vespasian suffers from leprosy. Gai recommends he undertake to avenge the Crucifixion, and sets off for Jerusalem as ambassador to demand tribute of Pilate. At the home of Jacob he meets Veronica, the woman who was cured of leprosy by a cloth bearing the imprint of Christ's face. She agrees to bring the cloth to Vespasian; Pilate refuses to send tribute.

   Back in Rome, Veronica performs her cure on the emperor on the occasion of his son's coronation. He swears to take vengeance on the Jews and promises to embrace Christianity. Vespasian's army besieges Haifa and then Jerusalem. The famine becomes so severe that a woman even eats her own child, an event prophesied several times in the course of the narrative. Pilate advises the Jews to ingest their gold and silver before they surrender. Roman soldiers kill all but sixty of the Jews to get at the swallowed treasures.

   When the army returns to Rome, a mass baptism takes place. After dinner, the senate sentences Pilate to be executed at Vienne. He hangs upside down for two years in a well before being thrown in prison and swallowed up into hell.

(5) ff. 91ra-132vb: [Bertrand de Bar-sur-Aube, *Girart de Vienne*], Francien with northern and eastern traits, around 1180 (Van Emden 1977, xxx-xxxiv, xciii-xciv), laisses of monorhymed decasyllables
   Incipit: [B]one chan con plait vos que je vos die
   Explicit: Explicit li romanz de gir art de vianne
   Editions: Bekker 1829; Tarbé 1850; Yeandle 1930; Van Emden 1977
   See also Louis 1947; Frappier 1955; Tyssens 1967.

Summary: After performing the filial duty of restoring the wealth and territory of their family, impoverished by Saracen raids, the four sons of Garin de Monglane, including Girart, set out to seek their fortunes. Renier and Girart travel together to the court of Charlemagne, where they are not treated well.

Renier eventually receives Geneva as his fief, but the king usurps the duchy of Burgundy, which he has promised to Girart, because he wants the widowed duchess for himself. Although the king has treated him badly, Girart remains loyal even when the duchess, preferring him to the king, tempts him to defy his lord and marry her. Spurned by Girart, she insults him by secretly substituting her own foot for him to kiss when he comes to the darkened royal bedchamber to pay homage to Charles for the fief of Vienne. The insult is revealed to Girart when the queen boasts about it to his nephew, Aymeri, and a war of vengeance ensues.

In the course of this war the king besieges Vienne for seven years, and his nephew Roland becomes acquainted with Girart's nephew and niece, Oliver and Aude. God intercedes by sending an angel to suggest the two forces join against the pagans instead of fighting each other. The pope (in other manuscripts, the archbishop) promises absolution to any who participate in an expedition against the Saracens in Gascony.

(6) ff. 133ra-172vb, 183r: [Gerbert de Montreuil, *Roman de la violette*], Franco-Picard literary dialect, 1227-29 (Buffum 1928, xxvii-xxviii, lxxiii), octosyllabic couplets
Incipit: [S]ens de povre home e*st* pou prisiez
Explicit: Ci fenist li romans de la violete
   Qui ci estoit *et* pure et nete.
Editions: Michel 1834; Buffum 1928
See also Gröber 1902, 532-33; Buffum 1904.
Summary: At the Easter court of King Louis, extravagantly described in its aristocratic splendor, the evil Lisiart provokes Gerart de Nevers to wager his domain on his lady's loyalty. Lisiart fails in his attempt to seduce the lady, Euriaut, but learns from a servant about the *violette*, a secret mark beneath her right breast. Believing she has betrayed him, Gerart abandons Euriaut in a forest, where she is rescued by the duke of Metz.

Disguised as a *jongleur*, he visits the court of Nevers, now held by Lisiart, where he learns by eavesdropping that his lady is innocent. He sets off in search of her, and a series of adventures ensues. Meanwhile, back at Metz, Euriaut has been framed for the murder of the duke's sister by a knight she has rejected. Gerart arrives just in time to serve as her champion against the treacherous accuser. Finally, a tournament provides the occasion for Gerart to accuse Lisiart of treason in the presence of the king and a great company.

After the judicial combat, the victorious Gerart returns to Nevers to celebrate his marriage with Euriaut.

(7) ff.173ra-182vb: [Aimon de Varennes, *Florimont*], Lyonnais dialect (Fourrier 1960, 471), 1188 (closing lines of the poem), octosyllabic couplets
Incipit: [C]il qui a cuer de vassalage
Explicit: puis q*ue* je n'en puis avoir pais
[more than 11,000 lines short of the ending]
Edition: Hilka 1933
See also Fourrier 1960.
Summary: The poem's hero, Florimont, is the grandfather of Alexander the Great. The story begins with the *amiralz* of Babilone (that is, Cairo) and king of Greece by marriage, who is the grandfather of Florimont's wife, Romadanaple. His second son, Philip, inherits the kingdom of Greece, founding the city of Philippopolis to commemorate his victory over a lion who had been laying waste to the land. In the course of a prosperous and peaceful reign, Philip marries, and his daughter, Romadanaple, is born. Camdiobras, king of Hungary, wishes to marry her and make Philip his vassal; Philip learns in a prophetic dream of a poor but wellborn knight who will become his champion against Camdiobras.

Here the narrative takes up the family history of Florimont: his parents are the duke of Albania and a Persian princess. B.N. f. fr. 1374 breaks off, incomplete, as the fifteen-year-old Florimont plans to confront a giant who has been ravishing the duke's land and people.[16] His education includes a liaison with the *Dame de l'Ile Selee*, who has magical powers, a sojourn at the court of the king of Slavonia, and the conquest of the evil giant. Eventually, he loses his lady's love when he betrays a vow of secrecy, and his fortune through an excess of *largesse*. He takes the name Povre Perdu and joins the company of a prince en route to help in Philip's war against Camdiobras.

Recognized by Philip as the champion of his dream, Povre Perdu distinguishes himself in battle against Camdiobras and courts Romadanaple. Once his identity is revealed, Florimont becomes Philip's commander in chief and then his son-in-law and heir. The firstborn of Florimont and Romadanaple is named Philip for his grandfather.

Camdiobras swears fealty to Florimont, and all goes well until news arrives

---

[16] Since it is likely the collection was intended to include the complete text (see p. 60), a summary of the lacking portion will be pertinent to my analysis of the combination.

that Florimont's father is being held hostage by the emir of Carthage. Disguised as merchants, Florimont and his men, including Camdiobras, obtain the release of the old duke. The emir eventually agrees to peaceful terms, promising his daughter as a bride for Florimont's son. She is to become Alexander's mother. After the emir dies of remorse, Camdiobras marries his widow. The poem ends with an epilogue extolling *largesse*.

4
Pious Hermits and Magical Helpers
Alternative Solutions for
Spiritual Problems

TEXTS

La Vie des Pères
Gautier de Coinci, prologue to the *Miracles de Nostre Dame*; *Vie de Théophile*
Jehan de Blois, *Le conte dou barril*
Les neuf joies Nostre Dame
La Passion Ihesu Crist
Life of Saint Catherine of Alexandria
L'estoire del Saint Graal
Merlin en prose and Vulgate continuation

The first text of Bancroft Library UCB 106 (ff. 1ra-92vb) is a large collection of short narratives in octosyllabic couplets known as the *Vie des Pères*. Tales from the collection occur in at least thirty-eight manuscripts. A few contain all seventy-four tales,[1] several have the first forty-two (the kernel of the collection), and some combine selected extracts with miracles of the Virgin and other texts. Bancroft Library UCB 106 is one of a number that lack the series 51-63.

Studies of the *Vie des Pères* have focused on the division between the first series (1-42) and the remainder of the collection and on the possibility of a third series separable from the other two (51-63). The division between the first and second series is supported by a general prologue at the beginning of tale 43. Edouard Schwan thought the third series was interpolated, since four of the manuscripts known to him lacked tales 51-63 (1884, 252). Morawski extended Schwan's hypothesis by attributing the third series to a third author: the rise of Marian devotion is reflected in the growing proportion of Marian miracles in the three series (eight out of forty-two in the first series, eight out

---

[1] For convenience, the tales are numbered according to their order in B.N. f. fr. 1546, assigned the siglum *A* by Weber (1876). A complete list of the tales in UCB 106, together with bibliographical information, is provided in table 6.

of nineteen in the second, and twelve out of thirteen in the third or "interpolated" series) (1935, 178). Bornäs suggests tales 51-63 were originally at the *end* of the collection, making it natural for them to be lacking from some witnesses. His material description of *A* (B.N. f. fr. 1546) accounts for a rearrangement of the order of a hypothetical model, which would have had the sequence 1-44, 64-74, 45-63, reflected in several extant manuscripts, including UCB 106 (*x*). While he does not contest the separate authorship of the first and second series of *Vie*s, he points out that the thematic differences of tales 51-63 do not necessarily indicate the contribution of a different poet but could be due to the evolution of the second author's thought (Bornäs 1968, 9-15). Translations of the Latin *Vitae Patrum* were made in verse by Henri d'Arci and in prose by Wauchier de Denain, among others (see Meyer, 1906b). The *Vie des Pères* is not a translation and cannot be explained by comparison with any one Latin collection. It is rather a composition based on the compilation of diverse material, including some Latin stories of desert fathers. Auméry Duval was not entirely mistaken in observing that "le titre de ce poëme n'en indique nullement le sujet. . . . Le plus souvent l'auteur ne raconte que les puériles aventures de personnages obscurs, connus de lui seul" ([1838] 1895, 857-58).[2]

According to the editor of the tenth story, Jacques Chaurand, the author of the first *Vie* was a Cistercian monk or novice, writing in the first half of the thirteenth century (1971, 3). Bornäs, who edits three tales from the second series (43, 64, and 69), fixes its date at around 1250, based on references to historical personages (1968, 22-23). Skeptical of Morawski's identification of the author as Ernoul de Laigni, named in one or perhaps two tales (see Morawski 1921, 381; Morawski 1935, 181 n. 2), he speculates that the stories "sont issus d'un milieu rattaché à l'un des deux grands ordres mendiants" but that the author was not himself a cleric: a friar perhaps explicated the Latin sources for the author's benefit (1968, 21). A methodical study of the style and language of all the stories would be needed to determine the actual number of contributors. The question of their milieux is complicated by the theological orientations of their ultimate sources and those of any intervening transmitters: the various mentions of a "blanche abbaye" or a "frère mineur," for example, do not necessarily indicate the collection's composition by a Cistercian or a Franciscan author.

The tales share many traits with Marian miracles, on the one hand, and with *fabliaux*, on the other. As I have mentioned, the *Vie des Pères* includes a number of miracle narratives and occurs together with selections from Gautier de Coinci in several manuscripts (including UCB 106). Collections of Marian miracles are more thematically

---

[2] A few decades earlier Legrand d'Aussy had opined that the author of the *Vie des Pères* was superior to Gautier de Coinci in choice of subjects, narrative skill, and art: "Il avait l'oreille vraiment poétique." He renounced the project of treating the *Vie des Pères* separately from the *Miracles* because the intermixing of the two collections in the manuscripts made it impossible for him to disentangle them ([1779] 1829, 5, 10-12).

consistent than the *Vie des Pères*: the Virgin's intervention assures salvation to any sinner who is capable of even minimal devotion to her (see Bornäs 1968, 7; Payen 1967, 516-17). Identical in form and similar in style, Marian miracles and tales of the *Vie des Pères* are usually considered together in relation to other genres.

The early publishers of these stories interspersed them with *fabliaux* (e.g., Méon 1823), and it is this genre they most closely resemble. In some cases it would be impossible to make a generic distinction between a *fabliau édifiant*, as Jean-Charles Payen characterizes the *Chevalier au Barisel* (1967, 516), and a *conte dévot*. A version of the same tale occurs, in fact, in the *Vie des Pères*.[3] Morawski points out that they borrow both form and style from the authors of *fabliaux* and share with them a taste for realism, a naïve tone, "l'absence de valeur — sinon de prétention — littéraire" (1935, 158).[4] The influence of romance has also been noted. Payen compares the complaint of Gautier de Coinci's Theophilus with monologues composed by Chrétien de Troyes (1967, 556-57). Also citing Chrétien, Chaurand points out that the use of proverbs so typical in *contes dévots* is common to secular literture as well as to sermons (1971, 73-74).

Many elements of medieval French society appear in the stories. Monks, friars, bishops, canons, deacons, priests, and, more generally, "clerics" represent the ecclesiastical population; lay characters include aristocrats, bourgeois, peasants, and outlaws. Hermits are the protagonists of many tales but often serve auxiliary roles in the spiritual lives of the main characters. Pagans and Jews furnish a number of opportunities for miraculous conversions, and the supernatural worlds are represented by the Virgin, a few angels, and crowds of devils.

What I have designated as the second text of the manuscript, although it appears as the sixty-first text since the title and decoration distinguish it little from the tales of the *Vie des Pères* preceding it,[5] is actually a combination of extracts from Gautier de Coinci's *Miracles de Nostre Dame* (ff. 92vb-101ra). The general prologue (incipit "A la loenge et a la gloire") serves as an opening for the life of Saint Theophilus, which follows it without any break or signal. This combination, omitting a series of lyric poems that follow the prologue in manuscripts containing the complete collection, also occurs in several other copies (see Ducrot-Granderye 1932, 244-48, 254-56).

In her study of the manuscript tradition of the *Miracles*, Arlette P. Ducrot-Granderye has divided the seventy-three extant copies into three groups: eighteen contain nearly all

---

[3] Payen speaks of the version edited by Lecoy, incipit "Entre Normendie et Bretaigne." A third version appears in UCB 106 and is discussed below (pp. 90-92).

[4] He gives *Saint Pierre et le jongleur* and the *Vilain que conquist paradis par plait* as examples of *fabliaux dévots* (Morawski 1935, 158 n. 3).

[5] The filigreed initial of the first line is six, rather than the usual four or five, lines high.

Gautier's *Miracles*, twenty have significant numbers of the eighty-six texts, and thirty-five include just a few of them (1932, 17). A total of thirty-three manuscripts preserve the life of Theophilus. Until Koenig undertook the project of editing the entire collection (1955-70, 4 volumes), it was accessible only in fragments and in the extensively "corrected" version of Abbot Poquet (1857). Koenig has used all the manuscripts *except* UCB 106 in his first volume (the prologue, the life of Theophilus, and intervening songs) but publishes the rest of the collection using only a few important ones: BN f. fr. 22928 (*L*) serves as his base for all the texts (1955, 1: xxxiv, xlvi).

Gautier de Coinci is one of the few authors of early medieval vernacular literature whose life is documented outside his own works. Born 1177-78, he became a monk in 1193 and served as prior of Vic-sur-Aisne and later of the abbey of Saint Médard. His milieu and audience, both clerical and lay, was aristocratic, and he suffered from ill heath (ibid., xviii-xxx).

Gautier's principal source for the *Miracles* was probably a Latin collection, no longer extant, although the opening lines of the life of Theophilus, which serve as a prologue, suggest that it and other tales may have circulated independently (see Koenig 1955, 1: xxv-xxvi, xxxi):

> Por ceus esbatre *et* deporter
> Qui se deporte*n*t en porter
> A l'onour cele qui Deu porta
> Miracles ou gra*n*t deporta.
> *Et* ou ie sovent me deport
> Rimoier voil de gra*n*t deport
> De cele qui fist la portee
> Q*ui* tote joie a raportee.
> En lui loer est mes depors:
> Q*uar* c'est la rive *et* li droiz pors
> Q*ui* toz les douz depors aporte,
> *Et* du ciel est *et* ponz *et* porte.
> (ll. 1-12 Koenig, f. 93vc23-34)

Ducrot-Granderye posits three stages in the composition of the collection, extending from 1218 to 1227, basing her position on the manuscript tradition as well as on the textual references.[6] Koenig maintains that these dates are not verifiable, suggesting a *terminus ad quem* of 1231 for the narrative portion of the *Miracles* and pointing out that Gautier's lyric production, including an annual Marian tribute, continued until his death in 1236 (ibid., xxix-xxx).

---

[6] Book 1, including the general prologue and life of Theophilus, around 1218; revision of book 1, 1222; book 2 and changes to book 1 in order to make a matched pair, 1223-27 (Ducrot-Granderye 1932, 159-71).

Gautier's originality distinguishes him from others who translated Latin miracle collections, and although he was no doubt familiar with earlier authors of Marian literature (Wace, Herman de Valenciennes), no direct influence can be confirmed (ibid., xxxii-xxxiii). Like the tales of the *Vie des Pères*, his work reflects a familiarity with the *fabliau* and the romance.

The legend of Theophilus combines the ancient and widespread tradition of the devil's associate with the class of Marian miracle that sets the Virgin in direct opposition to the devil. Among early Greek treatments of the first theme are the legends of Cyprian, Basilius, and Anthemios. The legend of Basilius, or the Servant of Proterius, seems to be a source of the Greek Theophilus miracle, which in turn serves as a model for Latin prose translations of the ninth century. Paul the Deacon's version, surviving in many manuscripts, probably lies behind the Western vernacular traditions (Plenzat 1926, 16-19). The story was versified by Hroswitha of Gandersheim, Marbode of Rennes, and Radewin of Freising in Latin, and by poets and dramatists in German, Dutch, English, Spanish, Italian, and Icelandic (ibid., 25-41). Anonymous French versions survive, as well as those by Adgar (in Anglo-Norman), Rutebeuf, and Gautier de Coinci (Plenzat 1926, supplement a1).

Gautier's version is among the longest (nearly 2,100 lines) and is ornamented throughout by his rippling, glittering wordplay. Although the selection and sequence of events differ little from the antecedent prose text by Paul the Deacon, Gautier expands on the description of Theophilus's worldly life and adds an epilogue criticizing the hypocrisy and pride of monks and prelates. He also emphasizes the vidame's devotion to the Virgin but provides no evil influence to motivate his initial rejection of God and his mother (see Plenzat 1926, 98-106).

UCB 106 contains one of two extant copies of the thirteenth-century *Conte dou barril* that follows the life of Theophilus (ff. 101ra-105ra). Robert Bates, who edited the tale in 1932, believes the scribe of this manuscript to have been Norman or to have copied a Norman model. He accounts for the text's Picard traits by positing a Picard ancestor in the manuscript tradition. The scribe has changed a number of words to suit himself, and perhaps rewrote one or two passages (ll. 1081-90, 1142-end) (Bates 1932, li, lx-lxii, 42-43). The other extant copy (B.N. f. fr 1807) makes references to the Albigensian Crusade at the point where the two texts diverge (on the grounds of which Bates dates the poem's composition at 1216-18). If these references were in the Norman scribe's model, he might naturally have altered them to suit a local audience (ibid., lxi). The author names himself twice in the other copy:

> D'un bel example et de cortais
> commaince ci Jouham de Blais
> (ll. 7-8; Bates 1932, 3)

> De cest conte vos ferai fin.
> Jouham le fist de la Chapele;
> Le *conte dou barril* l'apele.
> (ll. 1260-62; Bates 1932, 38)[7]

He gives no further information about himself, and Bates is left to deduce from textual references to Cistercians, his interpretation of the poem's theological bent, and the strong anti-Catharist position expressed in the poem that "Jouham de la Chapele de Blais" was a Cistercian monk (1932, xi-xiii). He may also have been a professional poet (ibid., xiv-xv).

The only extant Latin version of the story dates to the end of the thirteenth century and therefore could not be a source for the Old French versions. The plot seems to be a fusion of two types of exempla. First, the sinner readily accepts the task of filling the barrel, which he believes will be easy. This is analogous to the case of the man who hated leeks being forbidden to eat them, then finding that he suddenly craved them. Secondly, after expending a great deal of fruitless effort, the knight believes his task to be impossibly difficult, as did the man who was assigned to fill a container from a river running uphill:[8] tears accomplish the penance for both (they must flow upward from the heart to the eyes) (Lecoy 1955, xxiii).

The text contains two sermons, one on the Fall and Redemption of man (based on the Bible, patristic literature, and commonplaces of Cistercian thought), and the other an allegory of virtue as the arms of a knight (a popular tradition variously executed with no direct source) (Bates 1932, xix, xxi-xxii).

Three thirteenth-century verse versions and one fifteenth-century prose version of the tale survive. One of the verse tales occurs in the *Vie des Pères* (f. 54rb of this manuscript). Its plot is distinguished by the knight's willingness to repent, although he is reluctant to undertake a heavy penance. In the other two verse versions the main character, proud and insolent, must be persuaded to repent. There seems to be an affinity between these latter two: Bates sees the *conte* of Jouhan as less worldly and believes the other poet adapted it to suit a lay audience. Félix Lecoy, who edited the *Chevalier au barisel* in 1955, argues conversely that it served as a model for the aesthetically inferior *Conte dou barril*, which uses the plot merely as a frame for the two sermons it contains (1955, xix). But aesthetic defects do not constitute proof of

---

[7] UCB 106, which diverges from this text at line 1142, lacks the second reference.

[8] Cf. the fifth tale of the *Vie des Pères*, "Copeaux."

posteriority; redactors have been known to improve works. Payen, pointing out among other things that the *merveilleux* has a more important role in the *Chevalier au barisel*, and that the tendency was to add magic rather than reduce it, believes the *Conte dou barril* to be more archaic (1967, 542).

The "joys" of the Virgin Mary inspired no fewer than sixteen different Old French poems, mostly dating to the thirteenth century (Brayer 1970, 47-48) and mostly treating the five, seven, or fifteen joys. The fourth text of UCB 106 (ff. 105ra-105vc) is the only one known to the editor of the work, Tauno Mustanoja, to specify nine (1952, 10-11).

In the thirteenth century such poems were usually included in narrative collections; they later became a regular feature in Middle French books of hours (ibid., 12). Although the genre is most aptly described as an invocation, a potential for narrative lies behind each of the listed joys. These varied among the versions but included such events as the Annunciation, the Visitation, the leaping of the babe in Mary's womb, the Nativity, the Adoration of the Shepherds, the Epiphany, the Presentation of Christ in the Temple, the Finding in the Temple, the Marriage in Cana, the Feeding of the Five Thousand, the Crucifixion, the Resurrection, the Ascension, Pentecost, and the Assumption and Coronation of the Virgin (ibid., 11).

While the rubrics of most of its eighteen known copies refer to the poem as *Les neuf joies Nostre Dame*, the text in UCB 106 actually consists of an enumeration of the Virgin's names and symbols, ending with a list of her joys. The Latin exegetical tradition had given particular attention to the explication of the Virgin's life and qualities. Her symbols were a common subject for Latin hymns of the period, regarded in general as the French poet's source (ibid., 10; for a list of examples, see Diehl 1984, 115-16). The compositional principle of enumeration is characteristic of Marian poetry, represented by "Mary-Psalters" of 50, 100, and 150 elements as well as by various sorrows and joys of the Virgin (Diehl 1984, 113-16).

The poem was attributed to Rutebeuf by Paulin Paris and by Achille Jubinal, who published it in 1839. Although it occurs in manuscripts that also contain Rutebeuf's works, has a stanzaic pattern similar to one favored by him, and treats one of Rutebeuf's favorite subjects, the Virgin, Mustanoja's close analysis of the style, versification, and language fails to support the attribution (1952, 31, 36-40). He leans heavily on paleographical evidence of the extant manuscripts to suggest a date between 1250 and 1270 for the text.[9] Seven of the seventeen extant manuscripts are now held by English libraries, which, together with a few linguistic traits, leads him to situate its composition near the Channel coast of France (ibid., 36).

---

[9] UCB 106 was one of the two manuscripts he was unable to consult (Mustanoja 1952, 12, 35). With traits characteristic of the second quarter of the thirteenth century, its hands indicate a date nearer to 1250 as a *terminus ante quem* for the poem.

The editor describes the versification as "stanzas of eight octosyllabic lines rhyming abababab abababab cdcdcdcd cdcdcdcd" (ibid., 30). Given the sixteen-line rhyme scheme, his remark implies that the manuscripts divide the poem into eight-line segments. UCB 106, however, has paragraph marks at sixteen-line intervals, indicating each change in rhyme. It also omits stanzas 17 and 18 (as numbered in the edition) and has a different order: 19 and 20, which contrast Eve and Mary, appear between 2 and 3. The apparatus of the editor reflects considerable verbal variation, particularly for the final stanza (stanza 26), but the reordering of stanzas 19-20 in UCB 106 appears to be the only example of rearrangement.

Five of the six Old French verse versions of Christ's Passion cited by Edith Brayer (1970, 50) date to the thirteenth century, among them the version copied as the fifth text in UCB 106 (ff. 105vc-111ra). Printed by Frances Foster as background for her edition of the Old English *Northern Passion* (1916), it survives in at least twenty-one manuscripts,[10] with widely divergent endings and a few variations among prologues. In some cases, the Passion forms part of a biblical compilation (Foster 1916, 49, 58). It may be based on Latin commentaries or "Gospel harmonies" (continuous narratives interweaving the four Gospels), but no single Latin authority accounts for all cases of divergence from the Scripture itself (ibid., 47-48, 59).

Bancroft Library UCB 106 is one of five manuscripts containing the anonymous medieval French version of the life of Saint Catherine edited by Mary Trenkle (1976) (ff. 111rb-116va);[11] many of the other versions survive in unique copies. Ten of the fourteen medieval French verse versions of her life have been published (Trenkle 1976, xv-xvii, xxxi). The legend has been treated in Latin, Greek, Arabic, German, Hungarian, Czech, Polish, English, Irish, Welsh, Italian, Spanish, and French (ibid., xii). The earliest surviving record of the saint occurs in the late ninth-century *Menologium Basilianum*. She probably became known in France around 1030, when the traveler Simeon of Trèves deposited relics he had obtained from the monastery of Mount Sinai in a monastery near Rouen (ibid., vii-viii). Although the text of this version begins "Nos trovomes en nos escris," Trenkle remains silent on the question of sources.

Trenkle's comparison of the narrative elements of the published versions underscores the characteristics peculiar to this one. The narrative opens abruptly: other versions have prologues stressing the need for good models of Christian life. The topic of Catherine's marriage is treated more fully in some, and a hermit advises and converts her. In one case (published by Långfors 1910), the baby Jesus appears to Catherine in his mother's arms, and he accepts her as his spouse.

---

[10] Foster publishes *O*, Trinity College Cambridge O. 2. 14.

[11] Trenkle uses Brussels, Bibliothèque Royle 10295-304x as her base manuscript.

The story of Catherine resembles that of Saint Margaret and of other virgin martyrs and falls squarely within the generic boundaries of the saint's life. Catherine's dialogue with the orator belongs to the medieval tradition of poetic contests.[12]

The last two texts of UCB 106, taking up a total of 229 folios, or about two-thirds of the entire manuscript, are the *Estoire del Saint Graal* and the *Merlin*, the first two branches of the Arthurian vulgate cycle (vol. 1, ff. 117ra-191vb; vol. 2, entire).[13] The complete cycle was concluded by the *Lancelot propre*, the *Queste del Saint Graal*, and the *Mort le roi Artu* (referred to as a trilogy by the title *Lancelot en prose*).

The trilogy of the *Lancelot en prose*, composed between 1215 and 1230, was probably planned by the author of the *Lancelot propre*, although the authorship of the works remains uncertain. All three have been wrongly attributed to Walter Map.[14] The *Lancelot en prose* was expanded by the addition of the *Estoire del Saint Graal* as a "retrospective sequel" (see Frappier 1978, 585-86), and the *Merlin*, which has no essential narrative connection with the other branches, fills a chronological lacuna between the *Estoire del Saint Graal* and the *Lancelot en prose* and thus completes the cycle (Micha 1978, 593). The *Estoire del Saint Graal* and the *Merlin* were written after the *Lancelot en prose*, some time between 1227 and 1235, the *Merlin* perhaps even later (Grimm 1984, 117, 168). They belong to the vast surviving corpus of thirteenth-century prose romances, nearly all of which are Arthurian.

The *Estoire del Saint Graal* (vol. 1, ff. 117ra-191vb) draws on numerous episodes from Robert de Boron's *Joseph d'Arimathie* and develops background for certain elements of the *Queste del Saint Graal* (ibid., 118). It borrows from biblical apocrypha as well as from the legends of insular saints (see Lagorio 1970).

The fifty-six surviving copies can be divided into two groups of texts, varying in the amount of descriptive detail but not in the contents or order of episodes (Bogdanow 1960, 343-44). The incipit of the text in UCB 106 aligns it with the long version, probably closer to the original than the short version (Grimm 1984, 118).

The legendary personnage of Merlin, protagonist of the eighth text in UCB 106 (filling vol. 2), combines the Welsh popular tradition of a bard or chieftain named Myrddin with the character of Ambrosius, who appears in early Latin insular chronicles

---

[12] Wine against water, knights against clerics, and soul against body are among the principal subjects of this tradition, which occurs already in the comedies of Aristophanes. Many examples survive in Old Provençal (*tenso, joc partit*).

[13] The vulgate cycle has received a great deal of scholarly attention, particularly with regard to its genesis. This brief review is based on the work of Frappier (1968b, 1978a, 1978b); for a more detailed bibliographic account, see Woledge 1954 and 1975.

[14] The texts of the *Queste del Saint Graal* and the *Mort le roi Artu* allude to him in such a way as to imply Walter Map wrote the trilogy. The date of his death, some time before 1210, discredits these claims. See Grimm 1984, 169.

(Gildas, Bede, the anonymous *Historia Britonum*). Geoffrey of Monmouth introduces Merlin the magician in the *Prophetia Merlini* of 1134 (Micha 1978, 591-92; Zumthor [1943] 1973, 9-17).

He makes his first appearance in Old French in the verse *Merlin* of Robert de Boron, a sequel to that author's *Joseph d'Arimathie*. Only a fragment of the poem survives, but a prose translation comes down to us in forty-seven manuscripts and five fragments (Grimm 1984, 166).

The history of this text is complicated by the fact that it became part of two distinct cycles. The Robert de Boron cycle (so called because it was once thought to be written by him) includes *Joseph d'Arimathie*, *Merlin*, and *Perceval*. In the vulgate cycle *Merlin* follows the *Estoire del Saint Graal*, and a continuation (the *Suite-Vulgate*) fills the chronological gap between its final episode, Arthur's coronation, and the time of Lancelot's advent at the height of Arthur's power.

In his study of the manuscript tradition, Micha distinguishes between the α *Merlin* of the Robert de Boron cycle and a shorter, more recent ß redaction designed especially for inclusion in the vulgate cycle. UCB 106 contains the α version, represented by a total of thirty-nine manuscripts. This copy belongs to a subgroup of α that appears to be contaminated by the ß text. Most of the manuscripts containing the ß version indicate no break between the *Merlin* and the *Suite-Vulgate*; in UCB 106, as in several other α copies, the paragraph is marked by a filigreed initial slightly larger than the others (see Micha 1958, 154).

CODICOLOGICAL ARTICULATIONS

The material description of this manuscript (see pp. 101-10 below), including the irregularities in the composition of gatherings and the rubrication, offers a number of possibilities for the manuscript's confection.

First, the gatherings vary from the usual quaternion in three places: toward the end of the first text (vol. 1, gathering 10), in the section containing a series of shorter texts (gatherings 14 and 16), and again in the second half of volume 2 (gatherings 11, 13, 14, 17, 18, 19). Single folios are missing from gathering 10 of the first volume and from gatherings 11 and 13 of the second. In one case (vol. 1, gathering 16), a folio has been carefully glued onto a stub. Since the missing folios should have been at the front or back of the gatherings in question, we could suppose that they too were originally glued to form complete gatherings but came loose and were lost either before binding or when the manuscript was rebound in the nineteenth century. Despite the poor quality of the parchment itself, the care taken to mend its flaws, like that observed in the numerous textual corrections, reflects a general concern for wholeness. A scribe motivated by such a concern would prefer to work with complete quaternions and perhaps took the trouble to piece his scraps together while he waited for a new batch of larger skins. Planning in sequence, he estimated the amount of parchment he would need as he went along. He had almost an adequate supply of complete gatherings for the *Vie des Péres* as well as for the *Estoire del Saint Graal*. He may have supposed the *Merlin* would take the same number of gatherings as its sister branch, for it begins with ten regular quaternions.

Secondly, mistakes in the spacing left for the rubricator suggest a model for the *Vie des Pères* that had no rubrics (such as B.N. f. fr. 2094). If such was the case, it is surprising that more mistakes were *not* made, since the sermonizing prologues and epilogues of the tales often had little to do with the narratives. On folio 67rb (vol. 1) the epilogue of tale 43 is given a rubric; on folios 84rb and 85ra the rubrics for tales 73 and 74 appear *after* the prologues, as though the scribe was overcompensating for his previous error; on folio 92vb, two lines have been erased under the rubric for the beginning of the Gautier de Coinci text, indicating that the scribe had not noticed he was beginning a new one.[15]

Finally, no title announces the *Neuf joies Nostre Dame*, although space has been left for one at the bottom of folio 105ra. While in some manuscripts this would not necessarily imply an omission, other texts in UCB 106 do begin with titles at the bottoms of columns (for example, ff. 35vc-36ra, 54ra-b). Since the usual large filigreed initial and scalloped border mark the beginning of the text, it seems likely that the titles and initials were done in separate steps, perhaps by different persons.

ANALYSIS AND INTERPRETATION

Keeping in mind these codicological peculiarities, I begin my analysis of the texts by examining connections between them that may help to account for their sequence, before taking up the question of audience.

The debauchery depicted in the *fabliau*-like tales of the *Vie des Pères* is time and again surpassed in gravity by such offenses as murder, incest, infanticide, renunciation of faith, and despair. The theme of the monstrous sin is well represented in the collection and reappears in the life of Theophilus and in the *Conte dou barril*.

In "Ivresse," for example (7 [35], f. 9rc), the devil gives a hermit his choice from among drunkenness, fornication, and murder; having selected the first as least offensive,

---

[15] Supposing we can assume the model lacked titles, a detailed investigation of the titles supplied as interpretations of the tales would shed light on the interests of the rubricator for this manuscript. Since comparison with rubrics from other manuscripts would be necessary, such an investigation lies beyond the range of this study.

he is easily led into the other two at the home of his friend, the miller. "Inceste" (21 [40], f. 28rc) is the story of an otherwise pious widow who conceals her incestuous relationship with her son for ten years and murders their offspring. She augments her good works and honors the Virgin but does not confess her sin until the devil, in disguise, denounces her to the emperor. The devil no longer recognizes her after she has been absolved by the pope. "Meurtrier" (22 [12], f. 30rb) compares the soul of a thief who repents and wins salvation with that of a hermit who in a fit of jealousy despairs, renounces God, and kills himself.[16] In the second text, Theophilus's renunciation is rendered more damning by his pact with the devil and by the fact that he holds an official ecclesiastical position. Mary's intervention, a foreshadowing of the Harrowing of Hell motif that appears in both the *Passion* and the *Merlin* farther on in the manuscript, takes on a peculiarly realistic cast when she must actually retrieve the contract itself from hell. The chatelain in the *Conte dou barril* flaunts his complete indifference to the state of his soul as he vaunts his numerous sins, their monstrosity amplified by his attitude (cf. Payen 1967, 519-34).

The theme of the monstrous sin runs through the first three texts, overlapping with the shared allegorical mode of texts 2, 3, and 4. The names and symbols of the Virgin are sprinkled throughout Gautier's prologue, echoed by the *Neuf joies Nostre Dame*, a dense exposition of Marian types and figures ending with a succinct account of the joys. In addition, the Theophilus miracle contains an extended metaphor of conscience on the horse symbolizing the weakness of the flesh. The *Conte dou barril* lying between the two lacks Marian emphasis, but the hermit's long sermon analyzing the soul's spiritual armor applies a kind of symbolic interpretation resembling those of Gautier's prologue and the *Neuf joies Nostre Dame*.

The triumphs of Christ's life constitute some of Mary's joys; her sorrows, lists of which belong to a tradition of poetic complaint, focus primarily on the Passion (see Diehl 1984, 114; Brayer 1970, 46-47). In the absence of an enumeration of her sorrows, the *Passion*, text 5 of this manuscript, seems an appropriate sequel and companion piece to the *Neuf joies Nostre Dame*. The scene for the traditional Marian complaint is set in the *Passion*'s account of the Crucifixion:

> Jouste la croiz estoit Marie,
> La soe mere, esbahie.
> Si i ert Marie Cleophe
> *Et* Maria Maudelene [*sic*],
> *Et* plusors autres i estoient
> . . . .

---

[16] In medieval tradition Judas was ultimately damned for his despair and suicide, not for his betrayal of Jesus. Although this story narrates the thief's one day of charitable life in some detail, the rubricator has entitled it "De l'ermit qui se despera" (see Foster 1916, 60; Payen 1967, 521 n. 13).

> Sor toutes en estoit corocose [*sic*]
> La soe mere glorieuse.
> N'est me*r*veille s'estoit ire
> *Et* coroucie *et* empirie.
> (f. 110va46-b7)

This passage places Christ's Passion in the context of his mother's grief, just as the enumeration of her joys recounts the miracles of his life as Mary experienced them.

As the story of a martyr, the sixth text of UCB 106 is one of those saints' lives that particularly lend themselves to comparison with Christ's Passion. Both narratives place events in an urban setting at the time of a festival. Catherine's wheel of torture parallels the cross, although she is ultimately beheaded. Just as the sun darkens at the time of the Crucifixion, supernatural forces manifest themselves during Catherine's ordeal by shattering the wheel and rendering its fragments deadly missiles against the pagans.

The most striking parallel between the story of Catherine and the following text, the *Estoire del Saint Graal*, is a focus on conversion of the pagans. A reworking of Robert de Boron's life of Joseph of Arimathea, it complements the martyrdom of Catherine by narrating the works of a missionary.[17] If the compiler of UCB 106 was so sensitive to generic distinctions as to counterpoise Mary's joys to an account of her sorrows as represented in the text of the *Passion*, he may also have felt the need to balance the life of a virgin martyr with that of a confessor. The overall concern for completeness reflected in the manuscript's material description might well extend to the selection and juxtaposition of texts.

The link between the seventh and eighth texts hardly needs explanation, since they constitute the first two branches of the vulgate Grail cycle. It might be supposed that the entire cycle belonged with the collection, since the *Merlin* text refers to the opening of the *Lancelot*, just as the *Estoire del Saint Graal* ends with a miniature illustrating the beginning of *Merlin*. Either the last three branches filled a second volume or series of volumes now lost or the scribe's project was interrupted.[18]

In addition to sequential links between texts 6 and 7 and 7 and 8, the last two texts are connected with earlier ones in the manuscript by thematic echoes. The *Estoire del Saint Graal*, after describing the circumstances of its composition, opens with a reference to the *Passion*, expanding on the role of the holy vessel used in the Last Supper. The Harrowing of Hell figures in Mary's retrieval of Theophilus's contract with the devil as well as in the *Passion*, where it is emphasized by the devil's visit to Pilate's wife, and

---

[17] Valerie Lagorio (1970) has shown how the author of the *Estoire del Saint Graal* might have consolidated various legendary accounts of the actual conversion of Britain, attributing them to one person.

[18] A survey of Alexandre Micha's three articles on the manuscripts of the *Lancelot propre* failed to turn up any likely companion volumes (1960, 1963, 1964).

in *Merlin*, which opens with the devil's wrath against the forces of Good ("Molt fu dolenz li enemis").

While all the texts in UCB 106 treat themes that could be described as religious, the collection's emphasis on hermits' roles, its criticism of the official clergy, and the abundance of magical elements found in it respond to the concerns of a devout lay public inadequately served by ecclesiastical institutions.

In a society that had outgrown the frameworks both of the Church and of feudal government, the hermit's life provided a number of solutions (see Delaruelle 1962, 240-41). By becoming a hermit, an individual could follow a religious vocation without seeking the sanction of an official order. He could do so at any time of his life, whether or not he had received clerical training. Without social connections or material contributions, he could establish his own "rule," modeling himself after the liberty of Christ praying on the mountain. If none of the institutions available to him met his standards of piety, he could nevertheless devote his life to God in his own way. This function of late medieval anchoritism as an alternative to the official religious life culminates in the development of the mendicant orders (see Becquet 1962, 210). Unlike the anchorites of an earlier period, hermits such as those depicted in the *Vie des Pères*, the *Conte dou barril*, and the Arthurian vulgate cycle were in continuous contact with each other and with laypeople (Becquet 1962, 194). They met a need for noncanonical spiritual counsel in situations where the clergy were inaccessible or unacceptable.

The research of Jean Becquet (1962) concerning the actual lives of hermits in western France reflects this need for spiritual alternatives. The texts in UCB 106, depicting sinners of various kinds who win salvation either by retiring to hermitages or through the benefit of hermits' guidance, affirm the spiritual authenticity of unofficial confession, penance, absolution, and sacraments.

While the hermits' roles in the various texts represent alternatives to ecclesiastical institutions, the *Estoire del Saint Graal* also implicitly rejects them by offering an alternate account of the conversion of Great Britain (see Lagorio 1970), by having Josephe, son of Joseph of Arimathia and Britain's first bishop, appointed and consecrated by Christ himself, bypassing the human ecclesiastical hierarchy; and by explaining the Christian faith and sacraments to converts without any reference to the fathers of the Church or any other canonical authority. The *Merlin* also subtly degrades the official clergy by having the boy magician reveal the sins of two priests: one the natural father of the judge who had condemned Merlin's mother for fornication, the other the father of a child whose funeral Merlin and his companions happen upon. Much as a saint's miracles manifest God's favor, Merlin demonstrates his supernatural knowledge, in these instances at the expense of representatives of the Church. Although written by a monk, the life of Theophilus contains explicit criticism. Not only does it depict a bishop who attains his office by treating with the devil, but its concluding sermon ("queue") inveighs against the vanity and hypocrisy of the clergy.

In addition to legitimizing spiritual alternatives, the texts in UCB 106 respond to the audience's inability to reconcile the challenges of thirteenth-century society with a model of ascetic virtue. As I have mentioned (in chapter 2), Spangenberg correlates the rise of the Marian cult with the instability of social and ecclesiastical structures. Brigitte Cazelles sees the Virgin's role in the humanization of virtue and redemption ascompensating for a cosmic view of the battle between good and evil: her mediation puts sin into perspective by acknowledging the individual's vulnerability as a pawn in the battle. The overwhelmed believer puts his faith in the Virgin because he feels incapable of earning salvation for himself (Cazelles 1978, 12-16). Unlike B.N. f. fr. 2162, which stresses virtue, prayer, confession, and repentance while it avoids depicting dependence on magical help from the Virgin or any other saint, UCB 106 places in the foreground the devil's power over individuals and the roles of magical helpers, especially of the Virgin, in overcoming him.

Devils are featured in many tales of the *Vie des Pères*, often just for the sake of affirming their presence. "Image du diable" (11 [41], f. 14rb) relates how the devil, for revenge, corrupts a sacristan who had made a very ugly statue of him.[19] "Queue" (28 [15], f. 40vc) is an anecdote about Saint Jerome and a companion, who, visiting town one day, notice a devil hiding under the extravagant train of a lady's dress. When they call her attention to him, she shakes him off into the mud. "Vision de diables" (38 [23], f. 58rb) describes the experience of a young monk who sees a thousand devils surrounding the walls of his abbey, but only one embracing the nearby town. His abbot explains that the city, already given over to evil, needs only one guard, while the abbey with its virtuous inhabitants requires a mass assault.

Mary's opposition to the devil is paramount in the life of Theoophilus. The devil makes an appearance in the *Estoire del Saint Graal* when he tempts characters whose faith is being tested. The story of Merlin opens with the devils' plot leading to his conception. His powers as a magical helper, not unlike those of many saints (see Loomis 1948), are demonstrated throughout the text, as well as in one of the tales of the *Vie des Pères*: "Merlot" (25 [42], f. 35vc) narrates a peasant's dealings with a voice in the forest identifying itself as Merlin and promising the peasant ever greater favors in exchange for an annual visit.[20] The life of Catherine not only contains marvelous episodes but honors a saint often invoked as a magical helper. Her intellectual prowess against the emperor's sages, which C. Grant Loomis believes a medieval audience would have regarded as supernatural in a beautiful woman (ibid., 111), adds a dimension to the heavenly food

---

[19] It is easy to imagine that the sculptors of gargoyles may have actually feared such retribution.

[20] The story is no doubt a spin-off of the legend of Merlin's burial in the forest of Brocéliande.

she receives in prison, the stormy destruction of the torture wheel, and the miracles performed on her tomb.

The texts in UCB 106 answer the need for spiritual alternatives reflected in the hermits' roles, the rejection of church institutions, and the dependence on magical help. At the same time they offer models of spiritual success with whom a devout layperson could identify. The *Vie des Pères* contains many such examples of ordinary people who commit even monstrous sins and win salvation through sincere repentance, with or without magical intervention. "Goliard" (40 [28], f. 61rc), for example, is the touching story of a wicked young vagabond who enters a monastery for the sole purpose of making off with its treasure. He repeatedly postpones his escape to assuage his conscience with yet another day of prayer, until eventually he wins salvation through the torture of many years of temptation. "Prévôt d'Aquilée" (4 [32], f. 4vb) describes a married couple who live in chastity but subject themselves to the repeated temptation of sleeping together. "Rachat" (8 [36], f. 10vc) relates the bargaining success of a merchant who, having joined a Carthusian monastery, uses his worldly skills to serve God. The chatelain of the *Conte dou barril* reforms his ways not by retiring to a religious order or even to a hermitage but by living virtuously in the world and keeping his promises to the hermit who converted him.

The urban middle class would be a likely audience for such a combination of texts. When she examined manuscript UCB 106 in 1981 Marie-Thérèse d'Alverny said she thought the scribe was a layman, and that the texts were all ordered by the same man, perhaps at different times. The codicological and textual evidence together seems to suggest a wealthy bourgeois as the client.

MATERIAL DESCRIPTION: BANCROFT LIBRARY UCB 106

Generalities

This manuscript is bound in two volumes, numbered separately in pencil in a modern hand, with a total of 346 folios. The parchment is of poor quality, with some folios chalky in appearance, and too many holes and blemishes to note here. In addition, tears have occurred since the writing. It was repaired both before and after the text was written, with glue in some cases and with red or blue stitching in others. It is also in rather delicate condition, probably due to the procedures of the nineteenth-century binder.[21] The parchment of the second volume appears to have been gnawed on the lower outside corner, especially toward the back. Throughout the manuscript, the parchment appears to have been rolled or folded at some time along the spaces between columns.

The tan leather binding of each volume, embossed front and back with a geometric floral design in brown and gold, bears the signature "Lefebvre" (which I have not succeeded in identifying), and the following titles are embossed on the spines: "La Vie des Peres," "Theophilus," "La Passion," "La Vie de S. Katherine," "Joseph de Arimathee," "XIIIe siecle" (vol. 1); "Le St. Graal," "Merlin," "XIIIe siecle" (vol. 2). Both volumes have marbled end sheets and paper guard sheets with no watermarks; the edges of the parchment have been gilded.

The ink used for the text varies between dark brown and black; numerous contemporary corrections in a second hand are mostly in brown ink, either in the margins or written over erasures. The entire text is written in one regular, disciplined, even gothic bookhand with characteristics of the second quarter of the thirteenth century (see figure 19). Final *s* is mostly upright, although occasionally it is curved as though the scribe intended to make the round form but omitted the lower loop. The upper loop of *a* is consistently rounded and open. Round *r* occurs only after *o*, and the upright of *t* does not protrude above the crossbar. While contiguous *d* and *e* are sometimes joined, they are often separate, as are other adjacent curves. Miniscule *i* is occasionally marked with a convex hair stroke of the same shape as that which finishes *e* at line ends. No phonetic distinction is made between *u* and *v*, and *v* appears only as the initial of a word. Ascenders are of a regular and restrained height, topped with a hook to the left.

The hand adding corrections uses a fine quill and has a pointed, uneven appearance: the scribe apparently missed having the ruling to guide him. Ascenders are tall, some forked at the top. Round and upright *s* are both used in final position; *a* has a backward-leaning shaft and an open loop. Round *r* follows *o*, but the letters are kept separate. The upright of *t* does not extend above the bar. In some instances, the scribe of the text makes his own corrections. Guide letters for the person adding the filigreed initials are frequently visible in the margins.

The consistently poor quality of the parchment, the regular size of the writing block, the style of decoration, and the uniformity of the handwriting give the manuscript a homogeneous appearance.

Quaternions linked by horizontal, undecorated catchwords (lower right verso) are numbered by two modern sets of signatures. One set, made before the present binding divided the manuscript into two parts, counts the gatherings all together, 1-47 (lower left

---

[21] The hypothesis concerning the cause of the parchment's present condition, communicated to me by Anthony Bliss of the Bancroft Library, was suggested by Albert Derolez of the University of Ghent. Bliss dates the binding at around 1830.

recto, some partly concealed in the binding). The other set counts the gatherings separately for each volume, 1-26 and 1-19 (lower center verso).

Titles are rubricated, with the first letter in blue. Incipits of the texts are distinguished by filigreed initials four or five lines high, red on blue and blue on red, extending into vertical scalloped borders. These are characteristic of Parisian workshops of the second half of the century, suggesting that the decoration was added later or by someone younger than the scribe (see Walpole 1976, 62, 418-422). Decorated and historiated initials and small miniatures are painted in green, violet, brown, two shades of blue, two shades of red, orange, white, and gold (see description of detail, table 5). Marks in dry point or in red number the four bifolia of some of the gatherings ("1," "ll," "lll," "llll"). Many have worn off; more survive in the second than in the first volume.[22]

Particularities

At least two modern hands have annotated the manuscript in pencil on the paper guard sheets. One makes a lengthy commentary in English concerning the contents, referring to Méon (1823) and Legrand d'Aussy ([1779] 1829), on the verso of the second guard sheet, volume 1. It mentions that the manuscript contains about 57,000 verses; the computations are visible on the first back guard sheet of volume 1. This appears to be the hand that provides the foliation. Another hand seems more concerned with the organization of the volume, listing the irregular gatherings on the recto of the second guard sheet of volume 1. This person probably wrote the set of signatures on the lower center verso of what he believed to be the last folio of each gathering, and also inscribed the Phillipps shelf mark (3643) in each volume.

The text of the *Neuf joies Nostre Dame* contains paragraph marks, indicating the stanzas in alternating blue and red. These are also used in the prose texts to distinguish the last words of one paragraph from the first words of the next when these are combined on a single line. The life of Saint Catherine has a greater proportion of filigreed initials than the other texts, with twelve or thirteen per folio rather than four to six. The text of the *Conte dou barril* contains relatively few such decorations. Blank lines occur in volume 1, columns 99a, 100d, and 100f; two lines in column d are in a different hand. The first four lines of a tale of the *Vie des Pères* ("Demi-ami," 18 [39], vol. 1, f. 25) have been copied in the bottom margin of folio 191v of volume 1. It begins with the proverb "Tant as, tant vaus, *et* je ta*n*t t'eim" (see Morawski 1925, 83). Perhaps against the devils of whom he was about to write, the scribe recorded an invocation: "Sancti

---

[22] These have been helpful in indicating the position of the stitch, and thereby the original organization of the volume.

Spiritus assit nobis gratia" (column a) and "Assit principio Sancta Maria meo" (column b) in the top margin of the first folio of *Merlin*.

Meyer identified two notes in fourteenth-century hands and southern French dialect on folio 93v of volume 1 and folio 155v of volume 2, and a sixteenth-century note in English also on the latter of the two (1891, 155). There is a table of contents in fourteenth-century *lettres de forme* at the end of volume 2, which, along with the lower left recto signatures, indicates that the manuscript was originally bound in one volume.

The manuscript was listed for sale in the Motteley catalogue, Paris, 1824 (lot 875, ff. 701), and afterwards belonged to Robert Lang, who collected manuscripts of French romances. At the Evans sale of 17 November 1828 (lot 1962, L19) it became part of the Phillipps collection at Cheltenham and was sold to Messrs. William H. Robinson, Ltd., along with the remnants of that collection in 1946 (Koenig 1955, 1: xxxiv). The Bancroft Library acquired it at the Sotheby sale of 28 November 1967.

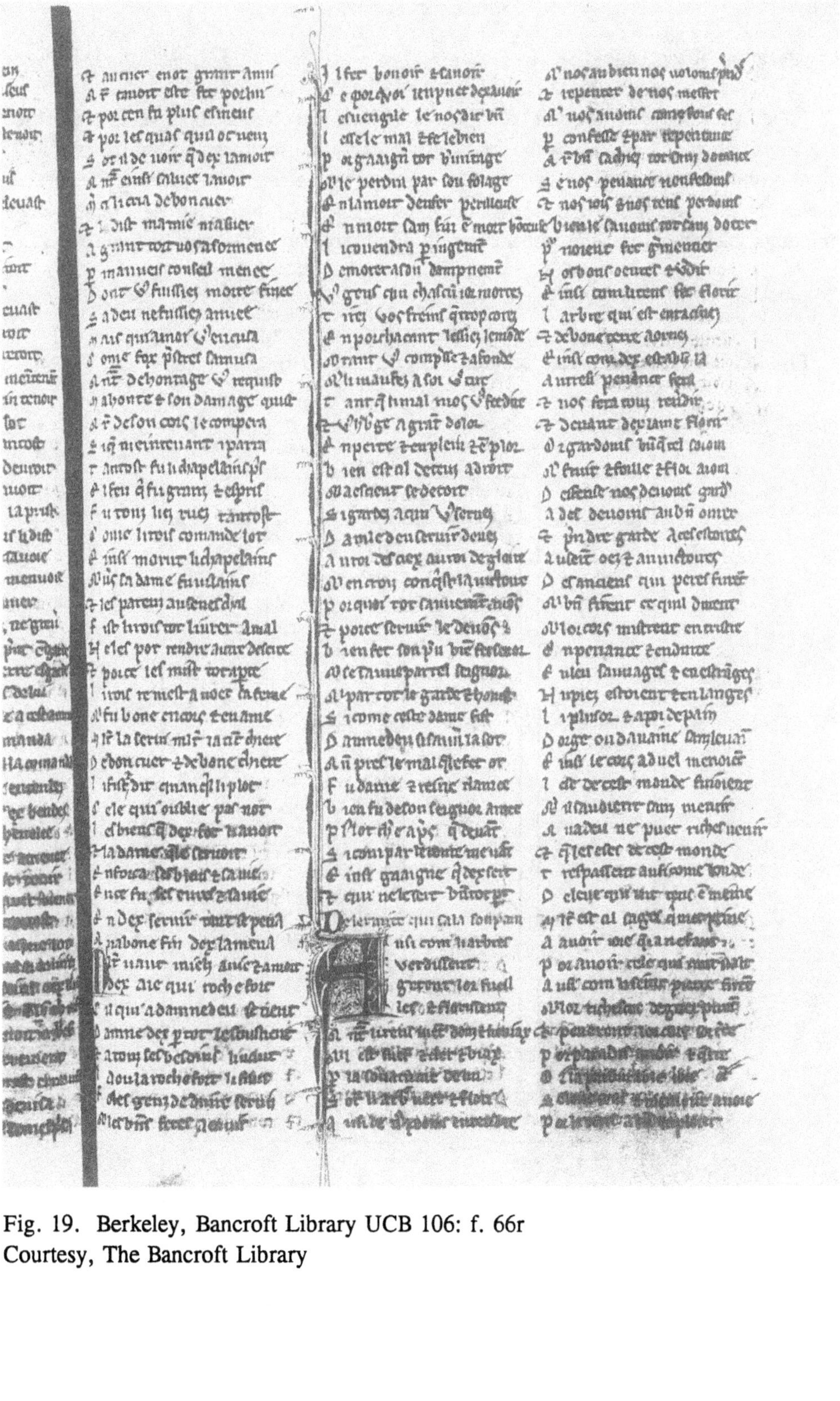

Fig. 19. Berkeley, Bancroft Library UCB 106: f. 66r
Courtesy, The Bancroft Library

Organization of the Page

Folios are ruled with dry point for forty-eight lines per column, both verse and prose. Prickings across the bottom of the folios in volume 1 and bottom and top in volume 2, more pronounced in the first few folios of each gathering, mark the spacing for vertical lines. None remain for the horizontal lines. The first gathering has rather large prickings, eleven across; the rest are barely discernible and only two to five across.

Folio dimensions: 328-35 x 219-26 mm

Fig. 20. Page layout, verse section (Vol. 1, ff. 1-116)

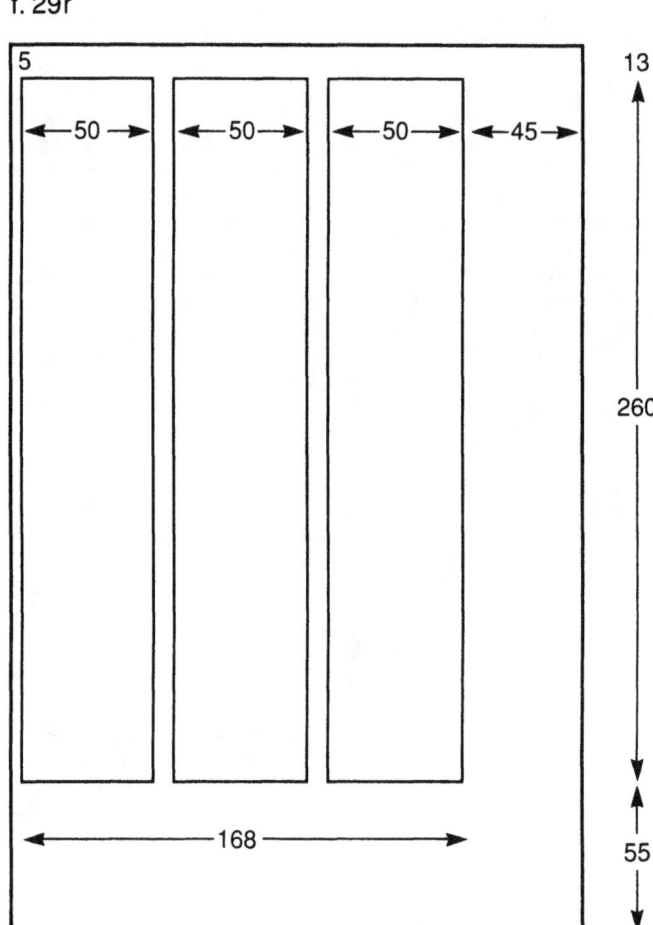

Justification:
3 columns, 260 x 168 mm

Fig. 21. Page layout, prose section (Vol. 1, ff. 117-191; Vol. 2, entire)

f. 137r

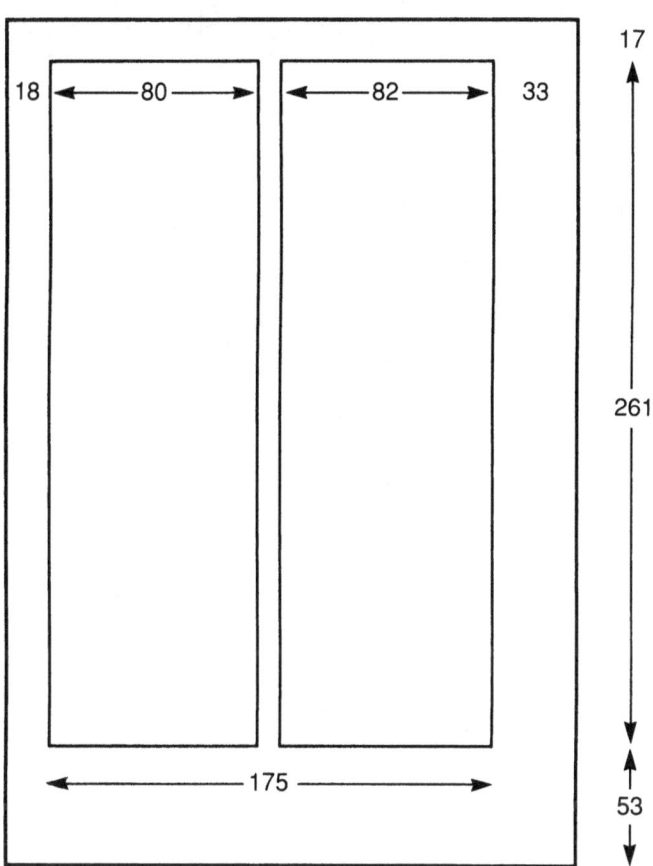

Justification:
2 columns, 261 x 175 mm

Table 4

Organization of the Volume: Vol. 1

Gathering	Type	Catchword	Signatures	Remarks	Texts
1 (1-8)	4/4	yes	1, LCV f. 8		*Vie des Pères*, f. 1ra
2 (9-16)	4/4	yes	2, LLR f 9; LCV f. 16		
3 (17-24)	4/4	yes	3, LLR f. 17, LCV f. 24		
4 (25-32)	4/4	yes	4, LLR f. 25, LCV f. 32		
5 (33-40)	4/4	yes	5, LLR f. 33, LCV f. 40		
6 (41-48)	4/4	yes	6, LLR f. 41, LCV f. 48		
7 (49-56)	4/4	yes	7, LLR f. 49, LCV f. 56		
8 (57-64)	4/4	yes	8, LLR f. 57, LCV f. 64		
9 (65-72)	4/4	yes	9, LLR f. 65, LCV f. 72		
10 (73-79)	4/3	no	10, LLR f. 73	folio missing between ff. 79 and 80	
11 (80-87)	4/4	yes	11, LLR f. 80; 10, LCV f. 87, LCV f. 80		
12 (88-95)	4/4	yes	12, LLR f. 88; 11 LCV f. 95		Gautier de Coinci, prologue to the *Miracles de Nostre Dame*, f. 92vb; *Vie de Théophile*, f. 93vc
13 (96-103)	4/4	yes	13, LLR f. 96; 12, LCV f. 103		Jehan de Blois, *Le conte du barril*, f. 101ra
14 (104-5)	2	yes	14, LLR f. 104; 13, LCV f. 105		*Les neuf joies Nostre Dame*, f. 105ra; *La Passion Ihesu Crist*, f. 105vc
15 (106-13)	4/4	yes	15, LLR f. 106; 14, LCV f. 107; 15, LCV f. 113	correction mistaken for catchword, f. 107v	Life of Saint Catherine of Alexandria, f. 111rb
16 (114-16)	1/2	no	16, LLR f. 114, LCV f. 116	f. 114 appears glued onto stub; f. 116vb and c blank	

Table 4 — Continued

Gathering	Type	Catchword	Signatures	Remarks	Texts
			Organization of the Volume: Vol. 1 (continued)		
17 (117-24)	4/4	yes	17, LLR f. 117, LCV f. 124	painted decoration, ff. 119c, 121d[a]	*L'estoire del Saint Graal*, f. 117ra
18 (125-32)	4/4	yes	18, LLR f. 125, LCV f. 132	painted decoration, ff. 125rb, 126rb, 132ra	
19 (133-40)	4/4	yes	19, LLR f. 133, LCV f. 140	painted decoration, ff. 134ra, 134rb, 135vb, 136rb, 137ra, 137va, 139vb	
20 (141-48)	4/4	yes	20, LLR f. 141, LCV f. 148	painted decoration, ff. 141vb, 143ra, 143va, 145va, 145vb, 147vb	
21 (149-56)	4/4	yes	21, LLR f. 149, LCV f. 156		
22 (157-64)	4/4	yes	22, LLR f. 157, LCV f. 164	painted decoration, f. 160vb	
23 (165-72)	4/4	yes	23, LLR f. 165, LCV f. 172	painted decoration, ff. 167vb, 168ra, 169ra, 170vb	
24 (173-80)	4/4	yes	24, LLR f. 173, LCV f. 180		
25 (181-88)	4/4	yes	25, LLR f. 181, LCV f. 188	painted decoration, 183ra, 184rb, 187rb, 188rb	
26 (189-91)	3	no	26, LLR f. 189, LCV f. 191	painted decoration, ff. 190rb, 191vb	

[a] Details concerning painted decoration appear below, table 5.

Continued on next page

Table 4 — Continued

Organization of the Volume: Vol. 2

Gathering	Type	Catchword	Signatures	Remarks	Texts
1 (1)	1	yes	no	belonged to gathering 26 before manuscript was divided; painted decoration, f. 1ra	Beginning of *Merlin*
1 (2-9)	4/4	yes	27, LLR f. 2; 1, LCV f. 9		
2 (10-17)	4/4	yes	28, LLR f. 10: 2, LCV f. 17		
3 (18-25)	4/4	yes	29, LLR f. 18: 3, LCV f. 25		
4 (26-33)	4/4	yes	30, LLR f. 26: 4, LCV f. 33		
5 (34-41)	4/4	yes	31, LLR f. 34: 5, LCV f. 41		
6 (42-49)	4/4	yes	32, LLR f. 42: 6, LCV f. 49		
7 (50-57)	4/4	yes	33, LLR f. 50: 7, LCV f. 57		
8 (58-65)	4/4	yes	34, LLR f. 58: 8, LCV f. 65		
9 (66-73)	4/4	yes	35, LLR f. 66: 9, LCV f. 73		
10 (74-81)	4/4	yes	36, LLR f. 74: 10, LCV f. 81		
11 (82-88)	4/3	no	37, LLR f. 82	folio missing between ff. 88 and 89 unmatched catchword	
12 (89-96)	4/4	yes	38, LLR f. 89: 11, LCV f. 96		
13 (97-103)	3/4	yes	39, LLR f. 97: 12, LCV f. 103	folio missing between ff. 96 and 97	
14 (104-10)	4/3	yes	40, LLR f. 104; 13, LCV f. 110		
15 (111-18)	4/4	yes	41, LLR f. 111; 14, LCV f. 118		
16 (119-26)	4/4	no	42, LLR f. 120; 43, LLR f. 124; 15, LCV f. 126		
17 (127-29)	3	no	no		
18 (130-34)	4/1	no	44, LLR f. 131		
19 (135-43)	5/4	yes	45, LLR f. 137; 17, LCV f. 143		
20 (144-51)	4/4	yes	46, LLR f. 144; 18, LCV f. 151		
21 (152-55)	4	no	47, LLR f. 152; 19, LCV f. 155		text ends, mid-column f. 155a

Table 5

Detail of Painted Decoration

Folio, page[a]	Type[b]	Measurements (mm)	Description
1ra	historiated "A"	63 x 40	Three tiers: Crucifixion with two Marys, two hermits in brown habits, Mary Magdalene with hermit holding basket
117ra, 3	historiated "C"	50 x 50	Author in brown habit seated with pen; angel displaying scroll
119va, 12	historiated "N"	58 x 55	Crucified Christ flanked by two thieves, two Marys; gold disk[c]
121vb, 20	historiated "O"	30 x 28	Joseph preaches to his relatives; gold disk
125rb, 29	historiated "O"	27 x 25	Joseph ponders the conversion of King Evalac while lying in bed; gold disk
126rb, 31	historiated "O"	43 x 40	Christ anoints Joseph his "sergans"; vessel on table; gold disk
132ra	decorated "O"	18 x 17	
134ra, 73	historiated "A"	38 x 40	Evalac's prisoner, King Tholomer, falls at his feet.
135vb	decorated "A"	21 x 21	
136rb, 83	historiated "O"	47 x 40	Josephe and his company take leave of the king and Nacien.
137ra, 86	historiated "O"	43 x 43	Arriving in the palace hall after church, the queen is frightened by the sight of knights lying passed-out on the floor.
137va	decorated "L"	25 x 27	
139vb	decorated "E"	16 x 18	
141vb, 107	historiated "O"	42 x 40	Calafer imprisons Nacien.
143ra, 114	historiated "O"	42 x 38	Nacien is rescued by a hand issuing from a cloud.
143va	decorated "O"	16 x 20	
145va, 130	miniature	109 x 80	Two tiers: Cain strikes Abel; the Tree of Life
145vb, 130	historiated "M"	33 x 30	Two tiers: the Tree of Life; three busts, the descendants of Adam and Eve

[a] Page numbers are given for the edition of *L'estoire del Saint Graal* where applicable (Sommer 1908-9).
[b] "Ornamental" initials are those distinguished in any way from the script of the text (by size or color, red or blue); "filigreed" initials are red ornamented with blue or blue with red; "decorated" initials have been painted in several colors; "historiated" initials contain representations of narrative; "miniatures" are separate from the text.
[c] Although it has been suggested that the gold disk represents the grail, a less concrete meaning is indicated by the iconographic and narrative context.

Continued on next page

Table 5 — Continued

Detail of Painted Decoration

Folio, page	Type	Measurements (mm)	Description
147vb	decorated "O"	15 x 18	
160v-b, 182	historiated "O"	37 x 34	Shipwrecked, the two messengers and the damsel come upon the tomb of Hippocrates.
167vb, 207	historiated "C"	37 x 29	Nacien prays for knowledge of his descendants.
168ra, 208	historiated "O"	37 x 35	Mordrain and Sarracinte ride to visit Flegentine; third figure is perhaps a lady-in-waiting.
169ra, 212	historiated "O"	32 x 30	Nacien in the boat with his scroll; gold disk
170vb, 219	historiated "O"	31 x 28	Duke Ganor dreams; gold disk
173vb	filigreed "O"	37 x 30	This space was probably intended for painting, since the initial is much larger than others like it.
183ra, 266	historiated "O"	33 x 35	Chanaan the murderer repents before dying; gold disk
184b, 270	historiated "O"	31 x 35	Peter arrives at King Orcan's island.
187rb, 281	historiated "O"	33 x 33	Josephe preaches the gospel; gold rectangle
188rb, 284	historiated "O"	37 x 35	Josephe crowns Galaad king of Hocelice (=Gales); gold disk
188vb, 285	historiated "O"	31 x 33	The death of Josephe, mourned by King Mordrain; gold disk
190rb, 286	historiated "O"	33 x 30	Mordrain and the very good knight; red cross shield
191vb	miniature		The Harrowing of Hell; Christ, clad in a red drape and holding a staff, opposite nude figures issuing from a serpent's mouth fringed with teeth and surmounted by a devil; paint badly worn, particularly from the devil's face

CONTENTS

(1) ff. 1ra-92vb: [*Vie des Pères*], first half of thirteenth century (Bornäs 1968, Chaurand 1971), octosyllabic couplets

Title: Ici comence la vie des Peres [rubr.][23]
Incipit: Aïde Dex, rois Jhesu Christ
Explicit: Et je pri Deu que il m'en oie. Amen.
Editions: Bornäs 1968; Chaurand 1971
See also Duval [1838] 1895; Tobler 1866; Weber 1877; Schwann 1884; Meyer 1906b; Morawski 1921, 1935, 1938; Del Monte 1966; Payen 1967.
Summary: Sin and redemption motivate most of the plots: the theme of the monstrous sin is a favorite (e.g., "Ivresse," 7 [35], f. 9rc).[24] The quality of contrition is emphasized in some stories, often demonstrated by magical tears ("Copeaux," 15 [5], f. 20rb). Salvation depends not on the extent of virtue or sin, but on the repentant individual's sincerity and devotion; several tales illustrate this principle by comparing hermits with other sinners, to the advantage of the latter ("Meurtrier," 22 [12], f. 30rb). The successful or failed resistance to temptation reflects similar concerns in other stories ("Prévôt d'Aquilée," 4 [32], f. 4vb).

Some plots center on supernatural events or visions, either of marvelous characters or of the afterlife ("Gueule du diable," 19 [29], f. 26rb). A few others focus on the hermits' role in converting pagans to Christianity ("Malaquin," 37 [22], f. 57rb). Without reference to particular sins, a number of tales illustrate the spiritual integrity of the simple or the rewards reserved for the especially devout ("Ave Maria," 27 [14], f. 40ra). Moralistic rather than spiritual lessons are conveyed in a few tales ("Demi-ami," 18 [39], f. 25ra).[25]

---

[23] See table 6 for a list of individual stories and editions.

[24] Gaston Paris provided capsule titles for the tales in a note to Schwann's article (1884, 240 n.5). I have used these titles in referring to them, with numbers indicating the position of each in the sequence of UCB 106 and, in brackets, in that of MS *A*.

[25] For a more specific indication of the stories' subjects, see the list of rubrics in table 6. A few summaries are included in the discussion of textual combination; see above pp. 96-97.

Table 6

Contents of the *Vie des Pères*

UCB 106 [A][a]	Begins (f.)	Subject[b]	Rubric	Incipit	Edition
1 [1]	1ra	Fornication imitée	De .ii. hermites dont li uns chai en fornication	Aide dex rois Jhesu crist	Méon 1823
2 [24]	2rb	Ermite accusé	De la damoisele qui mist sus l'ermite qu*i*l l'avoit engrossie	Dex q*ui* les repostailles voit	Méon 1823
3 [25]	3rb	Brûlure	De l'ermite qui la reine vot engignier qui ardi sa main	Qui tale*nt* a de bie*n* apre*n*dre	Keller 1840
4 [32]	4vb	Prévôt d'Aquilée	Du provost d'aquilee	Qu*ant* Damnedeu le monde fist	Méon 1823
5 [33]	6rc	Saint Paulin	De seint Paulin qui fu mis en la prison de sata*m*e	Dex q*ui* ses biens *n*os a doné	Le Coultre 1884
6 [34]	7va	Nièce	De l'ermite qui retorna sa niece de folie	Bien trueve q*ui en* bien se tie*nt*	
7 [35]	9rc	Ivresse	De l'ermite qui s'enyvra	Vielz pechiez fet novele honte	Méon 1823
8 [36]	10vc	Rachat	Del marcha*nt* qu*i* se re*n*di a chartrose q*ui* reai*n*t le pere *et* le filz *et* des.d'. au cove*nt*	M*u*lt est povres q*ui* ne voit	
9 [37]	12rb	Usurier	Du ch*re*tien qui dona sa fille au roi	Qui n'a qu'.i. oil sove*n*t le tert	
10 [38]	13va	Feuille de choux	De la nonain qui manga la flor del chol et si enraja	Mauveis est qui ne guerredone	Michi 1983
11 [41]	14rb	Image du diable	Du segrestain moine qui contrefist le diable	Desouz Bethleem en un prez	Méon 1823
12 [2]	15vc	Juitel	Del jutel qui fu mis el four de verre	Qui v*er*ges espargne si het son enfant	Wolter 1879

[a] Figures in brackets indicate the numbers of the tales according to their sequence in B.N. f. fr. 1546 (A), a conventional reference.
[b] Subject titles were assigned to the tales by Gaston Paris in a footnote to Schwan 1884, 240 n. 5.

Table 6 – Continued

Contents of the *Vie des Pères*

UCB 106 [A]	Begins (f.)	Subject	Rubric	Incipit	Edition
13 [3]	16vc	Sarrasine	De l'ermite qui renoia Deu por la sarrasine	De gr*a*nt franchise se demet	Keller 1840
14 [4]	18va	Renieur	Du borgois qui ne voust renoier Nostre Dame por avoir s'amie	De fol avoir a gr*a*nt tale*n*t	
15 [5]	20rb	Copeaux	Du prodom q*ui* geta les coispiax en le ble son voisin	Qui de loing garde de p*re*s ot	Weber (?) 1876
16 [6]	21vb	Thais	D'une damoisele q*ui* ot non Tays que	Ce n'est pasor q*ua*mque reluist	
17 [7]	23vb	Miserere	Du prodom qui disoit miserere tui Deus	Qui oreilles a *por* oir	Le Coultre 1884
18 [39]	25ra	Demi-ami	Del borgois de Rome q*ui* fist a son filz esprover ses amis	Tant as tant vas *et* je tant aim	
19 [29]	26rb	Gueule du diable	De l'ermite qui passa par la geule a l'enemi	D'e*n* [sic] dit q*ue* cil asëur boit	
20 [20]	27ra	Nöel	Del provoire q*ui* fist la vigille de Noel fornicacion	Tant grate chievre q*ue* mal gist	
21 [40]	28rc	Inceste	De la dame de Rome a q*ui* son filz gisoit que li maufez encusa vers l'empereour	Bien est gardez cil q*ue* Dex garde	Méon 1823
22 [12]	30rb	Meurtrier	De l'ermit q*ui* se despera	Pierre volage ne quert mousse	Méon 1823
23 [21]	31va	Vision d'enfer	De cele qui vit sa mere e*n* enfer *et* son pere en paradis	Formage mox ne pierre dure	
24 [11]	33rc	Impératrice	De l'emperice que li freres son seignor pria de aucitire	Fous est qui acroit sor ses piax	Wallensköld 1907
25 [42]	35vc	Merlot	Du vilain asnier a qui la voiz parla	Bien s'eshauce q*ui* s'umilie	Méon 1823

Continued on next page

Table 6 – Continued

Contents of the *Vie des Pères*

UCB 106 [A]	Begins (f.)	Subject	Rubric	Incipit	Edition
26 [13]	38ra	Sacristine	De la segrestaine qui lessa s'abeie et a Nostre Dame servir por luxure	Assez vaut mielz amis en voie	Méon 1823
27 [14]	40ra	Ave Maria	Du povre clerc qui toz jors disoit Ave Maria	Encore ne me puis je terre	
28 [15]	40vc	Queue	De sein Jeroime qui vit le diable sor la keue a la dame	En la cité de Bethleant	
29 [26]	41vc	Crucifix	Du juis qui feriret le crucefix de la lance et il seigna	Des bons ist le bien par nature	
30 [16]	42vc	Crapaud	De celi qui le boterax prist a la levre por son pere qu'il lessa avoir mesese	Dex de qui tote bonté ist	
31 [17]	44ra	Image de Pierre	Du borgois de Rome qui esposa l'ymage de perre	Salemons dist que tant est	Méon 1823
32 [8]	46rc	Jardinier	Du prodome qui se mahaigna parce que il se repenti de s'aumosne	Si come li fus souz l'escorche	Matile 1839
33 [9]	47rb	Haleine	Du roi qui voust fere ardoir le filz son seneschal	Vilains est qui fet a autrui	Méon 1823
34 [10]	50va	Fou	Du chivalier qui ocist le prestre dedens l'iglise seint Lourenz	Si come la terre brehaigne	Chaurand 1971
35 [18]	54rb	Baril	De celui qui ne pot emplir le barillet d'eve	Voir est q chascun cuer se preueve	Schultz-Gora 1919
36 [19]	55rc	Abbesse grosse	De l'abeesse [sic] qui fu enceinte qui Nostre Dame delivra	si come li soliax acuevre	Méon 1823
37 [22]	57rb	Malaquin	De l'ermite de la nigre montaigne qui converti le duc Malaquin	Autresi come la quintaine	Méon 1823
38 [23]	58vb	Vision de diables	De l'ermite qui converti les .ii. chastias dont il estoit en Egypte	Qui a .ii. seignors veut servir	

Table 6 — Continued

Contents of the *Vie des Pères*

UCB 106 [A]	Begins (f.)	Subject	Rubric	Incipit	Edition
39 [27]	60rb	Payens	Du sarrasin qui fu saus par la priere de l'ermite	L'escripture nos dist por voir	
40 [28]	61rb	Goliard	Du clerc gouliars qui voust rober l'abeie	Au tens que Salemon vivoit	Méon 1823
41 [30]	62va	Colombe	Des .iii. hermites dont li dui estoient viellart et li angre becoit lor viande et puis le perdirent et puis le recovrerent par lor bone foi	Cil qui Dex crient riens ne li faut	
42 [31]	63vc	Sénéschal	Du roi qui esposa la fille au chastlain	Qui sens et reson a ensemble	Méon 1823
43 [43]	66rb	Sel	De l'ermite qui sala son pain	Ausi com li arbres verdissent	Bornäs 1968
Epilogue	67rb		Del despit du monde	Cist contes vos enseigne bien	
44 [44]	67rc	Enfant jureur	De l'enfant que l'enemi enporta hors du giron son pere	L'escripture si vos enseigne	
45 [64]	69rb	Coq	De l'ermite que li diable conchia du coc et de la geline	Apres vos cont d'un seint hermite	Bornäs 1968
46 [65]	72vb	Mère	De Nostre Dame qui delivra l'enfant qui estoit pendus	Ia en arriers a Rome avint	
47 [66]	73vb	Patience	De l'ermite qui ne so vost curoucier por nule rien qu'on li fesoit	Iadis en hermitage estoit	
48 [67]	75ra	Infanticide	Du miracle comment Nostre Dame gari cele qui manga les .iii. yraignes	Il avint si som j'oi dire	
49 [68]	76vb	Piège au diable	De l'ermite qui voust prendre le diable au laz	D'un seint pere apres vos dirai	

Continued on next page

Table 6 — Continued

Contents of the *Vie des Pères*

UCB 106 [A]	Begins (f.)	Subject	Rubric	Incipit	Edition
50 [69]	78vb	Anges	De Nostre Dame qui vint au prael la ou la dame estoit	Jadis un chivalier estoit	Bornäs 1968
51 [71]	80vb	Image du diable	Iadis Nostre Dame qui retint le moine qui chaoit	Iadis estoit une abeie	
52 [72]	82ra	Ange & hermite	De l'ermite qui s'acompaigna al angle	Un seint pere en egÿpte avoit	Méon 1823
53 [73]	84rb	Pain	De l'enfant qui pessoit l'ÿmage Nostre Dame [rubric misplaced]	[Mal semmer fet sor pierre dure] Une cité fu bone et riche	
54 [74]	85ra	Sermon	De l'ermite qui se converti a son sarmon [rubric misplaced]	[Cil qui bien voit et le mal prent] En egypte .i. seint pierre avoit	
55 [45]	86rc	Image de N.D.	De l'enfant qui besa la mein Nostre Dame	Un miracle briement vos di	
56 [46]	87vb	Frères	Des .ii. freres qui durent aler a la bone cité	En essample vos voil retrere	
57 [47]	89rb	Crane	De la terre qui parla	Iadis en la terre d'egÿpte	
58 [48]	90ra	Renieur	De l'escuier qui ne voust renoier Nostre Dame	En France avint ce m'est avis	
59 [49]	90vc	Deux morts	[D]e l'ermite qui vit la bone ame et la mal departir du cors	Il ot en .i. desert d'egÿpte	
60 [50]	91vc	Confession	Del escuier qui ne pot morir jusqu'il fu confes	Or vos comenz le premier vers	

(2) ff. 92vb-101ra: [Gautier de Coinci, prologue to the *Miracles de Nostre Dame*; *Vie de Théophile*], "langue qui caractérise l'Ile-de-France" (Cazelles 1978, 2), 1218-36 (Koenig 1955, 1: xxv-xxx), octosyllabic couplets
    Title: De Theofle [*sic*] qui fist homage au diable
        por richesce et terrien honeour avoir [rubr.]
    Incipit: A la loenge et a la gloire
    Explicit: Et fera totes nos acordes.
    Edition: Koenig 1955, 1: 1-19, 50-176; see Ducrot-Granderye 1932, 10-15, for earlier editions
    See also Ducrot-Granderye 1932; Cazelles 1978; Plenzat 1926.
    Summary: Some 300 lines long, the general prologue is written in the first person. The speaker says he will translate and rhyme miracles he finds in Latin for the benefit of those who do not understand "the letter," that they might be inspired to serve the Virgin. Happy is the man who serves her; he who does not is hideously deceived. The devil trembles with fright whenever anyone half pronounces her name. The character of a persistent but ever disappointed enemy unfolds in the last third of the poem. The poet names himself in a prayer concluding the prologue.

    Having initially declined the bishopric fearing the corruption of high office, the worthy vidame Theophilus changes his mind and enlists the aid of a Jew to make a bargain with the devil. Because he had been devoted to her, the Virgin persuades her Son to restore Theophilus's good conscience. After forty days of tearful contrition, the Virgin appears in a vision to scold him but finally relents and eventually even recovers the written contract Theophilus had made with the devil. He gives up his spirit in the Virgin's chapel after making a public confession during mass and delivering a sermon on penitence, tearful prayer, abstinence, good works, and the Virgin's power against hell.

(3) ff. 101ra-105ra: Jehan de Blois (author's name in line 8), [*Le conte dou barril*], "souche normande . . . avec les dialectes de l'Orléanais, de la Champagne, de l'Ile-de-France et même de la Picardie" (Bates 1932, cxi), 1216-18 (ibid., xvii), octosyllabic couplets
    Title: Du baril qui fu rampli d'une larme [rubr.]
    Incipit: En bon essample raconter
    Explicit: Si qu'a sa mor puissons venir
        Amen amen. Amen.
    Edition: Bates 1932
    See also Lecoy 1955; Payen 1967.
    Summary: An evil and powerful Gascon chatelain, whose lands have been interdicted by the pope, accompanies his men to a hermitage where they wish

to confess. When he boasts of his sins and refuses to perform any of the usual programs of penance, the hermit asks if he would at least refill his water barrel. This task takes the chatelain on a quest of a year and one night. He returns, unsuccessful and disheveled, and miraculously fills the barrel with one tear of contrition. The hermit hears his confession and delivers a lengthy sermon, and the chatelain goes on to lead a reformed life, thus earning God's pardon.

(4) ff. 105ra-105vc: [*Les neuf joies Nostre Dame*], west or northwest France, 1250-70 (Mustanoja 1952, 35-36), regular stanzas of octosyllabic verses, *a b a b* changing every sixteen lines
   Incipit: Reine de pitie Marie
   Explicit: O les IX ordres mansion. Amen.
   Editions: Jubinal 1874; Mustanoja 1952; Faral and Bastin 1959
   See also Brayer 1970, 47-49.
   Summary: The first stanza addresses the Virgin in paradoxical terms and announces the poem's subject:

> Fille to*n* filz, mere ton pere,
> M*u*lt as de no*m*s en prophecie:
> Si n'a nul qui n'ait mistere.
> (f. 105rb6-8)

A proliferation of names and symbols follows, organized to give each stanza a kind of tension between concrete and abstract, organic and cosmic, human and divine, expansive and enclosed. Oblique references to the Fathers as well as to Scripture suggest an audience of clerics, but the poet's skill would be likely also to please listeners who were not familiar with the exegetical background of the poem. Wordplay and rich rhymes lend a musical quality to the language (one manuscript has musical notation), and a preponderance of light images adds to the visual impact of the poem's sensuality.

The names and symbols are too numerous to mention here without reproducing the entire text, and the poet claims he could continue his life long without exhausting them (st. 21, f. 105vb1-16). The Virgin's joys are described at the end of the poem.

(5) ff. 105vc-111ra: *La passion Ihesu Crist* [rubr.], no language study available, first third of the thirteenth century (Gröber 1902, 657), octosyllabic couplets
   Incipit: Oiez moi trestouz doucement
   Explicit: Amen, amen, fiat, fiat
       Ab hoste nos eripiat.

Edition: Foster 1916

See also Brayer 1970, 50.

Summary: The narrative proceeds with the gospel account of the Passion, beginning with the Council of the Jews and ending with the Resurrection. It includes legendary and apocryphal incidents such as John sleeping on his Master's breast at the Last Supper, witnessing a vision of heaven, while Judas steals the best morsel of fish from Jesus' plate; Judas waking while the Apostles sleep in Gethsemane; Judas damned not for treachery, but for his despair and suicide; the Jews' purchase of Calvary with Judas's thirty "deniers de traison"; a personal visit of the devil to Pilate's wife, complaining that Christ's death will undermine his own power and seeking her cooperation in keeping him alive; the Legend of the Cross identifying the wood as cypress; the forging of the three nails by the smith's evil wife, when his own hands are miraculously afflicted by leprosy; the interpretation of Christ's thirst as his desire to save men's souls; Christ's breaking the locks and the gates of hell; and the healing of the blind knight who pierced his side, followed by his contrition, prayer for mercy, and pardon (see Foster 1916, 60-65).

(6) ff. 111rb-116va: [Life of Saint Catherine of Alexandria], editor makes no comment on language or date, octosyllabic couplets

Title: Ci comence la vie s Katerine [rubr.]

Incipit: Nos trovomes en nos escris

Explicit: Ci faut la vie seinte Katerine.

Edition: Trenkle 1976

Summary: Catherine, a Christian and a king's daughter, scolds Maxentius, ruler of Alexandria, for commanding a pagan sacrifice of cattle and sheep. She converts Maxentius's master orator and his colleagues in the course of a formal debate, and they suffer martyrdom. The emperor wishes to make Catherine his lady and a goddess; when she refuses, she is imprisoned in a dark cell. Military business calls Maxentius away, and Catherine converts his wife and a company of knights in his absence. Upon his return, an evil counselor recommends a new form of torture: the wheel. Catherine prays for a miracle, and the wheel is destroyed by lightning. Catherine's converts suffer martyrdom before she herself is executed. Milk flows from her neck when her head is struck off, and a miraculous healing oil flows from her tomb at Mount Sinai.

(7) ff. 117ra-191vb: [L'*estoire del Saint Graal*], literary Francien, 1230-35 (Grimm 1984, 117), prose

    Incipit: Cil qui la hautesce et la seignourie de si haute estoire com est cele du Graal mist en escrit par le comandement du haut mestre, mande premierement saluz a tous ceus et a toz celes qui ont lor creance en la glorieuse Trinite. . .

    Explicit: Mais or se test li contes de totes les lignies qui de Celidoine issirent, et s'en torne a une branche que l'en apele l'estoire de Merlin, qu'il covient a fine force aioster a l'estoire du seint Graal, por ce que branche en est e i apartient. Si comence Merlin Robers de Borron en tel maniere. Mult fu iriez li enemis.

    Edition: Sommer 1908-9

    See also Frappier 1968b, 1978a, 1978b; Woledge 1954, 1975; Grimm 1984, 116-19.

    Summary: Joseph of Arimathea, a liege man of Pilate, retrieves the vessel used by Christ at the Last Supper and, following the victory of Vespasian and his own baptism, departs with his family to preach Christianity in foreign lands. En route, Joseph's company joins the cause of Evalac against his former liege lord, Tholomer. After Christ brings about the victory of Evalac's forces, he and his brother-in-law, Seraphe, are baptized as Mordrain and Nacien, respectively. They eventually arrive in Britain to participate in converting the pagans there, after experiencing a series of marvelous adventures involving King Solomon's ship. Nacien learns from a vision about the nine generations of his descendants ending with one who will eventually return to the East (Galahad). Joseph and his son, meanwhile, have been leading the missionary effort and performing many miracles. Among them is the transformation of one fish into a meal for an entire company; all the keepers of the Grail are henceforth known as "rich fishers." A newly converted pagan king, cured of leprosy by the bishop Alain, builds the Grail castle, "Corbenic." The text ends with genealogies tracing the descent of Galahad from the fisher kings through Pelles and of Lancelot from Nacien through Celidoine, the older Lancelot, and Ban.

(8) v. 2, entire: [*Merlin en prose* and vulgate continuation], 1227-35+ (Grimm 1984, 165-68), prose

    Incipit: Mult fu dolenz li enemis quant Nostre Sires ot este en enfer, et il en ot gete Adan et Eve et des autres tant come li plot. Et quant li enemi virent cen [*sic*], si en orent mult grant peor . . .

    Explicit: Quar il estoit bons chevaliers et loiax et ot .i. seneschal qu'il avoit norri d'enfance, a qui il avoit toute sa terre comandee apres la mort Pharien, et ce fu icelui qui le trai et par qui il perdi le chastel de Trebe, einsi come li contes le vos devisera ca avant.

En la marche de Gaule *et* de la petite Bretaigne[26]
Editions: Micha 1979; Cerquiglini 1981; Paris and Ulrich 1886; Sommer 1908-9
See also the works cited above in item 7.

Summary: Merlin is begotten by a devil on a virtuous young woman, whom God rewards by allowing the child to be born with the devil's powers, but without evil. The author establishes the text's authority by introducing Blaise, a learned cleric to whom the infant Merlin relates the story of Joseph and the Grail, an account of the devil's plan resulting in his own birth, and a prediction that Blaise will retire to Great Britain and periodically receive reports from Merlin. The book produced by these reports will eventually be joined to the book about Joseph.[27] Merlin's visits to Blaise are used subsequently throughout the text as a narrative device to recapitulate the loosely connected sequences of episodes (see Micha 1953, 208-9).

When King Constant of England dies, the seneschal Vortigern successfully plots to usurp the throne from his eldest son. The two younger sons, Uther and Pendragon, win it back. Pendragon dies in battle against the Saxons, and his brother adopts the name Uther Pendragon. The Round Table comes into being, and Arthur, born to Uther Pendragon and the duchess of Tintagel, Ygraine, is raised incognito through Merlin's devices.

After Arthur's recognition and coronation, he is defied by his vassals until the alien threat of the Saxons eventually forces them to reconcile with him. Interlaced with the battle accounts are stories of the incestuous conception of Mordred, the meetings of Merlin with Viviane and Morgan, the marriage of Arthur and Guinevere, the conflict between the knights of the Round Table and the "queen's knights," and Arthur's conquest of the Roman emperor, to mention just a few. Merlin's visits to Blaise and his periodic displays of magical prowess punctuate the narrative. It closes with his imprisonment by Viviane in the forest of Brocéliande.[28]

---

[26] Just as at the end of volume 1 the opening line of Merlin appears, so volume 2 ends with a catchword for the beginning of *Lancelot*, the next branch in the cycle. See pp. 98-99.

[27] This passage reveals the author's original plan for a *pair* of texts, rather than a trilogy, based on the model of the Old and New Testaments of the Bible. See Bogdanow 1978, 534-35.

[28] Legrand d'Aussy describes the popular tradition that Merlin's voice might still be heard by people passing near the spot in the forest where he was buried ([1779] 1829, 1: 152). The forty-second tale of the *Vie des Pères* ("Merlot") draws on this tradition.

5

Saint Francis and the Mother of God

An Ascetic Ideal for the Laity

TEXTS

La Vie Saint Francois [sic]
La Vie des Pères
Thirteen miracles of the Virgin
Paraphrase of Psalm 44, *Eructavit*
Les quinze signes du jugement
Descent of Saint Paul
Life of Saint Juliana
Dit de l'unicorne et du serpent
Unidentified fragment

    B.N. f. fr. 2094 begins with a version of the life of Saint Francis (ff. 1ra-50vb) derived from Thomas of Celano's *Vita prima* (1228). Two verse versions (*A* and *B*), represented by three manuscripts, are based on that life (Thomas [1942], 22-65). The version in B.N. f. fr. 2094 (*B*) seems to be a revision of the one in B.N. f. fr. 19531 (*A*) and probably dates to between 1257 and 1266, when Saint Bonaventure's *Legenda major* (1263) became the official biography (ibid., 25-53). Old French texts derived from Saint Bonaventure's *Legenda major* also survive: the Anglo-Norman verse version edited by Marcel Thomas, an Anglo-Norman fragment, a prosification of a lost verse legend, and several prose versions (ibid., 66-138).

    As background for his edition of the version preserved in B.N. f. fr. 13505, Thomas analyzed the various medieval French versions of the legend based on the Latin works of Thomas of Celano and Saint Bonaventure and on the anonymous compilation *Actus beati Francisci* (ibid., 6-21). He concludes that the variations among versions reflect the internal politics of the order (ibid., 138-41).

    Unique to version *B* is a description of the translation of Francis's relics to the Basilica of Assisi. Thomas cites the omission of this event from *A* as evidence that it was composed with a bias toward the Spiritual ("zelanti") party of the order, which favored strict adherence to the ascetic rule. The passage lists extravagant gifts made by

Pope Gregory IX to the new church on this occasion, which clashed with the Spirituals' ideal of poverty. The inclusion of the translation, together with certain other details, points to the anti-Spiritual inclination of the text, and to a *terminus a quo* of 1257, the year the Spiritualist minister general John of Parma died (ibid., 1942, 34-45). The translation passage corresponds with no extant Latin text and may be the only surviving witness of the corresponding sections, now lost, of Thomas of Celano's *Vita secunda* (ibid., 46-53).

Following the life of Saint Francis in B.N. f. fr. 2094 is a collection of tales from the *Vie des Pères* (ff. 51ra-150vb). Although it has eighteen tales in common with the text of the *Vie des Pères* occurring in UCB 106, the version of the collection in B.N. f. fr. 2094 reflects a distinctly different emphasis. The first forty-two tales, dominated, as we have seen, by the theme of the monstrous sin, are absent. Morawski has noted that the second and third series of *Vies*, of which this manuscript contains all but four tales (51, 52, 62, and 63 of manuscript *A*), have a greater proportion of Marian miracles than has the first *Vie* (see above, pp. 86-87).

The second *Vie* (tales 43-50 and 64-74) contains eight Marian miracles. The themes of the nineteen tales include conversion to Christianity, visions of the afterlife, worthiness of the lay estate, rewards for the devout, protection of the weak and innocent, and, in two stories, monstrous sin ("Coq," 3 [64], f. 57vb, and "Infanticide," 6 [67], f. 75ra). Children are featured prominently in four tales, and hermits in nine.

If we keep in mind the comparison with the *Vie des Pères* copied in UCB 106,[1] some particular characteristics of this version come to light. While a few of these tales deal with conversion and repentance ("Sac," "Prêtre pécheur," "Ame en gage"), most of them focus on Mary's human compassion ("Brandons," "Ave Maria," "Ame en gage," "Nom de Marie"), on her protection of the innocent ("Enfant pieux," "Fenêtre," "Ame en gage," "Enfant sauvé"), or on various ways of honoring her ("Enfant pieux," "Prêtre pécheur," "Ave Maria," "Femme aveugle," "Enfant sauvé"). The narratives pass over the details of the sinners' offences. The "prêtre pécheur," for example, falls prey to gluttony and lechery, but we do not learn how or with whom; the "femme aveugle" has been punished for being, simply, "folete." Mary's maternal concern for her human friends receives more attention than her power to mediate between the human and divine realms. The practices of Marian worship (e.g., the Saturday service, reciting *Ave Maria*, pilgrimage to Rocamadour) are emphasized more in these tales than the examination of a sinner's conscience, so essential to many stories of the first *Vie*.[2]

---

[1] Summaries of tales *not* shared with UCB 106 are included in the section listing the manuscript's contents, pp. 153-56.

[2] Speaking of "Sacristine," Payen refers to the "goût de la *Vie des Pères* pour la fine analyse de la mauvaise conscience et du scrupule" (1967, 531). He invokes Guiette and Petit de Julleville in maintaining that the stories' sinners "ont le plus étonné, disons le mot, scandalisé la piété plus éclairée d'une autre

At the close of the thirteen miracles following the tales of the *Vie des Pères* in B.N. f. fr. 2094, these lines appear, raising some important questions:

>[Q]uanqu'en escrit et quenqu'en taille
>D'ui a demain revient a falle,
>Que toutes choses vont a fin;
>Par ce de mon livre fais fin.
>XXX. miracles sont escrites
>En ces livre, que granz que petites,
>Et .X. autres contes ancore.
>Atant la fin vos en fais ore.
>Se Deu plait, uns autres vendra
>Qui l'autre livre antreprendra
>A faire des fez Nostre Dame.
>Onques tant riens ne sit a m'arme
>Com li servir se je seüse
>Et lou sans et memoire eüse
>De biau parler et de biau dire.
>Assez panse(r) avoir martire,
>Mas qui ne set ovrer ne puet;
>Alumer mie n'i estuet:
>Qui est sor l'evre i voit tres bien
>Se li ovrers fait mal ou bien.
>Se de ceste ovre sui blasm[ez],
>Je ne m'an sant mie anc[usez],
>Q u'au mioz que j'onques poi [...]
>Selonc l'antante que [...]
>(ll. 1-24 "Epilogue" Kunstmann, ff. 170vb24-171ra)

First, the speaker mentions a total of forty tales, when the *Vie des Pères* added to the miracles totals forty-one. How should we account for the imprecision of numbers? He makes a distinction between thirty "en ces livre" and "ten other tales besides." Is it possible he makes a generic distinction between miracles and other pious tales, or is he merely separating a collection of thirty copied from another manuscript from ten of his own invention? Is the speaker a scribe or an author or both?

Pierre Kunstmann, after Morawski, supposes that "trente miracles" refers to the twenty-eight tales of the *Vie des Pères* plus the first two of the subsequent group, which the author may have found in his model for the *Vie des Pères*. The eleven "other tales"

époque" (Guiette 1927, 416, citing Petit de Julleville 1896, 1:43). The tales Payen treats are predominantly taken from the first *Vie*.

(assuming "X" is a scribal error) are unique to this manuscript, except for a few fourteenth-century fragments (in MS Bibliothèque de Carpentras 106; see Kunstmann 1981, 1, and Morawski 1935, 179). Although in practice it was sometimes observed, I think it highly unlikely that the generic distinction between miracles and other pious tales would be remarked discursively in this period. By "autres contes" the speaker probably means more miracles, as he goes on to speak "des fez Nostre Dame" and pursues no argument depending on a divergence of themes. If Kunstmann and Morawski are correct, then, we might suppose the author of the eleven added tales had copied the first thirty from a single model and was therefore a scribe as well as an author. While nothing in the passage necessitates this interpretation, there is no reason why a scribe could not have appended his own composition to something he had copied.

The scribe's language is Burgundian (Kunstmann 1981, 26), and the dialectal traits of the rhymes, while vague, suggest eastern France (ibid., 28). It would be worthwhile to make a study of scribal errors to determine whether or not the scribe of this manuscript may have composed the eleven unique tales, but such an analysis lies beyond the scope of this study. He might have collected them from disparate sources, in which case detailed linguistic and stylistic comparisons would reveal differences among them. I will have occasion to return to the question of the copyists' roles in compiling the manuscript when I discuss codicological details and textual combinations (below, pp. 132-37).

However the scribe obtained them, the thirteen tales have diverse origins. Although eleven of the thirteen texts recorded here are unique, most belong to common taletypes with versions and analogues in Latin and French verse and prose. Kunstmann makes no allusions to their relative dates (ibid., 2-21). Several are found in the well-known collections of Adgar, B.N. f. fr. 818, Gautier de Coinci, Jean le Conte, Jean Miélot, and B.N. f. fr. 1881 (tales 2, 4, 10, 12, 13). Some of these exist in many Latin redactions as well (2, 10, 12, 13). One belongs to a widely distributed cycle but has few close analogues (4, "Fiancé de la vièrge"; see p. 17 above). Tales not found in the usual French collections exist in other contexts: an excerpt from the life of Saint Honorat (1), a true story (3), various Latin chronicles (5), a Latin collection of exempla (6), and Latin miracle collections *not* commonly vernacularized (7, 8, 9, 11).

Kunstmann dates the collection (or that portion of it beginning with the third tale) at about 1300, suggesting the death of Nicolas de Tournai (i.e., Nicholas of Gorran) in 1295 as a *terminus a quo*, and corroborating his estimate by the manuscript's presumed date of the late thirteenth or early fourteenth century (ibid., 2, 6-7; Morawski 1935, 183-84). The latest of the three hands, however, has characteristics of the fourth quarter of the thirteenth century, and the other two appear older (see p. 138 below). Since the biographers of Nicholas of Gorran give no support for their dating of his death (see Kunstmann 1981, 6), I would extend the approximation backward to include the last decade or two of the thirteenth century.

The most remarkable thematic trait of this group of Marian tales is the *absence* of the monstrous sin motif, which in other collections (such as UCB 106) provides excellent opportunities for the Virgin to demonstrate her powers. Three of the thirteen tales are analogous to others that emphasize the theme; they are adapted to understate the gravity of the sin.

Although its editor, T. Atkinson Jenkins, characterizes the work following the miracles in B.N. f. fr. 2094 (ff. 172ra-194vb) as a "metrical paraphrase" of *Eructavit* — Psalm 44 (1909), it would be much more accurate to describe it as the paraphrase of a compilation of glosses on the psalm. In addition to compiling, translating, and versifying the commentaries, the anonymous poet has provided a narrative frame derived from the Scripture. His principal Latin sources were probably Augustine's *Enarrationes in Psalmos*, Gregory the Great, the *Explanatio* of Haymon of Halberstadt, and Jerome's *Epistola ad Principiam* (ibid., xxv-xxvii). The poem belongs to a group of works that are based on exegetical tradition, as distinguished from biblical paraphrases or adaptations relying heavily on biblical or apocryphal narratives as sources (see Jauss 1970, 203-19). Dedicated to Marie, "ma dame de Champagne" (l. 3 Jenkins, f. 172ra5; "la gentil suer le roi de France," l. 2079, f. 194ra1), the poem can be dated to between 1181 and 1187 (Jenkins 1909, vii-x).[3] Its attribution remains uncertain.[4]

Fourteen copies survive, mostly from the thirteenth century. Two manuscripts preserve only excerpts, and several contain fragments. Jenkins proposes a stemma but apologizes for the lack of "mathematical precision" in his description of the filiation. B.N. f. fr. 2094 (*A*) appears relatively high in the stemma and is one of two written in territories bordering Champagne, where Jenkins believes the work was composed. None of the copies was made in Champagne, but *A* and *E* (London, British Museum Addit. 15606) have Burgundian traits (ibid., xxxi-xxxiv).

At least twenty-four manuscripts preserve the Old French *Quinze signes du jugement* (ff. 194vb-199rb), which follows the *Eructavit* paraphrase in this manuscript. The tradition of the fifteen signs before doomsday was widely and extensively developed in

---

[3] As regards the *terminus post quem*, Louis VII, Marie's father, died in 1180, making her brother the king (Philippe-Auguste). She lost her husband in 1181, which may have caused her to withdraw from worldly society, according to Jenkins. If the poem had been composed after 1187, it surely would have alluded to the capture of Jerusalem in that year.

[4] John Benton has demonstrated the unlikelihood of Jenkins's hypothesis that Adam de Perseigne, an important monastic author of the period, was Marie's chaplain (and therefore the poet), elsewhere identified as a canon (Benton 1961, 182-83).

Latin as well as in German, Irish, Welsh, English, Italian, and Occitan (Kraemer 1966, 3-4, 34-36). Probably composed between 1180 and 1225, this is the oldest surviving Old French version (ibid., 6-7). Its principal sources seem to be the apocryphal *Apocalypse of Thomas* dating to the fifth century (ibid., 14), the *Apocalypse of Saint John*, the Middle English debate between the body and the soul, Gregory the Great's *Homilia de tempore* as revised by Haymo, the Antichrist legend, the apocryphal *Assumptio Moyseos*, the Bible, and biblical commentaries. No direct source can be confirmed for the combination of signs, and the poet probably drew on oral tradition and his own imagination (ibid., 31-34).

The work is unusual for the complex textual tradition of its prologue. Thirteen of the twenty-two manuscripts lack the first forty lines. The first line ("Oez trestuit communement") also serves as the incipit of a version of the *Passion*,[5] and in two manuscripts (B.N. f. fr. 20040 and 24301) the same *Passion* is followed by the *Quinze signes du jugement* beginning with line 41.

The ending of the poem, like those of many other Old French texts, also yields a great many variants. One group of manuscripts concludes with a narrative of the Last Judgment and a prayer, while others end with a prayer alone. The grouping of copies by endings does not coincide with that based on the presence or absence of a prologue. All the copies have unique errors, variants, and lacunae, and neither of the two most recent editors has proposed a stemma (Kraemer 1966, 56; Mantou 1966, 125-26).

The manuscript tradition suggests that the work was performed in conjunction with other texts. It serves as the conclusion to the *Jeu d'Adam* preserved in Tours, Bibliothèque Municipale 927.[6] The *Bible des sept estats du monde* (thirteenth century, by Geufroi de Paris) includes this work as a sequel to the "miracles" of the Antichrist. Another version of the *Quinze signes* follows the *Passion* and the coming of the Antichrist (thirteenth century, by Berengier) in B.N. f. fr 1444. The debate of body and soul is also frequently associated with this theme — as, for example, in *Li ver del Juïse*, of the twelfth century (Kraemer 1966, 8-10).

The work's genre designation cannot be determined by analogy to any modern text type. Its combination with popular tales and other short texts intended for oral performance in many of the manuscripts (e.g., B.N. f. fr. 837 and 19152, Bern Burgerbibliothek 354, well-known *fabliau* collections) suggests a particular audience and setting. At the same time the work reflects a fascination with salvation history, particularly when grouped with such themes as the Passion, the coming of the Antichrist, the debate between body and soul, and the Last Judgment. Taking into account both the

---

[5] This work occurs in UCB 106. See above, p. 93.

[6] Several editions of the *Quinze signes du jugement* have been published as part of the *Jeu d'Adam* (Luzarche 1854, Palustre 1877, Grass 1891, Aebischer 1963).

performance aspect and the theme, it is convenient to characterize this type of work as "popular eschatology."

After the apocalyptic vision of the *Quinze signes du jugement*, B.N. f. fr. 2094 contains a narrated visit to hell itself (ff. 199rb-204rb). Ultimately derived from the text of 2 Corinthians 12: 2-4, in which the apostle claims to *know* someone who has experienced a vision of the "third heaven," the tradition of Saint Paul's descent to hell with the archangel Michael as his cicerone goes back to a Greek work of the third century. Seven of at least ten Latin translations survive, dating from the eighth century onward. A version particularly well suited to homiletic functions, known as the "fourth redaction,"[7] was most widely distributed and vernacularized. Prose versions survive in French, English, Danish, Italian, and Occitan; verse accounts exist in French and in English. Seven Old French poetic versions of Saint Paul's descent to hell have come down to us in a total of eighteen manuscripts (Owen 1958; Jauss 1970, 240-42).

The text of B.N. f. fr. 2094 is unique, and particularly important both for its long prologue criticizing poets' fictions as lies and for its departures from the surviving Latin versions. Redactions II, IIIa, IIIb, and IV have been suggested as sources, but no single one accounts for all the poem's peculiarities (Owen 1958, 42-44). Since the theme was certainly a popular sermon topic, it is not unlikely that the vernacular poet developed his text from one he had heard preached: the written sources he mentions might well have been those used by the preacher.

Saint Paul's descent is the oldest description of hell in the tradition that includes Brendan's voyage, Patrick's purgatory, Tundalus's vision, and numerous episodes of saints' biographies.[8] By virtue of its concern with the life to come, the theme relates to those of the Last Judgment, the Antichrist, and the fifteen signs before doomsday.

The version of the life of Saint Juliana dating to the early thirteenth century, which appears as the next text in B.N. f. fr. 2094 (ff. 204va-217vb), survives in at least seven manuscripts. One other version exists, composed a century later and represented by one manuscript (Meyer 1906a, 360). References to "escriture" and a "passioners" where the story is found suggest that the work was translated from a written source. The prologue goes on to support such a conjecture:

> Une chose vos vel descrivre:
> Assez l'avez tuit oï dire;
> Mais ne la pouistes entandre,
> Si vos en vel auques apanre.
> Li latins vos fu mont pesanz,
> Si vos voudrai dire in romanç.

---

[7] The classification system was established by H. Brandes (1885). See Owen 1958, 33.

[8] Saint Basil's vision in the life of Saint Jehan Paulus is a noteworthy example. See pp. 15-16 above.

> Vos qui latin apris n'avez,
> Lou plain romans or entandez.
> Qui l'entendra parfeitemant
> S'ame en avra bon sauvemant.
> D'une virge vos vel conter
> qu'an l'escriture oï numer.
> (f. 204vb9-20)

The last line of this passage invites us to revise the hypothesis of a direct translation from the Latin source to include an intermediary, perhaps a cleric who orally translated the story for the poet's benefit. The beginning of the prologue implies a listening audience:

> Or escoutez bon crestien:
> Qui m'antandra si fera bien.
> Et qui voudra a Dieu panser,
> De Dieu li iert a escouter.
> (f. 204va)

The text is a virgin martyr's legend similar to those of Margaret and Catherine of Alexandria (see pp. 19, 93-94) and like several other texts in this collection, it evokes a situation of oral performance.

The *Dit de l'unicorne et du serpent* (ff. 218ra-220vb) appears also in B.N. f. fr. 2162 and is discussed above (p. 18). The text in B.N. f. fr. 2094 ends thirty-nine lines short of the that printed by Jubinal (1842, 2: 113-23).

The last folio (f. 221) has twenty-six octosyllabic lines of another text. In this as yet unidentified fragment, the speaker familiarly scolds someone for neglecting his soul in favor of the body:

> Tu te farsiz, tu te saoules,
> [Tu] laiz t'ame morir de fein.
> (f. 221ra11-12)

The passage has a curiously inconsistent rhyme scheme and ends abruptly near the top of column b, as though the scribe was interrupted before he could finish.[9]

---

[9] Jean Sonet, editor of the Old French *Barlaam et Josaphat* from which the unicorn parable is excerpted, suggests this text may be an amplification by the copyist of the parable's moral (1949, 35-36).

CODICOLOGICAL ARTICULATIONS

The presence of this fragment is one of many challenges to be met in the process of globally interpreting B.N. f. fr. 2094.[10] Unlike the other codices under consideration, it has a heterogeneous appearance. Three distinct hands copy three separate sections of the manuscript, and the changes of hand correspond with breaks in the organization of the volume as well as with the introduction of two new series of texts, at folios 51 and 172. The ornamental and decorated initials reflect at least five different styles, all but one of which appear to be the work of amateurs. While as many as eight persons may have participated in the writing and decorating, then, the scribes possibly executed some of the painting themselves.[11]

Despite the variations in script and decoration, several factors point to the manuscript's codicological coherence. However, in contrast to UCB 106, the product of a professional scribe working for a single client, B.N. f. fr. 2094 appears to be the project of several individuals working toward a common objective.

First, the three hands, though easily distinguishable in appearance, have similar traits for individual letters, all characteristic of the second half of the thirteenth century (see below, p. 138).

Secondly, the scribes also share certain dialectal traits. I have noticed, for example, that all three render *multum > mont* (without confusion, as occurs in some squared gothic hands, between *u* and *n*).[12] All the scribes have been described as Burgundian by scholars who have treated texts in this manuscript (Thomas [1942], the life of St. Francis; Kunstmann 1981, the thirteen interpolated miracles; and Jenkins 1909, *Eructavit*). The editors of the *Quinze signes du jugement* suggest the scribe's language is Lorrain (Mantou) or simply "eastern" (Kraemer) (see the list of contents below, pp. 150-60).

Finally, the parchment is of the same coarse quality throughout, and the second and third sections, except for the eighth gathering, are written on parchment prepared with the same pattern of prickings, ruled for twenty-four lines with the same justification. Except for the beginning, the end, and the breaks between sections, the volume consists

---

[10] See table 7 for an overview of the volume's organization.

[11] This is likely in the third section (ff. 172-221), where all but the first are simple colored initials without decoration, and the few Latin verses added in red are copied in the same hand as that of the French text. The decoration of this section is uncompleted, with several blanks left for titles and verses from the psalm: only the twenty-fourth gathering has rubrics supplied. This hypothesis concerning the decoration is consistent with the sudden ending of the last text. The scribe perhaps painted initials as he went along, and planned to add the rubricated verses when he finished.

[12] *Progressive* nasalization is a characteristic of the eastern region (e.g. *ami > amĩ*). See Pope 1952, 167, 177.

of full quaternions. The folios at the breaks bear no indications that the sections ever circulated separately.

The codicological evidence is strong for the unity of the second and third sections: the organization of the page and the filigreed initials on 51a and 172a point to a common effort. The material connection between these two sections and the first seems more tenuous, however. I will defer speculation concerning the scenario that produced this codex as it has come down to us to the conclusion of my analysis of textual combinations.

ANALYSIS AND INTERPRETATION

The first section consists of a single text, probably based on a single Latin author (Thomas of Celano: see pp. 124-25 above). The second section contains texts all of which the scribe considers "miracles" ("Trente miracles sont escrites" f. 171; see pp. 125-28 above) and which reflect a certain thematic consistency. I have discussed the relative lack of emphasis on the monstrous sin motif in both the version of the *Vie des Pères* copied in this manuscript and in the thirteen added tales. This is even more striking in view of Hubertus Ahsmann's opinion that miracles in which Mary rescues a criminal are more common, in general, than those narrating her protection of the simple or innocent and those describing the various forms of Marian devotion (1930, 86).

Certainly the compiler of B.N. f. fr. 2162 aimed, by underplaying Marian piety, to discourage a too great dependence on Mary as a magical helper (see pp. 28-29 above). B.N. f. fr. 2094, in contrast, advocates an affective Marian piety not based on the hope of her aid in avoiding due punishment, but rather on her role in the humanization of God. In curing sickness, caring for children, and rewarding her devotees, she provides worldly solutions to worldly problems. The worship of Mary in these tales celebrates Christ's human nature, as well as her own compassion for the human condition. The emphasis on Christ's humanity corresponds with a new belief in the possibility of an ascetic ideal for laypeople.

Like the second section, the third is itself a collection. No contemporary or modern generic concept accounts for the selection of texts, but an analysis of the texts in sequence will provide a useful approach to interpreting the section as a whole.

The *Eructavit* and the *Quinze signes du jugement* (texts 4 and 5 of the manuscript) together provide a comprehensive eschatological vision. The poet's interpretation of the Old Testament text looks to the future New Law, with foreshadowings of the life to come represented both (synchronically) by David's view of heaven and (diachronically) by references to Judgment Day. The *Quinze signes du jugement*, which might be considered a version or a development of the New Testament Apocalypse, focuses on the Day of

Judgment itself and concludes with the final division between the blessed and the damned, with a brief description of hell.

The sixth text of B.N. f. fr. 2094, Saint Paul's descent into hell, expands on the ending of the previous text, giving details of various punishments inflicted for certain offences. The relatively commonplace virgin martyr narrative that follows it (text 7, the passion of Saint Juliana) describes the Last Judgment in its prologue and echoes the descriptions of hell in previous texts, this time placing it in the mouth of Satan. At Juliana's insistence, the devil provides instruction on how to avoid damnation. The manuscript ends with a parable in which death plays the principal role, a warning that the honey sweetness of earthly delights offers little compensation for the prospect of spending eternity in hell. The fragment on the last folio complains about the consequences to the soul of the body's indulgence in the worldly pleasure represented in the parable as droplets of honey.

In a broad sense, the texts in the third section represent a kind of popular authority on Christian eschatological doctrine. Each has a distinctly biblical motivation: the apocalyptic *Quinze signes du jugement* complements David's prophecy; the apostle Paul witnesses hell's torments; Juliana's martyrdom, as a passion narrative, commemorates Christ's Passion; and the unicorn parable also belongs to a characteristically biblical genre. While none of the texts offers a translation or even an adaptation of Scripture or of canonical authority, each is sustained, as though by an umbilical cord, by biblical tradition.[13]

Each of the three sections, then, has its own focus: the first combines significant events in the life (and afterlife) of an individual; the second combines several *vies* (its kernel being the *Vie des Pères*) and significant events in the lives of numerous individuals; and the third addresses various topics of salvation history in texts loosely derived from the Scriptures. Sections 2 and 3 have been shown to have codicological connections, so that a strong thematic link of either one with the first section would confirm the manuscript's essential wholeness. It will then remain to be seen who the participants in its confection might have been, and to what end they undertook their project.

In addition to the material consistency between sections 2 and 3, the epilogue of the thirteen interpolated tales ending the second section, which I have cited above (p. 126) contains a curious reference to "*the* other book":

> Se Deu plait, uns aut*res* vendra
> Q*ui* l'aut*re* livre antrep*re*ndra
> A faire des fez N*os*t*re* Dame.
> (f. 171a)

---

[13] I owe this metaphor to Alfred Adler, who makes the same analogy for Old French epic and the historical reality behind it (1975, 21).

The use of the definite article is significant: to what "other book" does the speaker refer if not the third section of the manuscript? Although he knows neither who will undertake the last part nor what it will include, the passage implies a project already planned, perhaps with several gatherings of parchment set aside.[14]

How, then, do the texts of the second and third sections connect with the life of Saint Francis? Their themes invite explanation in terms of Franciscan culture. For example, the particular character of Marian piety in the tales of the second section is consistent with Franciscan Marianism, in which the Virgin is honored more as Christ's means of entering the world than as a sinner's vehicle to paradise. Celano wrote of Francis that "toward the Mother of Jesus he was filled with an inexpressible love, because it was she who made the Lord of Majesty our brother" (Habig 1979, 521).

The biographer also mentions Francis's instructions to honor all priests, while he acknowledges their human failings. "Confession" (19 [50], f. 125ra), "Femme aveugle" (26 [59], f. 142va), and "Nom de Marie" (27 [60], f. 145va) witness the importance of an official confession, even for those loved by the Virgin; "Prêtre pécheur" (22 [55], f. 131va) narrates the spiritual rehabilitation of a debauched clergyman.

The author of the thirteen interpolated tales (text 3) had in mind the generic concept of the "miracle" when he composed his epilogue (see p. 126 above), and the inventory of miracles that concludes the first section may well have prompted the scribe to select a collection of miracle narratives as an appropriate sequel. The thirteen added tales include several examples of miraculous healing, the dominant motif in the catalogue of Saint Francis's wonderworks.

Francis's practical asceticism is mirrored by that of the hermits depicted in the *Vie des Pères*. The first tale of the second section ("Sel," 1 [43], f. 51ra) provides a particularly strong link to the life of Saint Francis by depicting a hermit immediately recognizable as a retrospective protofriar. Its prologue and epilogue, furthermore, emphasize the themes of penance and poverty, the principal Franciscan disciplines (see Fleming 1982, 38-40, n. 15). The epilogue contains an echo of Bonaventure's *Legenda major*, in which Francis addresses his body as "Brother Ass" while scourging himself to ward off temptation (Habig 1979, 665). A man who values his body more than his soul, says the speaker, displeases God:

> A celui lo vuil *com*parer
> Q*ue* veut deseur son col porter
> Son asne, q*ui* doit chevauchier.
> (f. 53rb2-4)

---

[14] This would be consistent with an identification of the scribe with the author/compiler of the thirteen interpolated tales, as I have suggested above, pp. 126-27. If the scribe of section 2 was *not* the author/compiler of the thirteen interpolated tales, then the person who *did* compose the epilogue must also have been involved in a collective compilation project.

The hermit in this story sins by softening his hard, black bread with water, seasoning it with salt, and then concealing his extravagant meal at the approach of a neighboring hermit; the biography of Francis in B.N. f. fr. 2094 describes how he repented of eating some chicken once when he was ill, and how he was in the habit of mixing ashes or cold water with his food to render it less appetizing. The anecdotes are analogous in the austerity of their asceticism, in the zeal of the characters' repentance, and in the theatrical effects of the hermit's hastily throwing his bowl under a basket and Francis's being dragged through the streets as a "gloton." The severity of the hermit's remorse seems out of proportion to the mildness of his offence, except in the context of the saint's ascetic fervor.

While eremitic themes connect the life of Saint Francis with the second series of the *Vie des Pères*, the affinity between the first and third sections hinges on the popular characterization of Saint Francis as "God's *jongleur*." His literary role includes both the composition and the performance aspects. He wrote a number of *laude* or praises, and an "Office of the Passion" composed mainly of verses from the Psalms (see Habig 1979, 123-55). The *Canticle of Brother Sun* was written in the Umbrian dialect, "in the manner of the prophet David" (Celano, cited in Fleming 1977, 180). As a preacher, he performed with spontaneity and vigorous movement, "making a tongue of his body," and "moved his feet as though he were dancing, not indeed lustfully, but as one burning with the fire of divine love" (Habig 1979, 290; see Fleming 1977, 119).

The first text of the third section purports to be the translation of a psalm, which John V. Fleming regards, in the form of *laude*, as a characteristically Franciscan genre (1977, 180-85).[15] It has a *jongleur* as its protagonist: the prophet David himself. The poet repeatedly evokes the narrative frame for his interpretation of the psalm in order to emphasize the *jongleur*'s role.

The other texts in the third section also reflect the oral performance situation in their prologues' references to hearing and listening. The speaker in Saint Paul's descent to hell calls attention to himself as a reformed "trouveor":

> Vos di ge, saignor, tout debout
> Que ge vel laissier la folie
> Et amander, se puis, ma vie.
> Ne vel pas de fable paller [*sic*]
> Ne mon tans en folie user.
> (f. 199vb14-18)

---

[15] Chaucer seems to have regarded this particular psalm, at least in jest, as a favorite of friars. Describing their habits, his Summoner remarks: "Hir preyere is of ful greet reverence,/ Whan they for soules seye the psalm of Davit;/ Lo, 'buf!' they seye, '*cor meum eructavit!*'" (ll. 1932-34 Robinson). I am grateful to Professor Anne Middleton for bringing this passage to my attention.

Such a one was Brother Pacificus: "He was called *The King of Verses*, because he was the most outstanding of those who sang impure songs and he was a composer of worldly songs" (Celano, *Second Life* 106, in Habig 1979, 449). In the *Legend of Perugia* Francis, excited by his own composition of "Brother Sun," wants Pacificus to go along on a preaching mission to sing it after each sermon. "At the end of the song, the preacher would say to the people: 'We are the jongleurs of God, and the only reward we want is to see you lead a truly penitent life'" (Habig 1979, 1022).

I do not mean to suggest that the texts of the third section, by virtue of this foregrounding of the performance situation, are necessarily Franciscan in origin. It is clear also that the tales collected in the second section come from very diverse sources. Their reception in B.N. f. fr. 2094, however, together with the life of Saint Francis, places them in a certain perspective: the combination conditions the reading of individual texts.

The collection as a whole would certainly have appealed to an audience interested in Franciscan teachings. It probably was not made as a reference for preaching: Latin collections of exempla were used even for vernacular sermons, and without any rubrics it would be a rather unhandy reference volume (see Schmitt 1977).

The Third Order, or "Order of Penance," mentioned in the first text of B.N. f. fr. 2094 as an order for "clergy and laity, men and women," was in the thirteenth century a formidable organization composed of individuals from all stations. For example, Saint Elizabeth of Hungary was a member, as was the Majorcan poet Ramón Lull (Iriarte 1983, 490-91). A list dating from 1252 of members in the Bologna fraternity includes "notaries, scribes, saddlers, barbers, shoemakers, carpenters, papermakers, bakers, apothecaries, furriers" (ibid., 1983, 487). The manuscript may have been written by a team of scribes belonging to this order or by a local group of Friars Minor for a lay audience. The cooperative effort reflected in the codicological details would have been in keeping with the Franciscan ideal of *fraternitas*.

MATERIAL DESCRIPTION: B.N. f. fr. 2094

Generalities

The leather binding of B.N. f. fr. 2094 has a red spine, a remnant of an earlier binding, and more recent brown front and back covers decorated in gold with the monogram of Napoleon: "N" embellished by an imperial crown, stars, and a garland. The title "Vie de S. François d'Assise, en vers &c" appears on the front. The end sheets are marbled in green, yellow, and rose. The shelf mark "fr 2094" and "reluire restaurée en 1971" are noted on the second of two front paper guard sheets. The foliation in ink is modern, in the upper right recto of each folio: two parchment guard sheets A and B, then 221 folios.

The parchment is unevenly prepared throughout, though without too many holes or repairs. Folios measure 152-58 mm across, with much greater variation in the vertical dimension: 180-204 mm. Many folios slant across the bottom or have imperfectly squared corners. Breaks in the volume's quaternion organization occur in gatherings 7 (four folios), 23 (a single leaf), and 3 (two folios). The first gathering is a senion.

The text is written in two columns, in three thirteenth-century bookhands. The first (ff. 1-50v, *La Vie Saint Francois*; see figure 22) has a loose, fluid, irregular appearance. Its *a* has an open upper loop and a sloping shaft; *s* is tall throughout except at line initials; round *r* is used most of the time after *o* and rarely after other letters. Uncial *d* is used, and *u* prevails over *v*, except in initial position, with no phonetic distinction. Curves of *h*, *d*, *b*, and *p* blend with following *o* or *e*, and *c* and *t* are ligatured to the next letter. The upright of *t* does not cross the horizontal bar. These traits suggest a date in the third quarter of the thirteenth century.

The second scribe (ff. 51r-171v, *Vie des Pères* and miracles; see figure 23) uses a rounded, expansive minuscule book hand with individual letters datable to the same period. The *i* is frequently marked with a hair stroke, but not systematically. Heads of ascenders are slightly clubbed, and in some cases those of the top line are extended, as in diplomatic or court script.[16]

The third hand (ff. 172r-221v, texts 4-9; see figure 24) is more compressed and angular than the others, with squared heads on some upright strokes. Round *s* sometimes appears in final position; tall *s* is sometimes broken. Minuscule *i* is sometimes marked with a hair stroke. Round *r* follows *o*, *p*, and rounded *d*; *v* is used only as a line initial; the loop of *a* is at times open, at times closed; the ascender of *t* penetrates the crossbar slightly. This hand seems somewhat later than the other two and may have belonged to a younger scribe.

The paleographic evidence suggests a date for the manuscript not earlier than around 1250. If the death of Nicholas of Gorran is taken as a *terminus a quo* (see above, pp. 127-28), the manuscript dates from the end of the thirteenth century. The characteristics of the third hand support this estimate.

Decoration is limited to initials; there are no rubricated titles, although the *Eructavit* (text 4) has spaces left for Latin verses of the psalm, some of which have been inserted in red (ff. 174va, 175vb, 176ra, 177ra, va, vb, 178ra, 179ra: only in gathering 24). Folios 1-6v have decorated initials in red and black, with blue added on folios 5v, 6r, and 6v. Folios 7-50v have red initials decorated with blue filigree. There is a denser

---

[16] Although Kunstmann remarks a change of hand at folio 59 (1981, 23), individual letters have the same characteristics as on folios 51-58v. A change in format from thirty to twenty-four lines per column gives the hand a more open appearance.

distribution of decorated initials beginning with folio 40r. Line initials are highlighted in red, folios 1r-51v. Folios 51r-171v have alternating red and blue initials, two to four lines high, filgreed in the contrasting color. The initial on folio 172r is elaborately decorated and similar to the one on folio 51r. Other initials on folios 172r-221r are two to three lines high, ornamental uncials alternating red and blue. The red paint used for decoration is geranium color, while the blue has faded toward green, except on folios 172r-221r. The variation in color seems to derive from a change in the thickness of application rather than from a different pigment: fine filigree strokes appear green, and whole letters are blue except where the paint has chipped or worn thin. The ink is brownish but very dark through folio 170v, then lighter.

Particularities

The guard sheets Av and B are covered with text in Latin in an early fourteenth-century cursive hand. Charles Faulhaber has identified it as a contract for the sale of some meadow land between a "Johannes" and a "Girardus." The edges have been trimmed, and no date survives. The recto of A bears script rendered illegible by rubbing or fading in a fourteenth-century gothic bookhand and two different cursives. The words "Explicit deo grat[ias]" appear. The verso of B had two capital *d*s with droleries and a capital *A* decorated in the same style as the initials of folios 1-5; there are also two indistinct words in late medieval cursive.

Folio 1 bears the shelf marks "760 Baluz." and "C. Reg. 7956 2," along with the oval stamp "bibliothe[cae] regiae." The bottom margin of 26v has, very faintly written, "Ci commonce [*sic*] la vie"; the signature on 46v (III) has been highlighted with doodling. A cat perches on the serif of a decorated *I* on folio 71a. On folio 97 the last line of column a is echoed in brown ink in the bottom margin. Folios 128v (bottom) and 129r (top) seem to indicate but do not supply corrections, "0a" and "0b," respectively. Folio 171, torn through the middle, has on the verso, in the same ink as that of the text, a sketch of Christ crucified flanked above the arms by the moon and the sun (see figure 25).[17] Folios 171v and 172r each bear pale mirror images of the other, probably caused by dampness.

Extravagant doodles taking off from line initials occur on folios 185v, 186r, 196v, 197r, 203v, 206v, 207r, 209r (including a face; see figure 26), 209v, 211v, 212r, 213r, and 215r. Folio 206v has a swastika, or "croix gammée," with three clockwise branches, wearing shoes, and one curved, rather than angled, counterclockwise (see Urech 1972, 51). Column 217d, left blank by the scribe of the third section, has six

---

[17] This iconography was common throughout the Middle Ages; there has not been any convincing explanation of its origin or meaning (Urech 1972, 168-69).

alexandrine verses in a different ink and hand from the text, apparently a prayer. Circular stamps "bibliothecae regiae" and "MSS bibliothèque nationale, RF" appear on 220 and 221, respectively. On 221 in the same ink as that of the text "domine labia mea aperies" is written below column b; it is repeated in the same place in a different ink and hand. Another cursive hand of the late thirteenth century writes something indistinct below, followed by "Guillaume Auleete [?] de Saint Leu." "Fr 2094" also appears, written in pencil. The verso of this folio, left blank by the scribe, has an illegible red oval stamp, the words "Explicit la vie" (an echo of f. A?), and several illegible remarks in at least two hands superimposed, washed, or rubbed off.

The parchment has holes on folios 18, 112, 137, 138, 200, 216, and 217. Folios 218-21 are very wrinkled. Stitched repairs have been made before the writing on 49, 104, 137, 142, and 169.

The manuscript was acquired by the Bibliothèque Royale from Baluze's estate, with his entire collection of manuscripts, in 1719 (Delisle 1868, 367). Two modern towns, both in Picardy, have the name "Saint-Leu," which is mentioned on folio 221r. Saint-Leu d'Esserent has a thirteenth-century church; the identity of "Guillaume Auleete" remains obscure.

... out euer li frere dolent   La pape honore lor estoit
Il amonesta doucement   A rate ou il seiornoit
Qui sofrit que lan li aidat   Et retur honorablemant
Et que len le medicinast   Tote lacort autrimant
Que il sotoit que la naue   Franç quant il fu uenuz la
Fi aunt de tout en tot perdue   Ot touz les aurres tenora
Par folie et por non sauoir   Ues qui euesques dore fu
Et plusors raisons lor mostroit   Ainz franç lauoir et lau
A son frere et li conmanda   Euant touz a pere a seignor
Que len fuit la uolente   E tout lordre gouernaor
Si il li uenroit a gre   Et le plaisir per le creant
Tieta li creantra quil meist   De la pape et c[...]sant
Enses yaux tout ce quil uosit   Us de tout a sa uolente
Plusor medecines li firent   Ane dex auoir de tint
Et plusors emplatres li mirent   Lapostoile de li frut
Et onques nul si bie ne li fir   Ainz franç maintenant hon
Amplatre queil i meist   Que tot apostoiles seroit
La maladie lengoisoit   Et quant letres li escriuoit
Et plus et plus li amproit   Ile solot nomer et dire
Oue lour a rate mene   E tout le mont euesque
Or querre aide de sante   et sire
Quar mout euer dolant li fi   Or poons bien apercouoir
Et or la maladie lor pere   Que saint franç profitoit uor
A franç lozer creantra   Que il fu pape apres
                                                   honore

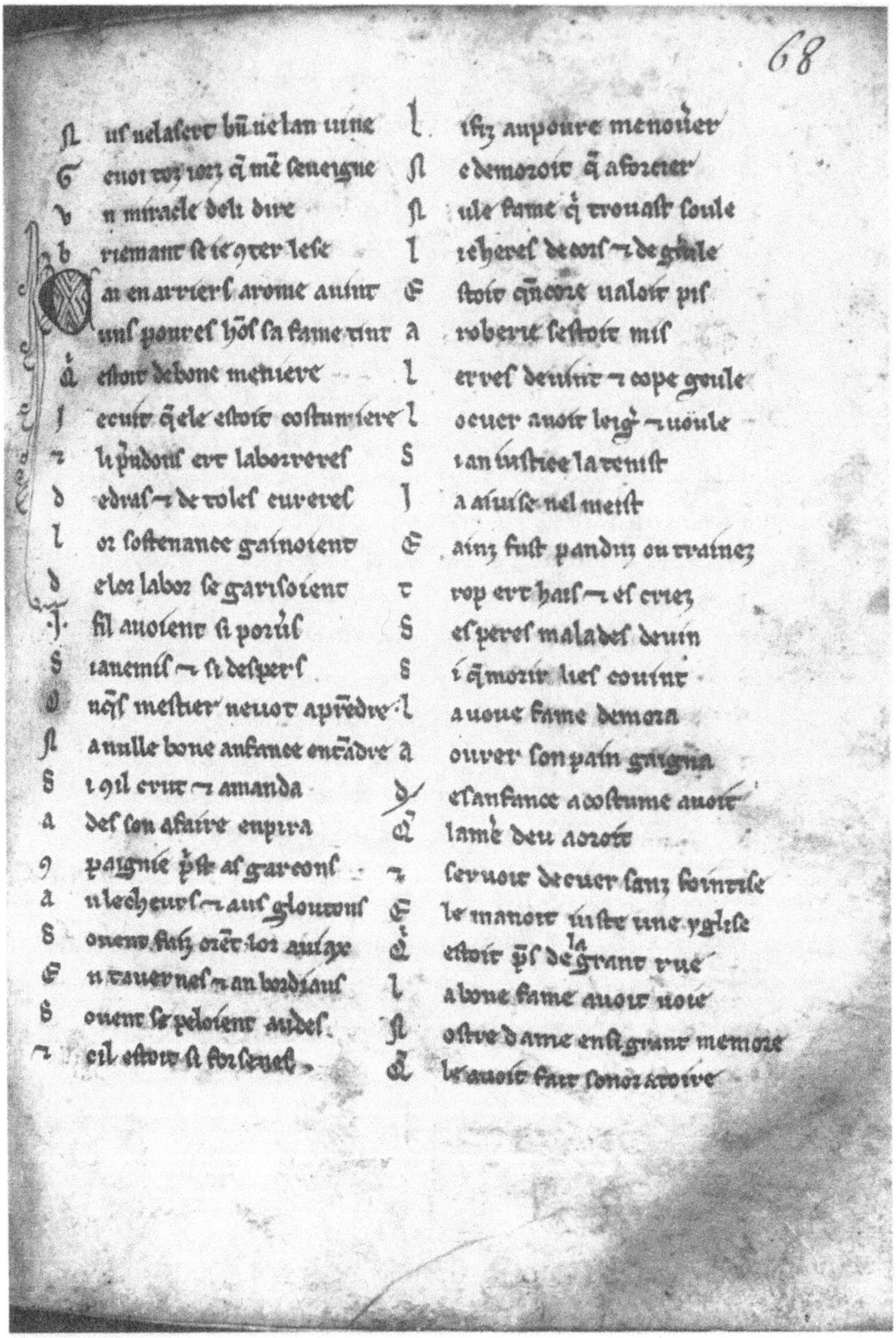

us ne la sert bn̄ ne lan uine	l fiz au poure menorier
enoi roi loi; q̄ me senergne	e demoroit q̄ afozerer
n miracle de li dire	ule fame q̄ trouast soule
riemant se ie grer le fe	l eheres de cors ⁊ de gule
an en arriers a rome auint	stoir encore ualoir pis
uns poures hō sa fame rint	robert se stoit mis
estoit de bone menieve	er ves denūt ⁊ cope goule
ecuit q̄ ele estoit costumiere	ocuer auoit leigī ⁊ uoule
li pudors ert laborerer	ian iustice la tenist
e dras ⁊ de roles euverer	a aiuise nel meist
oz sostenance gainoient	ainz fust panduz ou trainez
e lor labor se garisoient	rop ert hais ⁊ es criez
fil auoient si pozul	es peres malades deuin
ianemis ⁊ si despers	i q̄ mozir lies couint
n es mestier neuot apr̄edre	a uovre fame demora
a nulle bone anfance en cādre	ouuer son pain gaigna
i gil crut ⁊ amanda	e lanfance acostume auoit
des son afaire enpira	la me deu aozoit
paignie p̄st as garcons	seruoir de cuer sanz fointise
u lecheurs aus gloutons	le manoir iuste une yglise
onent sai; oier lor aulage	estoir p̄s de grant rue
n tauernes ⁊ an bordiaus	a bone fame auoir uoir
ouent se peloient au des	ostre dame en st grant memoire
cil estoit si fors enes	le auoit fait son ozatoire

Fig. 23. Paris, B.N. f. fr. 2094: f. 68r (hand 2)
Phot. Bibl. Nat. Paris

Qui toute lesperance auiue.   Parole ali mont doucemant.
Et le est nerf lui si enterine.   Si moustre son enseignemant.
Que riens ou siegle ne li plaist.   A chaiune arme crestienne.
Fors la douçor qui de lui naist.   Par ce que nest pas euienne.
Et lou roi riens tant nabelt.   Creantei si comme il furent.
Con feir lamors qui uient de li.   Qui la loi dieu auat ginurent.
Quant dauid ot cele meruoile.   Iaphete li patriarche.
Et oie con diex aparoile.   Adanz et noels qui fist larche.
Si se pourpanse quil fera.   Moyses et la grant lignee.
De la raigne chantera.   Cui la loi dieu fu enseignee.
Si la loeta en chantant.   Tuit cil uindrent ala iournee.
Que cele ioie quele atant.   Ainz que la fois fust atornee.
Bien fermemāt sa reigne ahẽde.   Se trauoilerent mout deuant.
Guart se bien quele ne la perde.   Quant ce uint au soloir leuant.
Que iamais en tout son aaige.   Se furent il ia tuit lassei.
Ne recouuerroit son demaige.   Et de cest siegle trespassei.
                                     Apres ce quil furent greuei.
                                     Quant diex or le soloir leuer.
                                     Son fil le haut roi ihesucrist.
                                     Celui quile siegle refist.
                                     Qui est droiz solautz ꝛ uerais.
Dauid qui sainte eglise apele   Qui en nos cuers espart ses rais.
Sa file cōme une pucele.   Lor fist li sires sourdre ꝛ naistre.
Qui de son parante fu nee   Sainte eglise qui deuoit estre.
Et de ses droiz hoirs angendree.

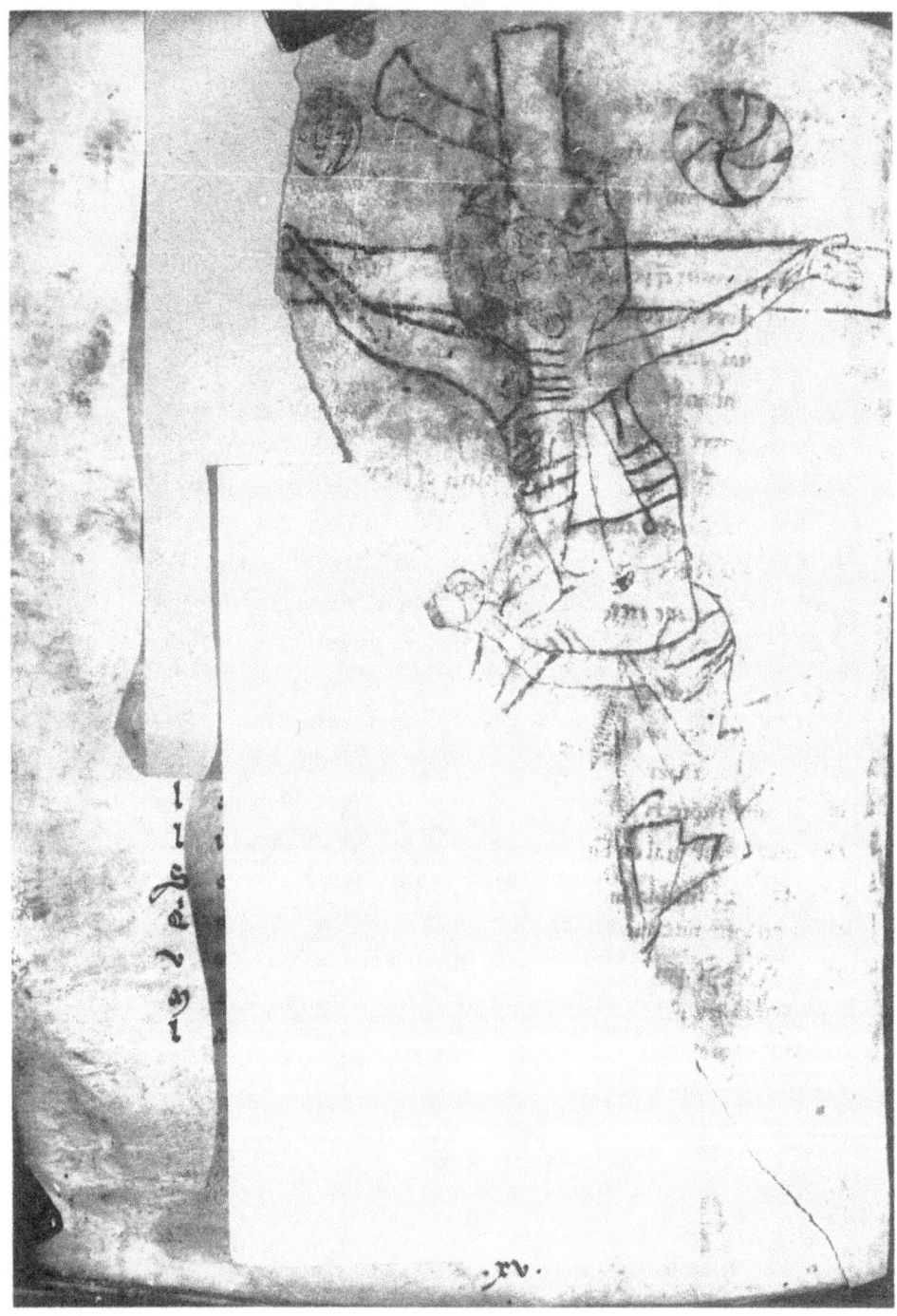

Fig. 25. Paris, B.N. f. fr. 2094: f. 171v (sketch)
Phot. Bibl. Nat. Paris

Par le omant filium patre.
Descent .j. anges en la chartre.
Qui gentement la acolee
& enseignié et confortee.
Dit li anges uirge mirable
Giete les meis pra ce deable.
Pran le felon dedeuant toi.
Venuz iest par male foi.
Qui te cuida asine sodurre
& ta uirginitei destruire.
Mas non fera li soudeanz.
Car damediex e tes garanz.
Pran la cheanne eau col as.
Et li ou sien buer le feras.
Puis enferas tout to uolor.
Jamais naura uers toi poor.
Site dira quanq bon tiert.
Et qui il est et que il quiert.
Quat la pucele entat la uoi.
S or li forma la sainte croiz.
Vers le deable uint errant.
A ucol li gita le charchant.
Or la formant encheeinnei.
Mais tout ce tiet il an uiei

Ont rutemat prist abraidir.
& atriper et a saillir.
Par sa force sen cude aler.
& la chartre toute effondrer.
Mais ne fera ne li uaut rien.
Car la uirge le tient mot bien.
Et le le tient plou chainon.
Ile torche ome .i. guaignon.
Onques matins q est en hart.
N ost de colees mies sa part.
Quant il se uit si confunduz.
& si honiz et si ueincuz.
La sainte uirge rapela.
Et a dire li commanca.
Julienne dit li maufez.
Mont par est forz uirginitez.
Ge fu coianz tramiuis a toi.
Que te cuidai traire uet moi.
De uoir le saiches toi cuidat.
G oute honir mais ne ferai.
G e ne te puis feire enobzier.
Car damediex te uaut aidier.
Deables sui lai mau suir.
Ne quier mais atoi reuenir.

Organization of the Page

Prickings have been made on the outside edges and on the tops and bottoms of folios. Ruling appears both in dry point and in plummet, but not consistently even within distinct sections. The text is written in two columns throughout. The organization of the page, including the pattern of prickings, justification, and number of lines, remains constant from gathering 9 to the end of the manuscript.

Folio dimensions: 180-204 x 152-58 mm

Fig. 27. Page layout, ff. 1r - 50v

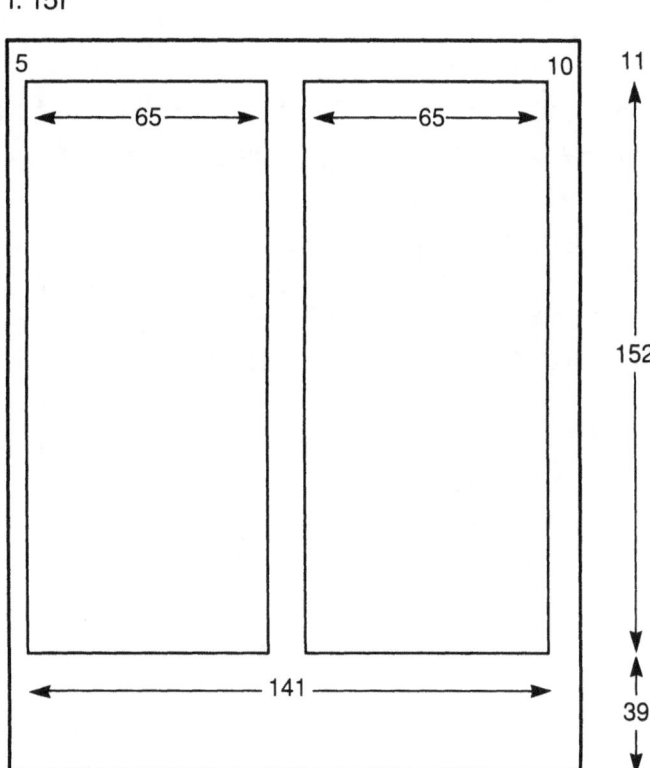

Justification:
25 lines, 148-55 x 130-35 mm

Fig. 28. Page layout, ff. 51r - 171v

f. 53r

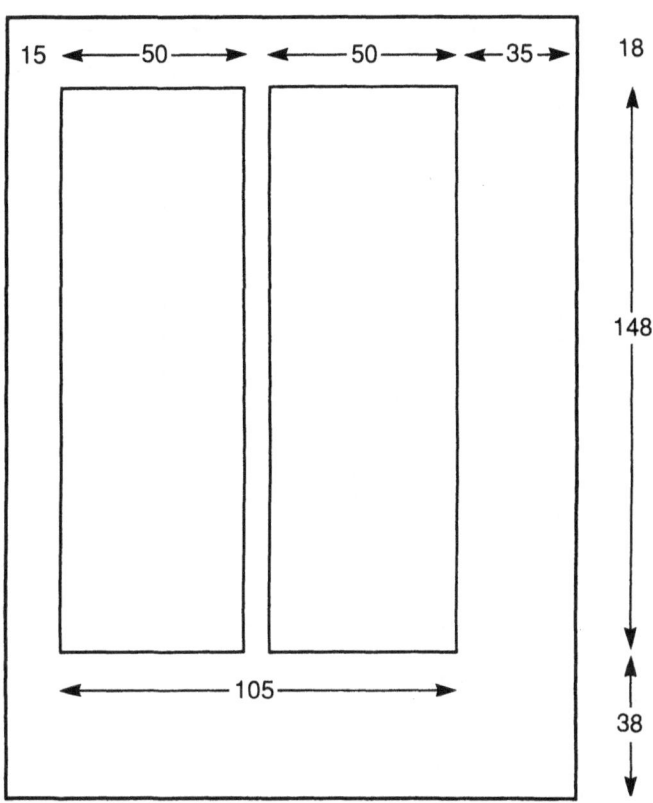

Justification, ff. 51r - 58v:
30 lines, 146-48 x 105 mm
Justification, ff. 59r - 171v:
24 lines, 146-48 x 105 mm

Fig. 29. Page layout, ff. 172r - 221v

f. 178r

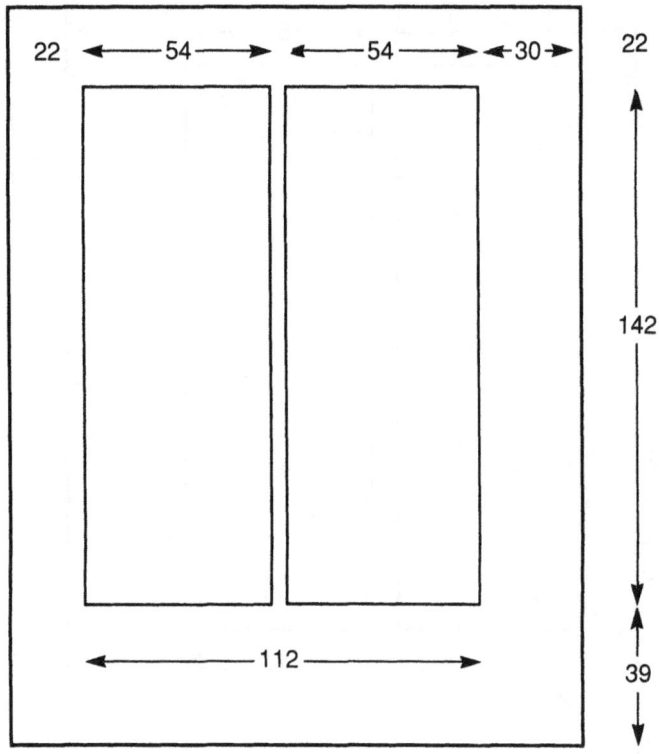

Justification:
24 lines, 142 x 112-18 mm

Table 7

Organization of the Volume

Gathering	Type	Catchword	Signatures	Remarks	Texts
1 (1-6)	3/3	yes	I		*La Vie Saint Francois*, f. 1ra
2 (7-14)	4/4	yes	II		
3 (15-22)	4/4	no			
4 (23-30)	4/4	no			
5 (31-38)	4/4	no			
6 (39-46)	4/4	no	III		
7 (47-50)	4/0	no		four folios torn out after f. 50	
8 (51-58)	4/4	no	I	hand 2, f. 51ra	*Vie des Pères*, f. f1ra
9 (59-66)	4/4	no	II	f. 59r, change in justification	
10 (67-74)	4/4	no	III		
11 (75-82)	4/4	no	IIII		
12 (83-90)	4/4	no	V		
13 (91-98)	4/4	no	VI		
14 (99-106)	4/4	no	VII		
15 (107-114)	4/4	no	VIII		
16 (115-122)	4/4	no	IX		
17 (123-130)	4/4	no	X		
18 (131-138)	4/4	no	XI		
19 (139-146)	4/4	no	XII		
20 (147-154)	4/4	no	XIII		Thirteen miracles of the Virgin, f. 150vb
21 (155-162)	4/4	no	XIIII	stub between ff. 162-63	
22 (163-170)	4/4	no	XV		
23 (171)	1	no		isolated folio, torn and repaired	
24 (172-179)	4/4	no		hand 3, f. 172ra	Paraphrase of Psalm 44, *Eructavit*, f. 172ra
25 (180-187)	4/4	no			
26 (188-195)	4/4	no		blank left for title	Les XV signes du jugement, f. 194vb
27 (196-203)	4/4	no		blank left for title	Descent of Saint Paul, f. 199rb
28 (204-211)	4/4	yes		blank left for title, bottom of f. 204b	Life of Saint Juliana, f. 204va
29 (212-219)	4/4	no		f. 217d, blank column	*Dit de l'unicorne et du serpent*, f. 218ra (incomplete)
30 (220-221)	1/1	no		at least one folio missing between ff. 220-21	fragment of unidentified text, f. 221r

CONTENTS

(1) ff. 1ra-50vb: *La Vie Saint Francois*, Burgundian, 1257-66 (Thomas [1942], 40-45), octosyllabic couplets

Incipit: A la loenge *et* a l'onor

Rubrics in text: Ci commancent li miracle (f. 21a)

                 Ci recommance la vie (f. 26b)

                 Ci commancent li miracle apres la mort (f. 40b)

Explicit: Ci faut la vie Saint Francois [rubr.]

Edition: ?

See Thomas [1942].

Summary: Francis of Assisi, son of a cloth merchant, lives a frivolous life until illness awakens his conscience and he dreams of becoming a knight of the Celestial King. He sells all his goods and returns the money to his father, who officially disowns him in the presence of the bishop. Francis ceremoniously removes all his clothes to return them to his father, obliging the bishop to cover his nudity with his own mantle.

    Dressed in rags, Francis goes through the woods singing God's praises in "French" [Occitan]. He rebuilds the church of San Damiano, and then the Portiuncula, dedicated to the Virgin. His ardent preaching attracts followers, whom he sends out, like new knights, to preach penitence. He founds three kinds of orders: the Friars Minor, the Good Ladies, and a third with clergy and laity, both men and women.

    Francis's soul appears to the brothers one midnight as a fiery chariot. He has miraculous knowledge of their hearts and of the future and often appears to them in visions. He leads an austere life, and once when obliged by illness to eat some chicken, has himself dragged through the streets by a brother proclaiming him a glutton. He burns with desire for martyrdom and visits Syria.

    Francis enjoys a special relationship with God's creatures and even preaches the word of God to his brother birds. Once when a flock of swallows disturbs his audience with the noise of their nest building, he admonishes them to be silent until he has finished speaking. The people honor him as a saint when they witness the miracle of the birds' obedience. Many miracles of healing are performed using Francis's clothing or other objects he has touched. He preaches to the crowd by day and seeks solitude for contemplation by night.

    Two years before his death, Francis experiences a vision of an angel, like a man crucified, but with six wings. He receives the stigmata, "Miracle gent/ C'omques nus hons plus bel ne vit" (f. 29rb22-24). He continues preaching, although he has become ill and weak. Brought to the city of [Rieti] in search of a cure for the sickness of his eyes, he is received by the pope. Hugolino, bishop of Ostia, honors him most, of all the papal court. With the pope's permission, Francis nominates Hugolino (later Pope Gregory IX) as governor of his order.

Francis's illness tortures him worse than any martyrdom. He has himself taken to the Portiuncula, where his life had first taken the way of perfection. When he dies, one of the brothers present (who will remain nameless to avoid renown) sees Francis's pure soul mount to heaven on a cloud, shining like the sun or the moon. The news spreads, and the townspeople flock to the spot. They see the stigmata, and the body, which had been thin and black, shines like snow, tender as a child's.

In the second year after Francis's death, Pope Gregory comes and, after hearing Francis's miracles read, declares him a saint. Records of the miracles and of the translation of Francis's body in 1230 conclude the narrative.

The text in B.N. f. fr. 2094 ends with forty-eight verses, probably added by the scribe, in unusual stanzas of four alexandrines with interior rhyme at the sixth syllable.[18] The passage begins with a prayer for God's favor and protection from the devil on behalf of anyone who reads, has someone else read, or dwells in the same place with this "romant." The speaker asserts its veracity but goes on to apologize for mistakes in the copy:

>   Por une sole letre
>   peut l'en cople fauser,
>   Por po ou por trop metre;
>   por ce est bon demander
>   Ne se doit entremettre
>   nus d'autre trop blamer.
>   Tex peut assez promettre
>   qui a po que doner.
>   (f. 50vb4-11)

(2) ff. 51ra-150vb: [*Vie des Pères*], second and third series,[19] around 1250 (Bornäs 1968, 22-23), octosyllabic couplets
   Incipit: Ansi *com* li arbre verdissent
   Explicit: A cui je doin mon cors et m'arme
   See Duval [1838] 1895; Tobler 1866; Weber 1876, 1877; Schwan 1884; Meyer 1906b; Morawski 1921, 1935, 1938; Del Monte 1966; Payen 1967.

---

[18] The passage is edited in Thomas [1942], 142-46.

[19] See table 8 for a list of individual tales and editions.

Table 8

Contents of the *Vie des Pères*

B.N. f. fr. 2094 [A][a]	Begins (f.)	Subject[b]	Incipit	Edition
1 [43]	51ra	Sel	Ansi com li arbre verdissent	Bornäs 1968
2 [44]	53va	Enfant jureur	L'escriture se nos enseigne	
3 [64]	57vb	Coq	Apres nos comte dou seint herm[ite]	Bornäs 1968
4 [65]	68ra	Mère	Cai en arriers a rome avint	
5 [66]	71ra	Patience	Jadis uns hermitage estoit	
6 [67]	75ra	Infanticide	Il avint si com j'oi dire	
7 [68]	76vb	Piège au diable	D'un saint pere [apres] vos [veil] dire	Bornäs 1968
8 [69]	82vb	Anges	Jadis uns chevaliers estoit	
9 [70]	87va	Sac	Fous est qui o siegle se fie	
10 [71]	91vb	Image du diable	Jadis estoit une abaie	Méon 1823
11 [72]	95rb	Ange et ermite	Un saint pere en egypte avoit	
12 [73]	101vb	Pain	Mal semer fait seur terre dure	
13 [74]	104ra	Sermon	Cil qui bien voit et bien antant	
14 [45]	108rb	Image N.D.	O miracle briemant vos di	
15 [46]	112va	Frères	Un essample vos voil retraire	
16 [47]	117ra	Crâne	Jadis an la terre de egypte	
17 [48]	119rb	Renieur	En France avint ce m'est avis	
18 [49]	122ra	Deux morts	Il ot en .I. dersert [sic] d'egipte	
19 [50]	125ra	Confession	Or comencez le premier viers	
— [63]	127rb	Vilain (prologue only)	Encor di ge que cui annuit	
20 [53]	127vb	Enfant pieux	Un borjois fu de grand renon	
21 [54]	129va	Brandons	Assez puet an troer matire	
22 [55]	131va	Prêtre pécheur	En engleterre .I. prestre ot ia	
23 [56]	134ra	Ame en gage	Apres d'on fevre vos recort	Méon 1823
24 [57]	139rb	Ave Maria	Un petit conte vos voil faire	
25 [58]	140vb	Fenêtre	Qui vodroit anquerre et cercher	
26 [59]	142va	Femme aveugle	Un novel comte avons apris	
—	145a	(Interpolated text)	Qi toz jors ot et rien n'antant	
27 [60]	145va	Nom de Marie	Tant a quis et tant reverchie	
28 [61]	148vb	Enfant sauvé	Assez puet an conter a dire	

[a] Figures in brackets indicate the numbers of the tales according to their sequence in B.N. f. fr. 1546 (A), the conventional reference.
[b] Subject titles were assigned to the tales by Gaston Paris in a footnote to Schwan 1884, 240 n. 5.

Partial Summary: An overview of the stories *not* shared with UCB 106 (see p. 113), including one tale from the second series and nine from the third, will help to clarify the thematic emphasis of the texts in B.N. f. fr. 2094. "Sac" (9 [70], f. 87va) has been omitted from the UCB 106 copy. The text begins with a four-column-long sermon on death.[20] The protagonist is a hermit living in the woods adjacent to a castle housing a group of young men who are in the habit of robbing and burglarizing everyone in the country. When they raid the hermitage one night, the frightened hermit prays in a corner. After they leave, he finds a sack under his cot that has escaped their notice. Assuming that their need must be greater than his, he delivers the sack to the castle. His humility and generosity arouse the thieves' pity and good conscience: they return all they have stolen and beg forgiveness. The epilogue discusses humility and pride and describes hell.

"Enfant pieux" (20 [53], f. 127rb) is about the child of a devout bourgeois couple who recites *Ave Maria* and speaks with an image of the Virgin. "Brandons" (21 [54], f. 129va) describes a hermit's vision of a lady who catches burning coals tossed at him by an angel: the lady represents the Virgin, who mitigates the consequences of our sins. "Prêtre pécheur" (22 [55], f. 131va) concerns Thomas Becket's chaplain, who had been led as a priest from gluttony into lechery. Although he had lived such a life for ten years, he never failed to sing the special Saturday service in the Virgin's honor. His congregation reports him to the archbishop, but he sincerely repents and becomes Thomas's chaplain after witnessing a miraculous vision of Mary.

"Ame en gage" (23 [56], f. 134ra) is the longest text in the third *Vie*, nearly 500 lines. A charitable goldsmith appeals to a hermit to pray for him: if he were to become wealthy, he would have more to give to the poor. The hermit does so, and when challenged by an angel, agrees to offer his own soul as a hostage in case the goldsmith should be corrupted by his new-found riches. When the hermit's soul is endangered by the goldsmith's behavior as a wealthy imperial courtier, the Virgin persuades the heavenly tribunal to give him another chance: he may choose hell for himself or the return of the goldsmith to his original status. His decision restores both his own and the goldsmith's souls to God. When he awakes from this vision, his body feels weak and sore.

---

[20] Both the theme and the length are unusual among the common sermonizing prologues of these tales, which typically go on for about a column, denouncing some specific sin, which may or may not be related to the tale thus introduced.

In its epilogue, the next tale makes a distinction between "corporal" and "spiritual" miracles, to the advantage of the latter. It gives examples of miraculous healing, but maintains

> Or laisomes ester les cors:
> L'arme de nos, c'est li tresors.
> (f. 140vb11-12)

The brief story ("Ave Maria," 24 [57], f. 139rb) relates how a secular student living a life of *luxure* in Paris benefits from a tender massage administered by the Virgin in a dream after he has repented and recited *Ave Maria* late into the night. The text implies that her touch, described in some detail, has restored his spirit.

"Fenêtre" (25 [58], f. 140vb) nevertheless describes a "corporal" miracle, in which Mary herself catches and saves the life of a child who has fallen from a high building. Its prologue distinguishes between miracles and stories sought from books stored in the "aumeres" of monasteries and those that have occurred in recent times (ff. 140vb-141ra).

The next miracle has been included in the collection at the request of a "Metre Hernaut," whom Morawski has supposed to be the author of the second *Vie*.[21] A pretty young woman whom God has afflicted with blindness as punishment for her being "folete" regains her sight upon praying to the Virgin and in gratitude undertakes a pilgrimage to Rocamadour. Not allowed in the church until she has confessed, she is obliged to cut her hair as penance. The church has a special holder ("*perce*") for the severed tresses of repentant women. On the way home the girl regrets the loss of her beautiful curls and prays to the Virgin for their restoration. Her prayer is answered, but at the cost of her sight. The epilogue exhorts beautiful women to avoid sin by covering themselves.

There follows a curious little discourse of forty-four lines that I have not succeeded in identifying (ff. 45a-45c).[22] It is unusual for its rhyme scheme:

---

[21] Morawski 1921, 381; Morawski 1935, 181 n. 2. See above, pp. 86-87. The context does not support Hernaut's identity as the author: "Por la priere metre Hernaut/ Sera en nostre livre escriz/ Cis miracle." The author, it would seem, has been the one to comply with the request of the compiler, the client, or a superior named Hernaut. Morawski's hypothesis depends on a correlation of this name with an "Ernoul de Laingni" mentioned in the epilogue of tale 5 [66], "Patience," in the second *Vie*. In my opinion the style as well as the themes of the third series, distinctly different from those of the second, point to a separate author.

[22] Its incipit, "Qui toz jors ot *et* rien n'a*nt*ant," is absent from Gröber 1902, Långfors 1917, and Beyer and Koppe 1970.

every fourth line ends in *-ie* (i.e. *a a a b c c c b d d d b* and so on).²³ The speaker meditates on the wisdom and folly, truth and falsehood, of his subject, and on the ambivalence of his audience. Although the sense of the passage is independent of any particular tale (it refers to "matire" and "discors"), it appears as a prologue to "Nom de Marie" (27 [60], f. 145va).

The opening of the tale itself credits the Virgin with bringing the story to the speaker's mind, as it otherwise might have been lost. One summer day, a wealthy and valiant count devoted to the Virgin sees a crowd of beautiful ladies gathered for recreation. He falls in love with one of them and sends his seneschal to investigate and negotiate. He purchases her favors for 2,000 *livres*, although she is a virgin. He learns her name, Mary, only when they are at last in bed together. His reverence for the name inhibits his amorous intent, much to the girl's chagrin:

> Ensi pechiez m'a deceüe,
> *Et* cil qui m'avoit achetee
> M'a mise arriere *et* degetee.
> Si fui pecheresse sanz fet!
> (f. 147ra16-19)

She joins a religious order, and her would-be lover is subsequently killed in a tournament. Since he had not confessed to a priest, he is buried outside the city. A year passes. Wishing to honor the count's body, the Virgin visits a hermit and gives instructions for a stately procession and reburial. The hermit hesitates to believe his visitor is really Mary, but she promises the count's flesh will be miraculously uncorrupted and a red rose will be found in his mouth. She persists until he is convinced, for, she says,

> Martire ot grant *par* lo mien no*m*:
> Plus grant jo sé de verité
> *Que* s'il eüst lo chief copé.
> (f. 148rb3-5)

"Enfant sauvé" (28 [61], f. 148d) opens with a prologue discussing truth and fiction, preferring authoritative Marian miracles to amusing tales of "Renart" or "Renoart." In a town by the sea, where two high tides each day deposit fish on the beach, lives a "borjoise cortoise" devoted to the Virgin.

---

²³ Naetebus (1891) cites only one poem, from the late thirteenth or early fourteenth century, with stanzas of eight lines rhyming *a a a b c c c b*. I have found no reference to a nonstanzaic pattern with this scheme, which resembles the Spanish *zéjel* (*a a : b b b a*) and occurs in poems of the Provençal troubadours Guillaume IX and Marcabru. See Navarro 1956, 24-27.

of "Renart" or "Renoart." In a town by the sea, where two high tides each day deposit fish on the beach, lives a "borjoise cortoise" devoted to the Virgin. She has only one child, whom she loves dearly and teaches to recite *Ave Maria*. Playing on the beach one day, he and his little friends are overwhelmed by the tide; all drown except him. As the grieving parents retrieve their children's bodies, the bourgeoise's son is found asleep: his soul has paid a visit to heaven in the Virgin's company. In a long epilogue the speaker maintains the advantages of devotion to Mary and compares God and his mother with King Louis and his mother: "la viele roine Blain*c*he . . . de son fil est dame *et* mestrosse" (f. 150rb12, 16).[24]

(3) ff. 150vb-171rb: [Thirteen miracles of the Virgin], eastern France (?) (Kunstmann 1981, 28), 1280-1300 (see above, p. 138), octosyllabic couplets
  Incipit: De la mere Deu hennorer
  Explicit: Ici li livres ex. . . [folio torn]
  Edition: Kunstmann 1981
  See also Morawski 1935.
  Partial summary: The ninth tale is a variation on the pact-with-the-devil motif. A rich bourgeois attacked by highway robbers returns home poor to be disowned by his family. In desperation he renounces his faith in exchange for the restoration of his wealth and station but loses everything again when he balks at the devil's demand that he renounce the Virgin as well as her Son. He subsequently repents, and Mary intercedes to gain God's pardon for the sinner by exposing the breasts he had fed upon to arouse his filial devotion.[25]

  Another near renunciation is related in the second tale: a merchant uses his Christian faith as collateral for a loan from a Jew but fails to return to his country by the specified date. He entrusts the money to the sea with a prayer, and it is magically transported into the usurer's possession. When the merchant returns and the truth is revealed by means of a speaking image of the infant Christ, the Jew adopts the Christian faith and receives baptism.

  The eleventh miracle narrates the dream of a debauched cleric devoted to the Virgin. In a vision of Judgment Day, his unspecified sins, listed on the

---

[24] On the basis of this and one other passage, Bornäs suggests a *terminus ad quem* of 1252, when Blanche of Castile died, for the second *Vie* (1968, 23).

[25] Another version of this story occurs in the *Vie des Pères* (17 [48], f. 119rb), with a young squire as its hero, but similarly focusing on his refusal to renounce Mary.

devil's roll, far outweigh the record of his good deeds, until Mary literally seats herself on the balance. In the dream she thus rescues his soul but admonishes him to add more good works to the list. When he awakes, the cleric finds the roll in his hand. While it is reminiscent of miracles in which the Virgin uses her power to save the worst sinners against all odds, this story neither dwells on the gravity of the cleric's crimes nor claims that Mary actually overwhelms the tribunal.

Other tales in the collection treat the magical provision of food (1), the avoidance of temptation (3, 4, 10), the restoration of lost limbs (6, 13), the cure of disease (8), the resuscitation of the dead (7), and military anecdotes (5, 12).

(4) ff. 172ra-194vb: [Paraphrase of Psalm 44, *Eructavit*], Burgundian (for this manuscript and one other) but written in Champagne, 1181-87 (Jenkins 1909, vii)
Incipit: Une chancon que David fist
Explicit: A lui loer et beneir. Amen.
Edition: Jenkins 1909
See also Jauss 1970; McKibben 1907; Benton 1961.
Summary: In a vision, David finds himself seated outside the entrance to heaven with his *vielle*, wishing to sing for the king. The door is opened to him when he cajoles the *hussier* by revealing that the Son of God will be born of a virgin of his own lineage. His song for the king consists of the "translation" and commentary on Psalm 44. The narrator's voice resumes from time to time to recall the setting of the *jongleur* and king, as well as to give additional interpretations of the psalm's verses.

Beauty is the keynote of the first section, in praise of the king (representing Christ). Then the king's bow and arrows are treated at length, and the meanings of the throne, the scepter, and the king's garments follow. The bride (that is, the Church) enters at this point, and David addresses his song to her, speaking again of the king's beauty and admonishing her to love him with *fine amor*. On Judgment Day she will be crowned and called to the *chambre celée* to enjoy the king's embraces.

The poet momentarily transfers his typology of the bride from the Church to the Virgin Mary, prophesying Christ's incarnation: the bride's jewels represent the Virgin's *inner* beauty. He returns to the bride: Church allegory, speaking of the happy souls of the faithful, the orders of angels, and the queen's sons, martyrs and apostles. Where the psalm speaks of the queen's everlasting name, the poet extends the metaphor of God's son as a fountain. The stream issuing from it is the Holy Spirit, dwelling among us. The flesh is weak; God rather than earthly bread is our true sustenance. Death was conquered when Life was crucified. David concludes by emphasizing that the crowd praises the Lord for all eternity. The poet adds an address to his lady ("ma dame de Champagne") and an expanded *Gloria patri, et filio, et spiritui sancto*.

(5) ff. 194vb-199rb: [*Les quinze signes du jugement*], no predominant dialectal traits (Mantou 1966, 135; Kraemer 1966, 59), 1180-1225 (Kraemer 1966, 6-7), octosyllabic couplets

Incipit: Oez trestuit *com*munema*nt*

Explicit: Que Diex l'otroit li fiz Marie

Edition: Kraemer 1966 (using this manuscript); Mantou 1966

See also Jauss 1970; Heist 1952.

Summary: In the prologue the speaker complains of man's ingratitude toward God, whom even the dumb beasts serve as they ought. Full of "covoitise," man would rather hear about the fight between Roland and Oliver than about the Lord's Passion.[26] Were he not afraid of disturbing his listeners, he says, he might tell about the end of the world, as prophesied by various biblical characters, whom he names. Each of the daily signs, except the first and third, is indicated by an ornamental initial. The poet lists the portentous catastrophes, beginning with a rain of blood and ending with a general conflagration, then describes the Last Judgment. God will separate the sheep from the goats. To the good he will promise reward for having served him through service to the poor and the sick, while the sinners will never lack torments in the stinking pit.

(6) ff. 199rb-204rb: [Descent of Saint Paul], dialect of the Ile-de-France, thirteenth century (Jauss 1970, 242), octosyllabic couplets

Incipit: Li autre trouveor *qui* trueve*nt*

Explicit: In seculorum secula. Amen.

Edition: Kastner 1906

See also Jauss 1970.

Summary: The speaker begins by distinguishing himself from other poets who care less about truth than about pleasing audiences with their skill. Their fables and tales are no better than lies, and they will burn in hell for not having

---

[26] Lines 23-28 Kraemer (f. 195ra21-b2r) suggest that the prologue was originally composed for a text combining the Passion with the *Quinze signes du jugement* (see Kraemer 1966, 12).

served God. Their suffering will be such that if the speaker had a hundred tongues, he could not describe it in a hundred years.

For the love of Saint Paul, God sends Michael to him with instructions to lead him into hell. Specific pains are inflicted on souls depending on their particular sins. In hell there are seven principal torments: snow, ice, fire, heat, toads and serpents, smoke, and a disgusting odor.

Paul sees sinners plunged into a flaming river up to various levels. The faithless are devoured by serpents in a dark, bottomless pit. Michael wonders why Paul weeps for pity? Because these might have been saved, since Jesus had ransomed them with his blood, except for their own will.

As the two saints watch, a new arrival is plunged into the boiling tide. The angels in heaven weep. "Do the souls get what they deserve?" asks Michael. Paul answers in the affirmative, and along with the damned they witness the reception of a worthy soul in heaven. Distressed by this sight, the sinners appeal to God for mercy. He scorns their prayer but relents when they have asked Michael and Paul to intercede for them: on Sundays they will have respite from their punishment. Whoever rests on this day will be rewarded for it!

(7) ff. 204va-217vb: [Life of Saint Juliana], octosyllabic couplets
   Incipit: Or escoutez bon crestien
   Explicit: Jhesu le fil sainte marie
   Edition: Feilitzen 1883
   See also Meyer 1906a.
   Summary: Daughter of a wicked pagan, Juliana has become Christian and promised her chastity to God. She suffers torture and imprisonment when she refuses to marry a pagan prince, and the devil confronts her in her cell. Instructed by an angel, Juliana captures him, and a long dialogue ensues: each time he begs her to release him, she asks a question.

   He identifies himself as Satan, boasts of his successes (e.g., Eve and Cain), describes the torments of hell, lists the martyrs whose tormentors he has incited, and recounts the fall of the rebel angels. He says he succeeds best at distracting believers in church and reluctantly explains how one can avoid his influence by sincere prayer and confession.

   Juliana is able to convert a great many pagans by revealing the chagrined devil to them and by miraculously rendering renewed torture ineffective through prayer. Though the pagan emperor kills the new Christians, he is powerless against Juliana, until Satan advises him to decapitate her. She is received in heaven with joy.

(8) ff. 218ra-220vb: [*Dit de l'unicorne et du serpent*], Francien, thirteenth century (Jauss 1970, 204), octosyllabic couplets
   Incipit: Mont par est fos cil q *ui* s'a*n*tant
   Explicit: Quant eles sunt aparellies.
   Edition: Jubinal 1839-42, 2: 113-23
   See also Långfors 1917, 227; Jauss 1970, 204.
   Summary: See above, p. 49.

(9) f. 221ra-b, [unidentified fragment], octosyllables, peculiar rhyme pattern: *aabbbabbacdedfeefeefghiggi* and so on
   Incipit: Que ta charoigne si la dane
   Explicit: Tu eusses tout lou tormant.
   See Sonet 1949.

6

Conclusion

Codicology and Reception History in the Interpretation of Pious Vernacular Literature

The bibliometric evidence uncovered in the first phase of this study reveals a separation between the traditions of Latin and of thirteenth-century Old French hagiographic manuscripts. Latin collections reflect the "card-index mentality" C. S. Lewis attributes to medieval man, while the vernacular corpus resists categorization. Indeed Lewis shows his awareness of heterogeneity when he introduces the *South English Legendary* as "better evidence than any learned production could be for the Model as it existed in the imagination of ordinary people" (Lewis [1964] 1967, 98). If the medieval image of the universe was shared by both learned and ordinary people, however, it need not follow that the mentality of codification, system building, and indexing was also shared. Whatever their points of contact, the two cultures of which these manuscripts come down to us as artifacts must have been different in some essential ways. We can suppose that pious Latin manuscripts had an educated public, and that they functioned within the ecclesiastical sphere. The audience for vernacular literary manuscripts, whether secular or pious, is less well defined.

Each of the four manuscripts I have analyzed addresses a specific segment of the thirteenth-century French-speaking public, and each combination of texts represents a specific literary function. B.N. f. fr. 2162 appeals to an audience seeking spiritual guidance in an environment that renders the ascetic life impracticable. The selection of texts emphasizes the Virgin less than might be expected for the period. It favors the alternatives of avoiding temptation and of sincere confession and penance rather than a dependence on her mercy for salvation. The manuscript dates paleographically to the second quarter of the thirteenth century, and its texts were composed predominantly in northern dialects: Picard, Francien, and Walloon.

B.N. f. fr. 1374 contains texts that imply an aristocratic audience and that have in common an unusual degree of realism in geographic detail, particularly of the eastern Mediterranean area. The evidence suggests it was intended for the entertainment of Crusaders, veterans, or colonists in the Middle East. Compiled around 1275, the texts have northern or eastern dialectal traits, although three editors have characterized the scribes' language as southern.

The contents of Bancroft Library UCB 106 emphasize hermits' roles, criticize the official clergy, and abound with magical elements, responding to the concerns of a devout lay public inadequately served by ecclesiastical institutions. The style of decoration is typical of the Parisian region, and the codicological and textual evidence together indicates the manuscript was produced in the middle of the thirteenth century by professionals, perhaps for a wealthy bourgeois client.

A life of Saint Francis begins B.N. f. fr. 2094, which contains other texts prominently featuring either hermits or *jongleurs*. Dating to the end of the thirteenth century, the manuscript was compiled for an audience interested in Franciscan teachings, possibly by a team of friars or Franciscan tertiaries. Francien and eastern dialectal traits have been recognized in some of the texts.

The study of these four manuscripts suggests a typological approach that might be applied in further research on the subpopulation I have defined. Three of the four respond to an audience's concern with the means of salvation: they offer a range of alternatives for the Christian facing the challenges of urban life. One could observe the Church's official sacraments (B.N. f. fr. 2162), rely on the Virgin or other saints for magical solutions to spiritual dilemmas (UCB 106), or follow the example of Saint Francis in asceticism and charity (B.N. f. fr. 2094). Significantly, the one among the four that does *not* emphasize the struggle for salvation is that which would have appealed to an audience of Crusaders (B.N. f. fr. 1374), who perhaps considered their own salvation to be guaranteed by their enterprise.

In the absence of generic distinctions, then, manuscripts can be characterized by reference to the audiences and the implied problems they address. Rather than collecting specific texts or types of texts, it appears that the scribe sought materials to serve a particular function and included whatever he found suitable to that function regardless of genre. I suspect that there are many more categories represented in the subpopulation than the ones illustrated by these four examples, and each new analysis will enhance our understanding of medieval modes of piety.

In addition to these glimpses of the vernacular literary system at work, the study offers a sample of pious works transmitted and received in conjunction with saints' lives. Certain traits common to these works support the interpretation of thirteenth-century French culture as heterogeneous.

First, in many cases, the texts bear little resemblance to the assumed sources, or the Latin analogues are later than the French versions. The *Bible* of Hermann de Valenciennes, many of the miracles and pious tales, the *Neuf joies Nostre Dame*, the *Ver de Couloigne*, the *Pater Noster* and *Eructavit* glosses, the works of Gautier de Coinci, the *Quinze signes du jugement*, and the *Passion* are examples of works reflecting indirect or otherwise tenuous relationships with their Latin analogues. The few works attributable to direct sources, such as the life of Alexis in B.N. f. fr. 2162, undergo significant transformations in the process of vernacularization. Certainly a great deal of research has yet to be done to identify sources and analogues for these works, particularly for collections such as the *Vie des Pères*. The evidence so far, however, shows fewer examples of source identification than of loose connections and dead ends. Although the aleatory nature of manuscript survival may well account for many missing antecedents, if vernacular works were systematically derived from monastic or other ecclesiastical sources, a greater proportion of them ought to be traceable.

Secondly, if pious vernacular literature were essentially derivative, we should expect ecclesiastical institutions to have played an important role in its dissemination, and the manuscript traditions would be likely to lend themselves to stemmatic interpretations. In fact, the witnesses reflect a high degree of autonomy on the part of the transmitters of these texts, challenging modern editors to account for variants, redactions, and versions created by the scribes' active intervention. In this way, the manuscript traditions of pious texts resemble those of secular genres, whether or not we even consider the question of orality. While critical editions have yet to be undertaken for a great many works, the open traditions of the *Bible* of Hermann de Valenciennes, the *Vie des Pères*, the *Eructavit* gloss, and the *Quinze signes du jugement* have all frustrated attempts at manuscript classification.

The complexity of manuscript traditions is consistent with the paucity of direct sources. Works that *are* translations and have some basis in ecclesiastical authority would undergo relatively little interference in the transmission process. Prose translations of Latin hagiographic collections offer an example.[1] Predominantly in verse, the pious works in these manuscripts, on the other hand, appear as the creative products of a living tradition: each transmitter intentionally reshapes the material to suit his own audience and situation, rendering the construction of a *stemma codicum* based on common error impracticable.

Finally, if the pursuit of sources and the difficulties of editing lead to frustration in interpreting pious vernacular works, their affinities with vernacular genres offer a fertile field for scholarly inquiry. Alison Elliott has established a link between vernacular epic and hagiography beginning with their common situation of oral performance. She compares the use of formulaic language in examples from the two genres (1977). The prologues of many of the works combined with saints' lives in the manuscripts address

---

[1] See Meyer 1906a, 378-458 ("Légendes en prose"). I would expect the corpus of pious vernacular prose works to be largely derivative, in contrast to the verse genres emphasized in this study.

listening audiences in the epic style.[2] Other prologues cite proverbs, just as many secular texts do (see p. 88 above). *Contes dévots* are frequently indistinguishable from *fabliaux*, and the similarity of some hagiographic narrative to the romance has long been acknowledged:

> The hagiographic poems of France . . . reflect not only the typical form of verse romances (rhymed octosyllabic couplets), but also, and above all, the prevailing novelistic tone of these romances. The elegant preoccupation with details, the desire to "interlace" the narrative gracefully, the desire to appear both new and recognizably traditional are shared by both genres. (Dembowski 1976, 119)[3]

It can be argued that learned authors *borrowed* from popular tradition to adapt their works for a particular audience. The codicological evidence, however, is more difficult to explain in terms of clerical origins.

The analysis of textual combinations and the material details of each manuscript, leading to an identification of the audience's interests, corroborate the evidence for separation between Latin and vernacular literary traditions reflected in the bibliometric study and in the various characteristics of pious texts composed in Old French verse. This is most evident in the case of B.N. f. fr. 2094, a collection appealing to an audience interested in Franciscan tradition and beliefs. I have suggested that it would be inconvenient as a reference for preachers addressing such an audience. Schmitt's study of Latin manuscripts determines that Franciscan exemplum collections are typically *more* systematic in their organization than the collections compiled by members of other orders (1977). Even though many tales are based on popular sources and were destined for oral propagation in the context of sermons to the faithful, the collections are often indexed and cross-indexed. B.N. f. fr. 2094, then, though demonstrably Franciscan in its combination of themes, represents a definite contrast to the Latin productions of the same religious order.

Scholars who treat saints' lives complain frequently that the genre has been neglected, at the same time apologizing for its literary inferiority and asserting its value to the historian of medieval culture. S. C. Aston, for example, contends that

---

[2] For example, "Or m'entendes *et* clerc *et* lai" ("D'une none ki fu trop biele"), "Plaist v*os* a escoter d'un sai*nt* home la geste" (life of Saint Alexis) in B.N. f. fr. 2162; "Seignor et dames, entendez tuit a moi" (life of Saint Eustace), "[Or] m'entendez baron, chevaliers et serjant" (*Venjance Nostre Seigneur*) in B.N. f. fr. 1374; "Oiez moi trestouz doucement" (*La Passion Ihesu Crist*) in UCB 106; "Oez trestuit *com*munema*nt*" (*Les quinze signes du jugement*), "Or escoutez bon crestien" (life of Saint Juliana) in B.N. f. fr. 2094.

[3] See also Clogan 1975.

> although the literary value of the individual lives is far from uniform, and although the great majority are probably of more importance as historical, linguistic, and sociological documents than as literature in the true sense, the corpus as a whole is worthy of systematic and comprehensive research. (1970, xxvii)

Peter Dembowski has attributed this neglect to the anticlerical and positivistic biases of early scholarship (1976, 118). Implicit in his remark is the assumption of clerical origins for pious vernacular works. In his comprehensive study of the medieval religious lyric, Patrick Diehl asserts that lay poets contributed the greater part of the Old French corpus, with the exception of Gautier de Coinci, who was a Benedictine monk (1984, 247). It is likely that lay poets and scribes are also responsible for most of the output of pious narrative works in Old French. If Dembowski is right, then, our forefathers have passed on an unfortunate prejudice based on an ill-founded assumption. Both the assumption and the bias are in need of revision.

The view of thirteenth-century French culture as heterogeneous compels us to acknowledge the relative independence of pious vernacular literature from ecclesiastical control. It was within the cultural and economic means of the devout lay public to produce literary works answering spiritual needs not addressed by the official institutions of the Church. The assumption that pious works are derivative implies that the public would have no spiritual life if not instructed by trained clerics. The immediate success of the mendicant orders, however, is only one indication of how pious this neglected population was. In his study of Franciscan culture, Fleming observes that "the curious notion that the Christian clergy are, at any historical moment, more 'religious' than the Christian laity has no basis in history even though it is an apparent axiom of medieval and renaissance studies" (1982, 8-9, n. 12). A great deal of evidence concerning the mentality of the lay public comes to light in the interpretation of pious vernacular literature.

Dembowski recommends opening new avenues for scholarship in the form of critical editions of vernacular saints' lives (1976, 129). I concur, with two added suggestions. First, codicological reception studies should be used to complement textual criticism in approaching Old French hagiography, and secondly, the generic field should be expanded to include the whole spectrum of pious works enjoyed by the medieval laity.

By providing access to pious vernacular texts without depending on their rather tenuous relations with the contemporary official religious culture, the study of entire codices offers a context for the interpretation of pious works as the public experienced them. If we assume the essential heterogeneity of culture indicated by the bibliometric, literary, and codicological findings of this study, then such a means of approaching the texts is needed. My analysis of examples has shown how we might do much more than to characterize a collection of texts as "pious," as manuscript descriptions so often do. Diehl remarks in the introduction to his work on the lyric:

> "Religion," it seems, covers a multitude—of things, of peoples, of social classes, of institutional forms, of historic periods, and of attitudes and tastes and individual quirks—and it is necessary to keep this multitude in view when discussing it. (1984, 56)

Focusing on an individual manuscript, we are able to differentiate among the concerns of specific publics.

While this investigation has emphasized literary interpretations of the collections, language studies also provide valuable evidence of textual production, adaptation, and transmission. Jean Rychner has recently published such a study on Bern Burgerbibliothek 354, which contains a collection of *fabliaux*, showing how two copyists collaborated in adapting texts to suit

> l'amateur peut-être pas tellement cultivé auquel ils destinent leur recueil. Sous cet aspect, leur travail, bien plus projectif que rétrospectif, prend tout sa signification dans l'histoire des conditions matérielles où s'est produite la rencontre indispensable de la littérature et de ses publics. (1984, 218)

The linguistic adaptations made by the scribes in this compilation enable Rychner to draw inferences concerning the audience for which they intended it.

Thus, the less useful a manuscript tradition is in reconstructing the archetype, the more useful it is likely to be for reception history. Subtle variations of emphasis appear in the comparison of manuscripts containing versions of the same work. For example, the *Vie des Pères* of B.N. f. fr. 2094 reflects concerns quite distinct from that of UCB 106. The detailed investigation of manuscript traditions from a "projective," as well as a "retrospective," perspective will reflect the multiplicity of audiences in the history of a work's reception. Rychner's discussion of the *fabliaux*, *Variantes, remaniemants, dégradations* (1960), is a model for this kind of study, which might be undertaken for any vernacular work surviving in more than one manuscript.

In addition to the analysis of individual codices and the extended investigation of manuscript traditions, bibliometric studies comparing various corpora of manuscripts will help to illuminate the elusive profile of the audience for medieval literature. The sample population used as a basis for this study, for example, might be compared with manuscripts of earlier and later periods containing saints' lives in verse, or with other manuscripts of the thirteenth century containing any texts in Old French verse: the first would yield a diachronic survey of the reception of hagiography, and the second would focus on the literary system of a limited period. The possiblilties for such comparisons are limited only by the scholar's imagination and by the scope of his or her concerns.

Without denying the need for textual criticism and research concerning origins, the study of works in their manuscript context displaces the issues of derivation and influence between cultures in favor of an expanded view of the vernacular tradition. I have remarked that pious vernacular literature suffers neglect because of certain biases and assumptions of early scholarship. Moreover, literary historians observing traditional category boundaries pass over great numbers of works simply because they do not belong to any established classification. As a member of the historical family of "biography," the saint's life has received more attention than, say, the "discursive gloss" (e.g., *Pater Noster* in B.N. f. fr. 2162, *Eructavit* in B.N. f. fr. 2094). The codicological approach, without depending on generic notions, offers access to works that would otherwise lack context. As most are anonymous, they have not been included in studies of authors' *oeuvres*. Since they do not fall under obvious generic headings, they have been excluded from genre studies and from historical surveys. Editors' literary assessments of these works are limited by an avoidance of the genre question, which forces a reliance on source and influence research to provide context for discussion. The manuscript context provides a valuable alternative.

Bibliography

ABBREVIATIONS

GRLMA: *Grundriß der romanischen Literaturen des Mittelalters*
GRP: *Grundriß der romanische Philologie*
HLF: *Histoire Littéraire de la France*
PL: *Patrologia Latina* (Migne)
CCSL: *Corpus Christianorum Series Latina*

Adler, Alfred. 1974. *Episches Frage- und Antwortspiel in der* Geste de Nanteuil. Analecta romanica 36. Frankfurt: Klostermann.
____. 1975. *Epische Spekulanten*. Munich: Wilhelm Fink.
Aebischer, Paul. 1963. *Le Mystère d'Adam* (*Ordo representationis Ade*), *texte complète du MS de Tours publié avec une introduction, des notes et un glossaire*. Geneva and Paris: Droz and Minard.
Ahsmann, Hubertus Petrus Johannes Maria. 1930. *Le culte de la Sainte Vierge et la littérature française profane du moyen âge*. Paris: Picard.
Alexander, J. J. G. and M. T. Gibson, eds. 1976. *Medieval learning and literature: Essays presented to Richard William Hunt*. Oxford: Clarendon Press.
Allen, Louis. 1925. De l'hermite et del jongleour, *a thirteenth century "conte pieux."* Paris: Solsona.
Aston, S. C. 1970. The saint in medieval literature. *Modern Language Review* 65 (October): xxv-xlii.
Atiya, Aziz S. 1962a. *Crusade, commerce and culture*. Bloomington, Ind., and London: Indiana University Press and Oxford University Press.
____. 1962b. *The crusade: Historiography and bibliography*. Bloomington, Ind.: Indiana University Press.
Auvray, Lucien, and René Poupardin. 1921. *Catalogue des manuscrits de la Collection Baluze*. Paris: E. Leroux.
Baker, Alfred T. 1924. Saints' lives written in Anglo-French: Their historical, social, and literary importance. *Transactions of the Royal Society of the United Kingdom* 4: 119-56.

Baratier, Edouard, Maurice Agulhon, André Bourde, Max Escalon de Fonton, Pierre Guiral, Jean Remy Palanque, Louis Pierrein, Félix Reynaud, and Michel Vovelle. 1969. *Histoire de la Provence*. Toulouse: Privat.

Bates, Robert Chapman, ed. 1932. Le conte du barril: *Poème du XII*ᵉ *siècle par Jean de la Chapelle de Blois*. New Haven: Yale University Press.

Bateson, Gregory. 1966. Information, codification, and metacommunication. In Smith 1966, 412-26.

Bayot, Alphonse, ed. [1929]. *Le poème moral*. Brussels: Langue et littérature français de Belgique.

Becquet, Jean. 1962. L'érémitisme clérical et laïc dans l'ouest de la France. In Settimana internazionale di studio 1962, 182-211.

Bekker, Immanuel, ed. 1829. *Der Roman von Fierabras*. Berlin: G. Reimer.

Benton, John F. 1961. The court of Champagne as a literary center. *Speculum* 36: 551-91.

Bernheimer, Richard. 1970. *Wild men in the Middle Ages: A study in art, sentiment, and demonology*. New York: Octagon Books.

Beyer, Jürgen, ed. 1968. *La littérature didactique, allegorique, et satirique*. GRLMA 6:1 (Partie historique). Heidelberg: Carl Winter/Universitätsverlag.

―――, and Franz Koppe, eds. 1970. *La littérature didactique, allegorique, et satirique*. GRLMA 6:2 (Partie documentaire). Heidelberg: Carl Winter/Universitätsverlag.

Bogdanow, Fanni. 1960. The relationship of the Portuguese *Josep Abarimatia* to the extant French manuscripts of the *Estoire del Saint Graal*. *Zeitschrift für romanische Philologie* 76: 343-75.

―――. 1978. La trilogie de Robert de Boron: Le *Perceval en prose*. In Frappier and Grimm 1978, 513-35.

Bonnard, Jean. [1884] 1967. *Les traductions de la Bible en vers français au Moyen Age*. Geneva: Slatkine Reprints.

Bornäs, Göran, ed. 1968. *Trois contes français du XIII*ᵉ *siècle, tirés du recueil des* Vie des Pères. Etudes romanes de Lund 15. Lund: Gleerup.

Bowen, Willis H. 1946. The present status of studies in saints' lives in Old French verse. *Symposium* 1, no. 2: 82-86.

Boyle, Leonard E. 1984. *Medieval Latin paleography: A bibliographical introduction*. Toronto Medieval Bibliographies 8. Toronto: University of Toronto Press.

Brandes, Herman. 1885. *Visio s. Pauli, ein Beitrag zur Visionsliteratur*. Halle: Niemeyer.

Branner, Robert. 1977. *Manuscript painting in Paris during the reign of Saint Louis: A study of styles*. Berkeley: University of California Press.

Brayer, Edith. 1970. La littérature religieuse (liturgie et Bible). In Beyer and Koppe 1970, 19-80.

Bruce, James Douglas. 1923. *The evolution of Arthurian romance from the beginnings down to the year 1300*. Göttingen: Vandenhoeck and Ruprecht.
Buffum, Douglas Labaree. 1904. Le roman de la violette: *A study of the manuscripts and the original dialect*. Baltimore: J.H. Furst Company.
____. 1928. Le roman de la violette *ou de Gerart de Nevers par Gerbert de Montreuil*. Paris: Champion.
Cazelles, Brigitte. 1978. *La faiblesse chez Gautier de Coinci*. Stanford French and Italian Studies, 14. Saratoga, Calif.: Anima Libri.
____. 1982. *Le corps de sainteté*. Geneva: Droz.
Cazelles, Brigitte, and Phillis Johnson. 1979. *"Le vain siecle guerpir": A literary approach to sainthood through Old French hagiography of the twelfth century*. Chapel Hill, N.C.: University of North Carolina Department of Romance Languages.
Centro italiano di studi sull'alto medioevo. 1963. *La Bibbia nell'alto medioevo*. Settimana di studio del Centro italiano di studi sull'alto medioevo 10. Spoleto: Presso La Sede del centro.
Chaurand, Jacques. 1971. Fou, *dixième conte de la* Vie des Pères. Geneva: Droz.
Chaytor, Henry J. 1945. *From script to print*. Cambridge: Cambridge University Press.
Clogan, Paul Maurice, ed. 1975. *Medieval hagiography and romance*. Medievalia et humanistica, n.s. 6. Cambridge, London, and New York: Cambridge University Press.
____, ed. 1976. *Medieval poetics*. Medievalia et Humanistica, n.s. 7. Cambridge, London, and New York: Cambridge University Press.
Colloque internationale d'histoire monastique. 1979. *Saint-Thierry, une abbaye du VIe au XXe siècle*. Reims and Saint-Thierry: Association des amis de l'abbaye de Saint-Thierry.
Comité de publication des mélanges René Louis. 1982. *La chanson de geste et le mythe carolingien: Mélanges René Louis*. Mayenne, France: En depot au Musée regional.
Cormeau, Christophe, ed. 1979. *Deutsche Literatur im Mittelalter — Kontakte und Perspektiven: Hugo Kuhn zum Gedenken*. Stuttgart: Metzler.
Dain, Alphonse. [1949] 1964. *Les manuscrits*. Paris: Belles-Lettres.
Delaruelle, Etienne. 1962. Les ermites et la spiritualité populaire. In Settimana internazionale di studio 1962, 212-47.
Delaville LeRoulx, Joseph Marie Antoine. 1894. *Cartulaire général de l'Order des Hospitaliers de S. Jean de Jérusalem*. Vol. 3 (1261-1300). Paris: E. Leroux.
Delehaye, Hippolyte. 1962. *The legends of the saints*. New York: Fordham University Press.
Delisle, Léopold. 1868. *Le cabinet des manuscrits de la Bibliothèque Impériale*. Paris: Imprimerie impériale.

Del Monte, Alberto. 1966. Volgarizzamento senese delle "Vie des Pères." In *Mélanges Italo Siciliano* 1: 329-83. Florence: Biblioteca dell' «Archivum Romanicum».

Dembowski, Peter. 1976. Literary problems of hagiography in Old French. In Clogan 1976: 117-30.

Denholm-Young, Noël. 1954. *Handwriting in England and Wales*. Cardiff: University of Wales Press.

Diehl, Patrick S. 1984. *The medieval European religious lyric: An Ars poetica*. Berkeley, Los Angeles, and London: University of California Press.

Diringer, David. 1953. *The hand-produced book*. London and New York: Hutchinson's Scientific and Technical Publications.

Dolbeau, F. 1979. Typologie et formation des collections hagiographiques d'après les recueils de l'abbaye de Saint-Thierry. In Colloque internationale d'histoire monastique 1979, 159-82.

Dorst, John. 1983. Neck-riddle as a dialogue of genres: Applying Bakhtin's genre theory. *Journal of American Folklore* 96: 413-33.

Ducrot-Granderye, Arlette P. 1932. Etudes sur les Miracles Nostre Dame *de Gautier de Coinci*. Annales Academiae scientiarum fennicae, ser. B, no. 25. Helsinki: Suomalainen Tiedeakatemia.

Duval, Auméry. [1838] 1895. La vie des anciens pères. *HLF* 19: 857-60.

Ebel, Uda. 1965. *Das altromanische Mirakel*. Heidelberg: Carl Winter.

Elliott, Alison Goddard. 1977. Saints and heroes: Hagiography and epic. Ph.D. diss., University of California, Berkeley.

―――. 1980. The double genesis of *Girart de Vienne*. *Olifant* 8, no. 2 (Winter): 130-60.

―――, ed. 1983. *The* Vie de Saint Alexis *in the twelfth and thirteenth centuries: An edition and commentary*. North Carolina Studies in the Romance Languages and Literatures 221. Chapel Hill, N.C.: University of North Carolina Department of Romance Languages.

―――. 1987. *Roads to paradise: Reading the lives of the early saints*. Hanover, N.H., and London: University Press of New England.

Erdmann, Carl. 1977. *The origin of the idea of the crusade*. Princeton, N.J.: Princeton University Press.

Faral, Edmond, and Julia Bastin, eds. 1959. *Oeuvres complètes de Rutebeuf*. Paris: Picard.

Favati, Guido. 1967. Le *Cligès* de Chrétien de Troyes dans les éditions critiques et dans les manuscrits. *Cahiers de civilisation médiéval* 10: 385-407.

Feilitzen, Hugo von. 1883. *Li ver del Juïse*. Uppsala, Sweden: Akademiska Boktryckeriet, Edv. Berling.

Fleming, John V. 1977. *An introduction to the Franciscan literature of the Middle Ages*. Chicago: Franciscan Herald Press.

———. 1982. *From Bonaventure to Bellini: An essay in Franciscan exegesis*. Princeton, N.J.: Princeton University Press.

Foerster, Wendelin. 1884. *Chrétien von Troyes: Sämtliche Werke*. Vol. 1, Cligès. Halle: M. Niemeyer.

Folda, Jaroslav. 1976. *Crusader manuscript illumination at Saint-Jean d'Acre, 1275-1291*. Princeton, N.J.: Princeton University Press.

Ford, Alvin E. 1984. *La vengeance de Nostre-Seigneur: The Old and Middle French prose versions; The version of Japheth*. Toronto: Pontifical Institute of Medieval Studies.

Ford, J. D. M. 1931. The saint's life in the vernacular literature of the Middle Ages. *Catholic Historical Review* 17: 268-77.

Foster, Frances A., ed. 1916. *The Northern Passion: French text, variants and fragments, etc.* Early English Text Society, orig. ser., no. 147. London: Oxford University Press.

Fourrier, Anthime. 1960. *Le courant réaliste dans le roman courtois en France au moyen-age*. Paris: A. G. Nizet.

Fowler, Alastair. 1982. *Kinds of literature: An introduction to the theory of genres and modes*. Cambridge, Mass.: Harvard University Press.

Francis, Elizabeth A., ed. 1932. *Wace: La vie de Sainte Marguerite*. Paris: Champion.

Frank, István. 1953-57. *Répertoire métrique de la poésie des troubadours*. Paris: Champion.

Frappier, Jean. 1955. *Les chansons de geste du cycle de Guillaume d'Orange*. Vol. 1. Paris: Société d'édition d'enseignement.

———. 1968a. *Chrétien de Troyes*. Paris: Hatier.

———. 1968b. *Etude sur la* Mort le roi Artu, *roman du XIIIe siècle*. 2d ed. Geneva: Droz.

———. 1978a. Le cycle de la vulgate (*Lancelot en prose* et *Lancelot-Graal*). In Frappier and Grimm 1978, 536-89.

———. 1978b. La naissance et l'évolution du roman arthurien en prose. In Frappier and Grimm 1978, 503-12.

Frappier, Jean, and Reinhold R. Grimm, eds. 1978. *Le roman jusqu'à la fin du XIIIe siècle (Partie historique)*. GRLMA 4:1. Heidelberg: Carl Winter.

Geertz, Clifford. 1973. *The interpretation of cultures*. New York: Basic Books.

Gerould, Gordon Hall. 1904. Forerunners, congeners, and derivatives of the Eustace legend. *Publications of the Modern Language Association* 19: 335-448.

Grass, Karl. 1891. *Das Adamspiel: Anglo-normannisches Gedicht des XII Jahrhunderts, mit einem Anhang "Die fünfzein Zeichen des jüngsten Gerichts."* Halle: Niemeyer.

Grimm, Reinhold R., ed. 1984. *Le roman jusqu'à la fin du XIIIe siècle* (*Partie documentaire*). GRLMA 4:2. Heidelberg: Carl Winter.

Gröber, Gustav. 1902. *Grundriß der romanischen Philologie* 2:1. Strassburg: Karl J. Trübner.

Gryting, Loyal A. T., ed. 1952. *The oldest version of the twelfth-century poem* La Venjance Nostre Seigneur. Ann Arbor, Mich.: University of Michigan Press.

Guessard, F., and L. Larchey, eds. 1860. Parise la duchesse, *chanson de geste*. Paris: Vieweg.

Guiette, Robert. 1927. *La légende de la sacristine*. Paris: Champion.

———. 1953. D'une nonain ki issi de son abbeïe. *Romanica gandensia* 1: 7-22.

Guigard, Joannis. 1890. *Nouvel armorial du bibliophile*: *Guide de l'amateur des livres armoriés*. Paris: Emile Rondeau.

Gumbrecht, Hans Ulrich. 1979. Faszinationstyp Hagiographie: Ein historisches Experiment zur Gattungstheorie. In Cormeau 1979, 39-84.

———. 1981. Strangeness as a requirement for topicality: Medieval literature and reception theory. *L'esprit créateur*, vol. 21, no. 2: 5-12.

Habig, Marion A. 1979. *St. Francis of Assisi, writings and early biographies*: *English omnibus of sources for the life of Saint Francis*. 2d ed. London: Society for Promoting Christian Knowledge.

Haidu, Peter, ed. 1974. *Approaches to medieval romance*. Yale French Studies 51. New Haven: Yale University Press.

Hartman, Richard, and Dorothy L. Schrader. 1982. Parise la duchesse: The editorial itinerary of a unique manuscript. *Manuscripta* 26: 177-85.

Heist, William W. 1952. *The fifteen signs before doomsday*. East Lansing, Mich.: Michigan State College Press.

Hilka, Alfons, ed. 1933. *Aimon von Varennes*: Florimont, *ein altfranzösischer Abenteuerroman*. Gesellschaft für romanische Literatur 48. Göttingen: Max Niemeyer.

Holtz, Louis. 1977. La typologie des MSS grammaticaux latins. *Revue d'histoire des textes* 7: 247-69.

Huot, Sylvia. 1987. *From song to book*: *The poetics of writing in Old French lyric and lyrical narrative poetry*. Ithaca, N.Y., and London: Cornell University Press.

Institut de Recherche et d'Histoire des Textes. 1977. *Guide pour l'élaboration d'une notice de manuscrit*. Série informatique et Documentation textuelle: bibliographies, colloques, travaux préparatoires. Paris: Centre Nationale de la Recherche Scientifique.

Iriarte, Lazaro. 1983. *Franciscan history*: *The three orders of St. Francis of Assisi*. Chicago: Franciscan Herald Press.

Jauss, Hans Robert. 1968. Entstehung und Strukturwandel der allegorischen Dichtung. In Beyer 1968: 146-244.

———. 1970. Genèse et structure des genres allégoriques. In Beyer and Koppe 1970, 203-80.

———. 1982. *Toward an aesthetic of reception*. Minneapolis: University of Minnesota Press.

Jenkins, T. Atkinson. 1909. Eructavit: *An Old French metrical paraphrase of Psalm XLIV published from all the known manuscripts and attributed to Adam de Perseigne*. Gesellschaft für romanische Literatur 20. Dresden: Max Niemeyer.

Jolles, André. 1956. *Einfache Formen: Legende, Sage, Mythe, Rätsel, Spiel, Kasus, Morabile, Märchen, Witz*. 2d ed. Tübingen: Niemeyer.

Joly, Aristide, ed. 1879. La vie de Sainte Marguerite, *poème inédit de Wace*. Paris: Vieweg.

Jubinal, Achille, ed. 1839-42. *Nouveau recueil de contes dits fabliaux et autres pièces inédits des XIIIe, XIVe, et XVe siècles, pour faire suite aux collections de Legrand d'Aussy, Barbazan et Méon*. 2 vols. Paris: E. Pannier (vol. 1); Challamel (vol. 2).

———, ed. 1874. *Oeuvres complètes de Rutebeuf: Trouvère due XIIIe siècle*. 2d ed. 3 vols. Paris: Paul Daffis.

Karl, Louis. 1913. La légende de Saint Jehan Paulus. *Revue des langues romanes* 56: 425-45.

———. 1928. Notice sur la *Vision de Saint Basile* dans la *Légende de Saint Jehan Paulus*. *Revue des langues romanes* 65: 304-23.

Kastner, L-E. 1906. Les versions françaises inédits de la *Descente de saint Paul en enfer*: Version anonyme du manuscrit français 2094 de la Bibliothèque Nationale. *Revue des langues romanes* 49: 49-62.

Keller, H., ed. 1840. *Zwei Fabliaux einer Neuenburger Handschrift*. Stuttgart: Ebner & Seubert.

Kelly, Douglas. 1976. *Chrétien de Troyes: An analytic bibliography*. London: Grant and Cutler.

King, E. J. 1931. *The Knights Hospitallers in the Holy Land*. London: Methuen.

———. 1934. *The rule statutes and customs of the Hospitallers, 1099-1310*. London: Methuen.

Kirchner, J. 1966. *Scriptura gothica libraria*. Munich: R. Oldenbourg.

Kleineidam, Hartmut, ed. 1968. *Li ver de Couloigne*; *Du bon ange et du mauves: Un ensaingnement*. Beiträge zur romanischen Philologie des Mittelalters 3. Munich: Max Hueber Verlag.

Kleinhenz, Christopher, ed. 1976. *Medieval manuscripts and textual criticism*. University of North Carolina Studies in Language and Literature Symposia 4. Chapel Hill, N.C.: University of North Carolina Department of Romance Languages.

Koenig, Frédéric. 1937. Le Comte de Poitiers, *roman du treizième siècle*. Paris: E. Droz.

———, ed. 1955-70. *Les Miracles de Nostre Dame par Gautier de Coinci.* 4 vols. Geneva and Lille: Droz and Giard.

Kraemer, Erik von. 1966. *Les quinze signes du jugement dernier; Poème anonyme de la fin du XIIe ou du XIIIe siècle.* Commentationes humanarum litterarum, vol. 38, no. 2. Helsinki: Societas scientiarum fennica.

Kunstmann, Pierre, ed. 1981. *Treize miracles de Notre Dame tirés du Ms. B.N. fr. 2094.* University of Ottawa Medieval Texts and Studies 6. Ottawa: University of Ottawa.

Lacy, Norris J. 1970. Form and pattern in *Cligès. Orbis litterarum* 25: 307-13.

———, ed. 1972. *Medieval French Miscellany.* University of Kansas Humanistic Studies 42. Lawrence, Kan.: University of Kansas Publications.

Lacy, Norris J., Keith Busby, and Douglas Kelly, eds. 1987. *The legacy of Chrétien de Troyes.* Vol. 1. Amsterdam: Rodopi.

Lagorio, Valerie M. 1970. Pan-Brittonic hagiography and the Arthurian Grail cycle. *Traditio* 26: 29-61.

Långfors, Arthur. 1910. La vie de Sainte Catherine par le peintre Estienne Lanquelier. *Romania* 39: 54-60.

———. 1912. Les traductions et paraphrases du *Pater* en vers français du moyen âge. *Neuphilologische Mitteilungen* 14: 35-45.

———. 1917. *Les incipit des poèmes français antérieurs au XVIe siècle; repertoire bibliographique.* Paris: Champion.

Lazar, Moshé. 1972. Satan and Notre Dame: Characters in a popular scenario. In Lacy 1972, 1-14.

Le Clerc, Victor. [1856] 1895. Poésies morales. *HLF* 23: 235-65.

Leclercq, Jean. 1963. L'écriture sainte dans l'hagiographie monastique du haut moyen âge. In Centro italiano di studi sull'alto medioevo 1963, 103-28.

Le Coultre, Jean Jules. 1884. *Contes dévots tirés de la Vie des anciens pères.* Neuchatel: J. Attinger.

Lecoy, Félix. 1955. *Le chevalier au barisel: Conte pieux du XIIIe siècle.* Paris: Champion.

Le Goff, Jacques. 1964. *La civilisation de l'occident médiévale.* Paris: Arthaud.

Legrand d'Aussy, Pierre Jean-Baptiste. [1779] 1829. *Fabliaux ou contes, fables et romans du XIIe au XIIIe siècle.* Vol. 5. Paris: J. Renouard.

Lewis, C. S. [1964] 1967. *The discarded image.* London and New York: Cambridge University Press.

Loomis, C. Grant. 1933. King Arthur and the saints. *Speculum* 8: 478-82.

———. 1948. *White magic: An Introduction to the folklore of Christian legend.* Cambridge, Mass.: Mediaeval Academy of America.

Louis, René. 1947. *De l'histoire à la légende: Girart, Comte de Vienne.* Auxerre: Aux bureaux de l'imprimerie moderne.

Luzarche, Victor. 1854. *Adam, drame anglo-normande du XIIe siècle, publié pour la première fois d'après un manuscrit de la Bibliothèque de Tours.* Tours: Imprimerie de J. Bouserez.

McKibben, G. F. 1907. *The* Eructavit, *an old French poem.* Baltimore: J. H. Furst Company.

McNeal, Edgar H., and Robert Lee Wolff. 1969. The Fourth Crusade. In Wolff and Hazard 1969, 153-86.

Maddox, D. L. 1973. Critical trends and recent work on the *Cligès* of Chrétien de Troyes. *Neuphilologische Mitteilungen* 74: 730-45.

Mantou, Reine, ed. 1966. Les quinze signes du jugement dernier: *Poème du XIIe siècle: Edition critique.* Memoires et Publications 80. Hainaut: Société des sciences, des arts et des lettres.

———. 1967. Le thème des *Quinze signes du jugement dernier* dans la tradition française. *Revue belge de philologie et d'histoire* 45: 827-42.

Margolin, Uri. 1973. The concept of genre as historical category. Ph.D. diss., Cornell University, Ithaca, N.Y.

Martonne, G. F. de, ed. [1834] 1969. *Li romans de Parise la duchesse.* Geneva: Slatkine Reprints.

Matile, M., ed. 1839. Du jardenier qui donnoit la moitié de son gaing pour Dieu. *Revue suisse* 2: 297.

Medvedev, P. N., and M. M. Bakhtin. 1978. *The formal method in literary scholarship: A critical introduction to sociological poetics.* Baltimore: Johns Hopkins University Press.

Mehne, Friedrich. 1900. Inhalt und Quellen der Bible des Herman de Valenciennes nach der Maihinger Handschrift und dem ms. B.N. fr. 2162. Ph.D. diss., Friedrichs-Universität, Halle-Wittenberg, Germany.

Méon, Dominique. 1823. *Nouveau recueil de fabliaux et contes inédits des poètes français des XIIe, XIIIe, XIVe, et XVe siècles.* Paris: Chasseriau.

Meyer, Paul. 1891. Notices sur quelques manuscrits français de la bibliothèque Phillipps à Cheltenham. *Notices et extraits des manuscrits de la Bibliothèque Nationale et autres bibliothèques*, vol. 34, no. 1: 155-67.

———. 1904. Notice du MS Med. Pal. 141 de la Laurentienne (Vies des saints). *Romania* 33: 1-49.

———. 1905. Fragments de manuscrits français. *Romania* 34: 444-45.

———. 1906a. Légendes hagiographiques en français. *HLF* 33: 328-458.

———. 1906b. Versions en vers et en prose des *Vies des Pères*. *HLF* 33: 254-328.

Micha, Alexandre. 1953. La composition de la vulgate du Merlin. *Romania* 74: 200-20.

———, ed. 1957. *Cligès.* Paris: Champion.

____. 1958. Les manuscrits du *Merlin en prose* de Robert de Boron. *Romania* 79: 78-94.
____. 1960. Les manuscrits du *Lancelot en prose*. I, *Romania* 81: 145-87.
____. 1963. Les manuscrits du *Lancelot en prose*. II, *Romania* 84: 28-60; III, 451-77.
____. 1964. La tradition manuscrit du *Lancelot en prose*. *Romania* 85: 293-318; 478-517.
____. [1939] 1966. *La tradition manuscrit des romans de Chrétien de Troyes*. Paris and Geneva: Droz.
____. 1978. L'estoire de Merlin. In Frappier and Grimm 1978, 590-600.
Michel, Francisque, ed. 1834. *Roman de la violette, ou de Gérard de Nevers*. Paris: Silvestre.
Michi, Christine. 1983. Edition du conte 38 de la *Vie des pères*: "De la nonain qui menja la fleur du chol ou li deables s'estoit mis, si qu'ele devint hors du sens." *Médiévales* 3: 111-35.
Migne, Jacques Paul, ed. 1844-1902. *Patrologiae cursus completus*. Paris: Migne.
Morawski, Jean. 1921. L'auteur de la second *Vie des Pères*. *Romania* 47: 381-82.
____. 1935. Mélanges de littérature pieuse (Parts 1 and 2). *Romania* 59: 165-209, 316-50.
____. 1938. Mélanges de littérature pieuse (Part 3). *Romania* 64: 454-88.
____. 1947. *La vie de Saint Jehan Paulus*: Origine et évolution d'une légende médiévale. *Lettres romanes* 1: 9-36.
Morawski, Joseph. 1925. *Proverbes français antérieurs au XVe siècle*. Paris: Champion.
Mustanoja, Tauno F., ed. 1952. Les neuf joies Nostre Dame: *A poem attributed to Rutebeuf*. Annales Academiae scientiarum fennicae, ser. B, vol. 73, no. 4. Helsinki: Suomalaisen Tiedeakatemian.
Naetebus, Gotthold. 1891. *Die nicht-lyrischen Strophenformen des Altfranzösischen*. Leipzig: S. Hirzel.
Navarro, Tomás. 1956. *Métrica espanola: Reseña histórica y descriptiva*. Syracuse, N.Y.: Syracuse University Press.
Ott, Andreas C. 1912. Das altfranzösische Eustachiusleben (L'Estoire d'Eustachius) der Pariser Handschrift Nat.-Bibl. fr. 1374. *Romanische Forschungen* 32: 481-607.
Owen, Douglas David Ross. 1958. *The vision of St. Paul*: The French and Provençal versions and their sources. *Romance Philology* 12: 33-51.
____. 1971. *The vision of hell: Infernal journeys in medieval French literature*. New York: Barnes and Noble.
Palustre, Léon. 1877. *Adam, mystère du XIIe siècle, texte critique accompagné d'une traduction*. Paris: Dumoulin.
Paris, Gaston. 1903. Le cycle de la gageure. *Romania* 32: 480-551.

Paris, Gaston, and Ulysse Robert, eds. 1876-93. *Miracles de Notre-Dame par personnages*. 8 vols. Paris: Société des anciens textes français.

Paris, Paulin. 1840. *Les manuscrits français de la Bibliothèque du Roi*. Vol. 3. Paris: Techener.

———. 1852. Parise la duchesse. *HLF* 22: 659-67.

Parkes, M. B. 1976. The influence of the concept of ordinatio and compilatio on the development of the book. In Alexander and Gibson 1976, 115-41.

Payen, Jean-Charles. 1967. *Le motif du repentir dans la littérature française médiévale*. Geneva: Droz.

Perry, Ben E. 1967. *The ancient romances: A literary-historical account of their origins*. Sather Classical Lectures 37. Berkeley and Los Angeles: University of California Press.

Petersen, Holger. 1924. Deux versions de la vie de Saint Eustache. *Mémoires de la Société néophilologique de Helsingfors* 7: 51-240.

———. 1925. Les origines de la légende de Saint Eustache. *Neuphilologische Mitteilungen* 26: 65-86.

Petit de Julleville, Louis. 1896-99. *Histoire de la langue et de la littérature française des origines à 1900*. 8 vols. Paris: A. Colin.

Philippart, Guy. 1977. *Les légendiers latins et autres manuscrits hagiographiques*. Typologie des sources du Moyen Age occidental, fasc. 24-25. Turnhout, Belgium: Brepols.

Pickens, Rupert T. 1975. *Estoire, lai* and romance: Chrétien's *Erec et Enide* and *Cligès. Romanic Review* 66: 247-62.

Plenzat, Karl. 1926. *Die Theophilus Legende*. Germanische Studien 43. Berlin: Emil Ebering.

Plouzeau, May. 1986. Parise la duchesse (*chanson de geste du XIIIe siècle*): *Edition et commentaires*. 2 vols. Publications du C.U.E.R.M.A., Senefiance 17 and 18. Aix-en-Provence: Université de Provence.

Pope, Mildred K. 1952. *From Latin to Modern French with especial consideration of Anglo-Norman*. Manchester: Manchester University Press.

Prawer, Joshua. 1972a. *The Latin kingdom of Jerusalem*. London: Weidenfeld and Nicolson.

———. 1972b. *The world of the Crusaders*. New York: Quadrangle Books.

Riley-Smith, Jonathan. 1967. *The Knights of St. John in Jerusalem and Cyprus c. 1050-1310*. London: Macmillan.

Riquer, Martín de. [1957]. *Les chansons de geste françaises*. 2d ed. Paris: Librairie Nizet.

Ross, D. J. A. 1952. Methods of book production in a XIVth century French miscellany. *Scriptorium* 6: 63-75.

Royer, George M., ed. 1970. Edition critique des contes 51 et 52 extraits des Vies des Pères. Master's thesis, University of Ottawa.

Rychner, Jean. 1960. *Contribution à l'étude des fabliaux: Variantes, remaniements, dégradations.* Geneva: Droz.

———. 1984. Deux copistes au travail: Pour un étude textuelle globale du manuscrit 354 de la Bibliothèque de la Bourgeoisie de Berne. In Short 1984, 187-218.

Schmitt, Jean-Claude. 1977. Recueils franciscains d'exempla et perfectionnement des techniques intellectuelles du XIIIe au XVe siècle. *Bibliothèque de l'Ecole des Chartes* 135: 5-22.

Schultz-Gora, O. 1919. *Zwei altfranzösiche Dichtungen.* Halle: Niemeyer.

Schwan, Edouard. 1884. La vie des anciens pères. *Romania* 13: 233-63.

Segre, Cesare. 1970. Les formes et traditions didactiques. In Beyer and Koppe 1970, 97-201.

Settimana internazionale di studio, 2d, passo della Mendola. 1962. *L'eremitismo in occidente nei secoli XI e XII.* Miscellania del Centro di studi medioevali 4. Milan: Vita e pensiero.

Setton, Kenneth M. 1969. *A History of the Crusades.* Madison, Milwaukee, and London: University of Wisconsin Press.

Short, Ian, ed. 1984. *Medieval French textual studies in memory of T. B. W. Reid.* London: Anglo-Norman Text Society.

Short, Ian, and Brian Woledge. 1981. Liste provisoire de manuscrits du XIIe siècle contenant des textes en langue française. *Romania* 102: 1-17.

Smeets, John Robert. 1968. Les traductions, adaptations et paraphrases de la Bible en vers. In Beyer 1968, 48-57.

———. 1970. Les traductions, adaptations et paraphrases de la Bible en vers. In Beyer and Koppe 1970, 81-96.

Smith, Alfred G., ed. 1966. *Communication and culture: Readings in the codes of human interaction.* New York: Holt, Rinehart, & Winston.

Société Rencesvals, 4e congrès international, 1969. *Actes et mémoires.* Studia romanica 14. Heidelberg: Carl Winter.

Sommer, H. O., ed. 1908-09. *The vulgate version of the Arthurian romances.* Washington, D.C.: Carnegie Institution.

Sonet, Jean. 1949. *Recherches sur la tradition manuscrite latine et française. Le roman de Barlaam et Josaphat*, Vol. 1. Paris: Vrin.

Spangenberg, Peter-Michael. [1980]. Das altfranzösische Mirakel — ein Modus der Wirklichkeitserfahrung im späten Mittelalter. Unpublished paper.

———. [1982]. Transformations du savoir et ambivalences fonctionelles: Aspects de la fascination hagiographique chez Gautier de Coinci. Unpublished paper.

———. 1987. *Maria ist immer und überall: Die Alltagswelten des spätmittelalterlichen Mirakels.* Frankfurt: Suhrkamp.

Speer, Mary B. 1980. Wrestling with change: Old French textual criticism and *mouvance*. *Olifant* 7, no. 4 (Summer): 311-26.

Spiele, Ina. 1975. *Li romanz de Dieu et de sa mere*. Leyde: Presse universitaire de Leyde.

Stebbins, Charles E., ed. 1974. *A critical edition of the 13th and 14th centuries Old French poem versions of the* Vie de Saint Alexis. Beihefte zur Zeitschrift für romanische Philologie 145. Tübingen: Max Niemeyer.

———. 1978. Une étude comparative des trois grandes versions en vers de la *Vie de Saint Alexis* conservés en vieux français. *Revue des langues romanes* 83: 379-403.

Stempel, Wolf-Dieter. 1979. Aspects génériques de la réception. *Poétique* 39: 353-62.

Suchier, Walther. 1900. Uber das altfranzösische Gedicht von der Zerstörung Jerusalems (La venjance Nostre Seigneur). *Zeitschrift für romanische Philologie* 24: 161-98.

———. 1901. Uber das altfranzösische Gedicht von der Zerstörungs Jerusalems (La venjance Nostre Seigneur). *Zeitschrift für romanische Philologie* 25: 94-109, 256.

Tarbé, Prosper, ed. 1850. *Le roman de Girard de Viane*. Reims: Imprimerie de Regnier.

Thomas, Marcel Henri Germain. [1942]. Recherches sur les légendes françaises de Saint François d'Assise. Thesis, Ecole des Chartes, [Paris].

Tobler, Adolf. 1866. Eine handschriftliche Sammlung altfranzösischer Legenden. *Jahrbuch für romanische und englische Literatur* 7: 401-36.

Trenkle, Mary Patricia. 1976. A critical edition of *Le vie me damme Sainte Kateline vierge*, Ms. 10, 295-304x, Bibliothèque Royale, Bruxelles, a versed Old French Passion of Saint Catherine of Alexandria, known as an anonymous version. Ph.D. diss., University of Alabama, Tuscaloosa, Ala.

Tyssens, Madeleine. 1967. *La geste de Guillaume d'Orange dans les manuscrits cycliques*. Paris: Belles-Lettres.

Uitti, Karl D. 1967. The Old French *Vie de Saint Alexis*: Paradigm, legend, meaning. *Romance Philology* 20: 263-95.

———. 1975. The clerkly narrator figure in Old French hagiography and romance. *Medioevo romanzo* 2: 394-408.

Urech, Edouard. 1972. *Dictionnaire des symboles chrétiens*. Neuchâtel: Delachaux et Niestlé.

Van Emden, Wolfgang. 1969. Hypothèse sur une explication historique du remaniement de *Girart de Vienne* par Bertrand de Bar-sur-Aube. In Société Rencesvals 1969, 63-70.

———, ed. 1977. Girart de Vienne *par Bertrand de Bar-sur-Aube*. Paris: Société des anciens textes français.

———. 1982. *Girart de Vienne* devant les ordinateurs. In Comité de publication des mélanges René Louis 1982, 663-90.

Wallensköld, A. 1907. *Le conte de la femme convoitée par son beau-frère: Etude de littérature comparée*. Helsingfors: Societatis scientiarum fennicae.

Walpole, Ronald N. 1976. *The Old French Johannes translation of the Pseudo-Turpin chronicle: A critical edition*. Supplement. Berkeley: University of California Press.

Wattenbach, Wilhelm. 1896. *Das Schriftwesen im Mittelalter*. Leipzig: S. Hirzel.

Weber, Alfred. 1876. *Untersuchungen über die* Vie des anciens pères. Handschriftlichen Studien auf dem Gebiete Romanischer Literatur des Mittelalters 1. Frauenfeld: J. Huber.

____. 1877. Zu den Legenden der *Vie des pères*. *Zeitschrift für romanische Philologie* 1: 357-65.

Williams, Charles Allyn, and Louis Allen. 1935. *The German legends of the hairy anchorite, with two Old French texts of La vie de Saint Jehan Paulus edited by Louis Allen*. Urbana, Ill.: University of Illinois.

Woledge, Brian. 1954. *Bibliographie des romans et nouvelles en prose française antérieurs à 1500*. Geneva: Droz.

____. 1975. *Bibliographie des romans et nouvelles en prose française antérieurs à 1500: Supplément, 1954-1973*. Geneva: Droz.

Wolff, Robert Lee, and Harry W. Hazard, eds. 1969. *The Later Crusades, 1189-1311*. Vol. 2 of Setton 1969.

Wolter, Eugen. 1879. *Der Judenknabe: 5 Griechische, 14 Lateinische und 8 Französiche Texte*. Bibliotheca normannica 2. Halle: Max Niemeyer.

Yeandle, Frederic G., ed. 1930. *Girart de Vienne*. New York: Columbia University Press.

Zink, Michel. 1976. *La prédication en langue romane avant 1300*. Paris: Honoré Champion.

____. 1987. Chrétien et ses contemporains. In Lacy et al. 1987, 5-32.

Zumthor, Paul. 1972a. *Essai de poétique médiévale*. Paris: Seuil.

____. 1972b. Classes and genres in medieval literature. In Lacy 1972, 27-36.

____. [1943] 1973. *Merlin le prophète: Un thème de la littérature polémique, de l'historiographie et des romans*. Geneva: Slatkine Reprints.

www.ingramcontent.com/pod-product-compliance
Lightning Source LLC
Chambersburg PA
CBHW080733230426
43665CB00020B/2726